YOU ARE
DEADPOOL

WRITER

Al Ewing

ARTISTS

Salva Espin (#1, #3, #5) & Paco Diaz (#2, #4)

COLOR ARTIST

Guru-eFX

LETTERER

VC's Joe Sabino

COVER ART

Rahzzah

ASSISTANT EDITOR

Annalise Bissa

EDITOR

Jordan D. White

CHARACTER NOTES

Collection Editor: **Jennifer Grünwald**   Book Designers: **Adam Del Re** with **Nick Russell**
Assistant Editor: **Caitlin O'Connell**
Associate Managing Editor: **Kateri Woody**   Editor in Chief: **C.B. Cebulski**
Editor, Special Projects: **Mark D. Beazley**   Chief Creative Officer: **Joe Quesada**
VP Production & Special Projects: **Jeff Youngquist**   President: **Dan Buckley**
SVP Print, Sales & Marketing: **David Gabriel**   Executive Producer: **Alan Fine**

YOU ARE DEADPOOL. Contains material originally published in magazine form as YOU ARE DEADPOOL #1-5. First printing 2018. ISBN 978-1-302-91238-3. Published by MARVEL WORLDWIDE, INC., a subsidiary of MARVEL ENTERTAINMENT, LLC. OFFICE OF PUBLICATION: 135 West 50th Street, New York, NY 10020. Copyright © 2018 MARVEL No similarity between any of the names, characters, persons, and/or institutions in this magazine with those of any living or dead person or institution is intended, and any such similarity which may exist is purely coincidental. **Printed in Canada.** DAN BUCKLEY, President, Marvel Entertainment; JOHN NEE, Publisher; JOE QUESADA, Chief Creative Officer; TOM BREVOORT, SVP of Publishing; DAVID BOGART, SVP of Business Affairs & Operations, Publishing & Partnership; DAVID GABRIEL, SVP of Sales & Marketing, Publishing; JEFF YOUNGQUIST, VP of Production & Special Projects; DAN CARR, Executive Director of Publishing Technology; ALEX MORALES, Director of Publishing Operations; DAN EDINGTON, Managing Editor; SUSAN CRESPI, Production Manager; STAN LEE, Chairman Emeritus. For information regarding advertising in Marvel Comics or on Marvel.com, please contact Vit DeBellis, Custom Solutions & Integrated Advertising Manager, at vdebellis@marvel.com. For Marvel subscription inquiries, please call 888-511-5480. **Manufactured between 8/3/2018 and 9/4/2018 by SOLISCO PRINTERS, SCOTT, QC, CANADA.**

10 9 8 7 6 5 4 3 2 1

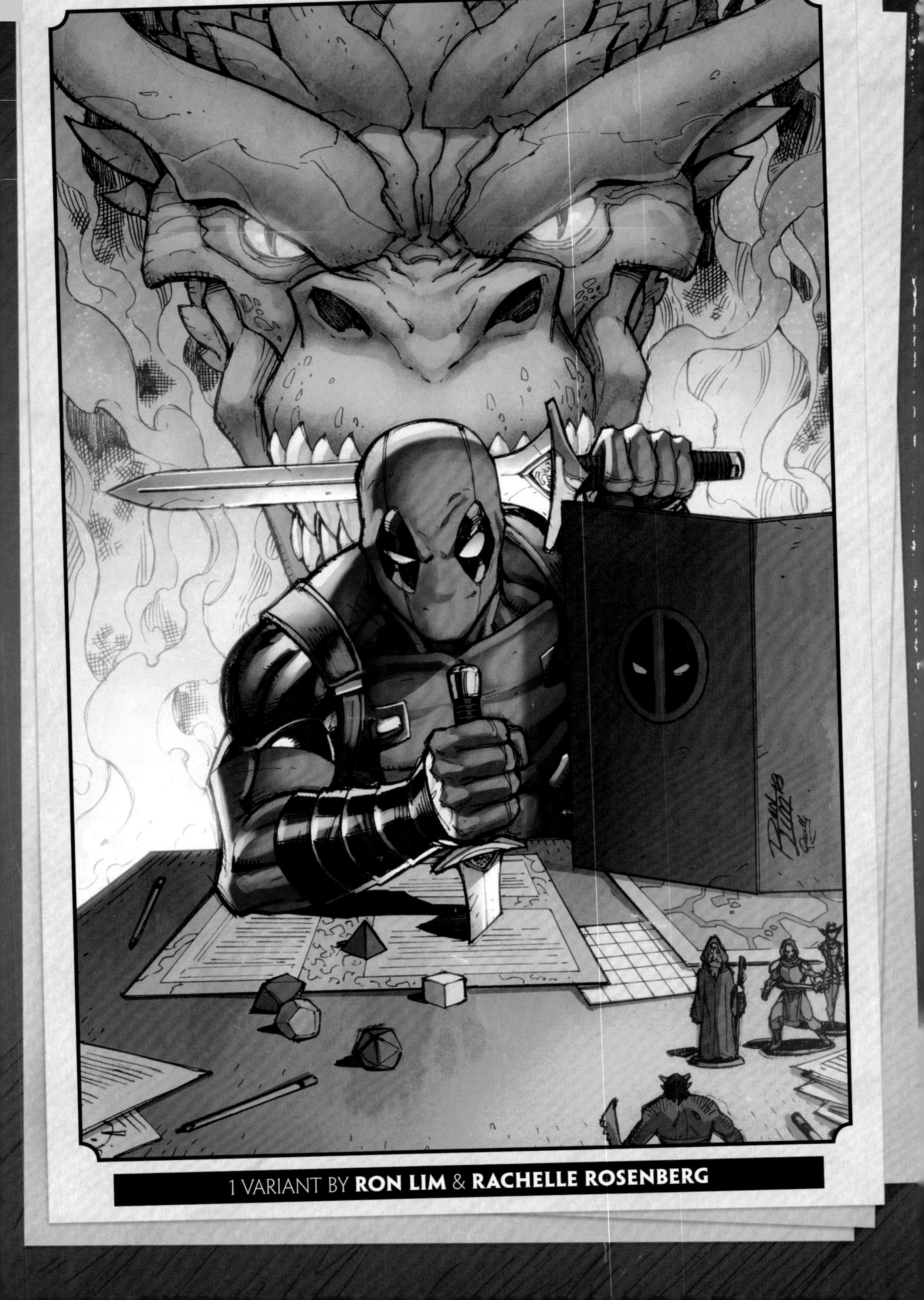

1 VARIANT BY **RON LIM** & **RACHELLE ROSENBERG**

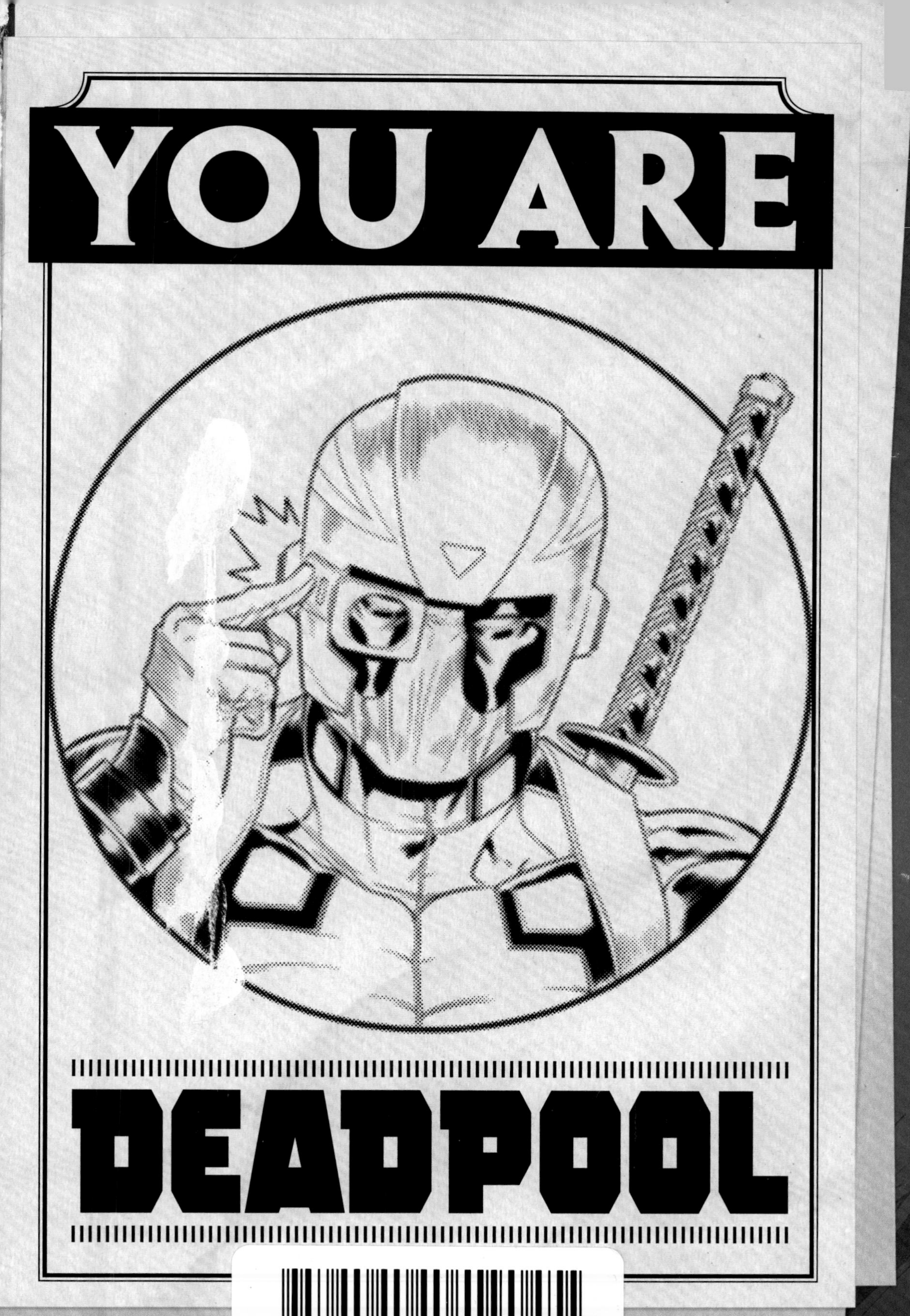
YOU ARE
DEADPOOL

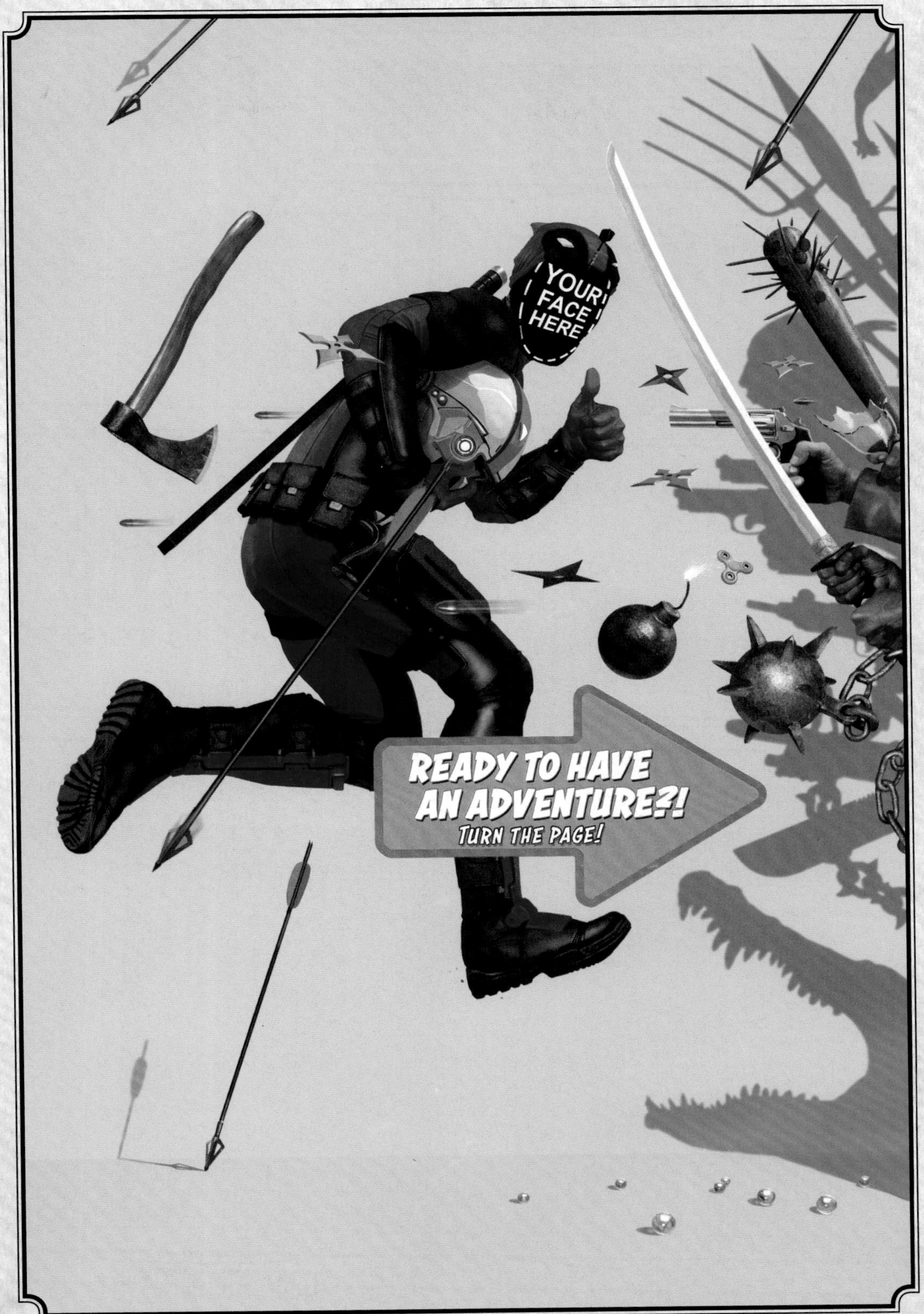
YOUR FACE HERE
READY TO HAVE AN ADVENTURE?!
TURN THE PAGE!

YOU ARE
DEADPOOL

NAME
Deadpool

CLASS
very little

ALIGNMENT
chaotic sassy

BACKGROUND

Deadpool, A.K.A. Wade Wilson, is a Level 3 Mercenary with Weapons Mastery (Amazing), Unarmed Combat (Incredible), Sad Clown Syndrome (Melancholy), Healing Factor (Shift-X) and Nasty Face (Shift-Ecch). He may or may not be a very tall hobbit. Currently, he's chilling at home waiting for you to turn the page and begin the tutorial.

RULES

Did I mention the tutorial? We put a lot of work into the tutorial. If you want the rules, you should probably play through it. I mean, you can skip it if you like, but it's your dollar. You should familiarize yourself with the boxes below, too – you'll be using them to keep stuff in.

SADNESS SCORE

BADNESS SCORE

INVENTORY

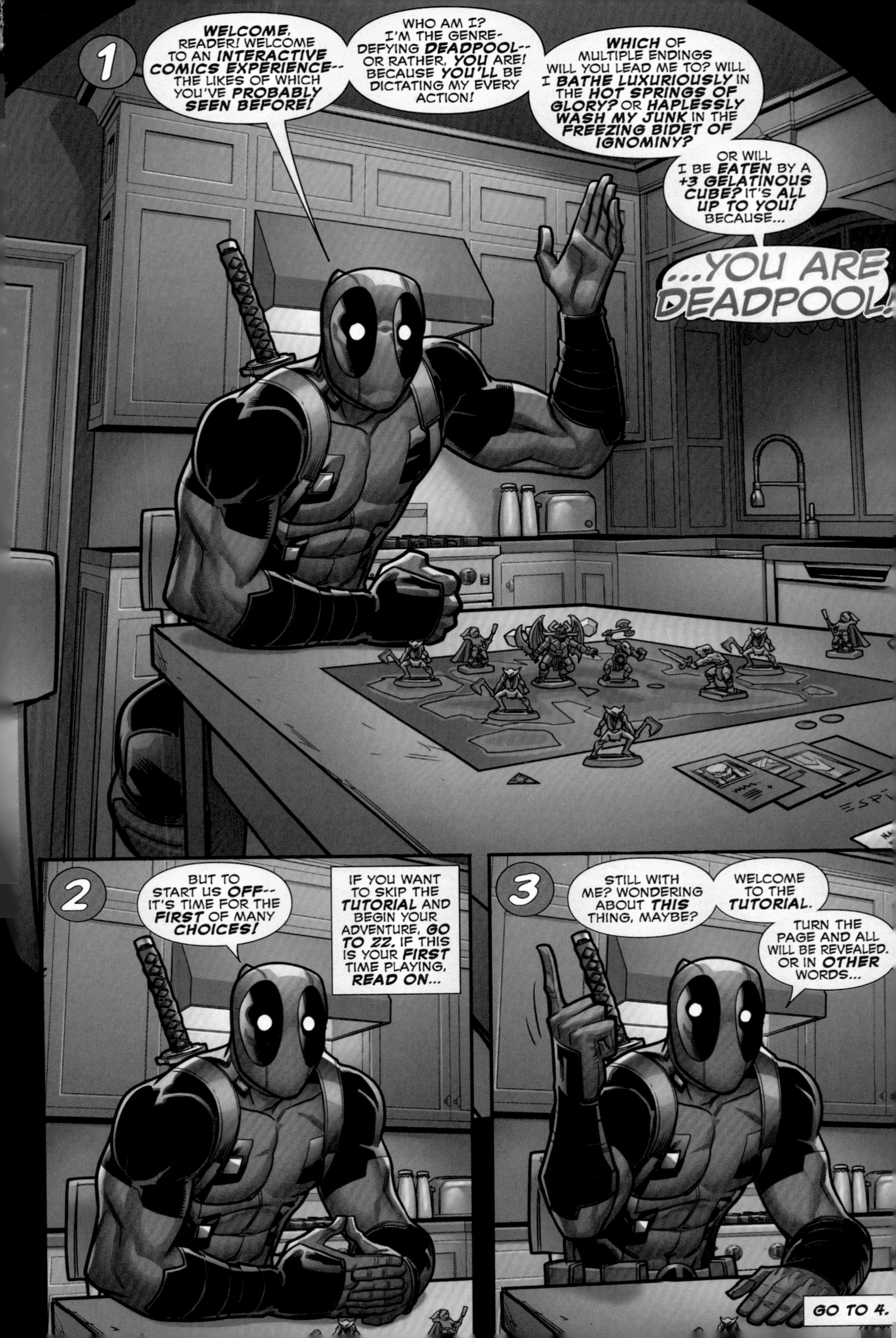
1
WELCOME, READER! WELCOME TO AN INTERACTIVE COMICS EXPERIENCE-- THE LIKES OF WHICH YOU'VE PROBABLY SEEN BEFORE!
WHO AM I? I'M THE GENRE-DEFYING DEADPOOL-- OR RATHER, YOU ARE! BECAUSE YOU'LL BE DICTATING MY EVERY ACTION!
WHICH OF MULTIPLE ENDINGS WILL YOU LEAD ME TO? WILL I BATHE LUXURIOUSLY IN THE HOT SPRINGS OF GLORY? OR HAPLESSLY WASH MY JUNK IN THE FREEZING BIDET OF IGNOMINY?
OR WILL I BE EATEN BY A +3 GELATINOUS CUBE? IT'S ALL UP TO YOU! BECAUSE...
...YOU ARE DEADPOOL!
2
BUT TO START US OFF-- IT'S TIME FOR THE FIRST OF MANY CHOICES!
IF YOU WANT TO SKIP THE TUTORIAL AND BEGIN YOUR ADVENTURE, GO TO 22. IF THIS IS YOUR FIRST TIME PLAYING, READ ON...
3
STILL WITH ME? WONDERING ABOUT THIS THING, MAYBE?
WELCOME TO THE TUTORIAL.
TURN THE PAGE AND ALL WILL BE REVEALED. OR IN OTHER WORDS...
GO TO 4.

4 "GO TO 4." AND HERE'S A LITTLE BOX MARKED **4**, MEANING **THIS** IS **PANEL 4.**

NEEDLESS TO SAY, IF YOU'RE **NOT** EXPLICITLY TOLD TO GO TO A PARTICULAR PANEL, YOU CAN MOVE RIGHT ON TO THE NEXT ONE, AS NORMAL. DO THAT NOW.

SORRY IF I'M BEING **PATRONIZING.** I'VE GOT TO GET EVERYBODY UP TO SPEED AT ONCE HERE.

TUTORIAL LEVELS, AM I RIGHT?

5 SO LET'S TRY IT AGAIN. I'LL USE MY **INTERNAL MONOLOGUE** TO OFFER YOU A SIMPLE **CHOICE...**

FOR A THUMBS-UP, **GO TO 8.** FOR A THUMBS-DOWN, **GO TO 6.**

6 THUMBS-DOWN! **EDGY!** WATCH YOUR **BADNESS SCORE**, PAL!

WE'LL GET TO THAT SOON.

TO GO BACK AND CHOOSE AGAIN, **GO TO 5.** IF YOU'VE GOT IT NOW, **GO TO 9.**

DON'T READ ON.

7 AAAHH! I'M **ADRIFT IN TIME!** EVENTS ARE HAPPENING **OUT** OF ORDER!

WHY DID WE NOT FOLLOW SIMPLE INSTRUCTIONS?

GO TO 11.

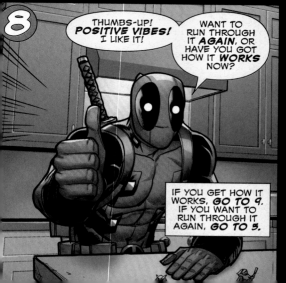

8 THUMBS-UP! **POSITIVE VIBES!** I LIKE IT!

WANT TO RUN THROUGH IT **AGAIN**, OR HAVE YOU GOT HOW IT **WORKS** NOW?

IF YOU GET HOW IT WORKS, **GO TO 9.** IF YOU WANT TO RUN THROUGH IT AGAIN, **GO TO 5.**

9 THEN I THINK WE'RE **DONE!**

(OH, THAT PANEL **ABOVE** ME? IT'S...PROBABLY NOTHING.)

WHEN YOU'RE **READY**--FOLLOW ME TO THE NEXT **STORY PAGE!**

THAT'S PANEL **10**, BY THE WAY.

10

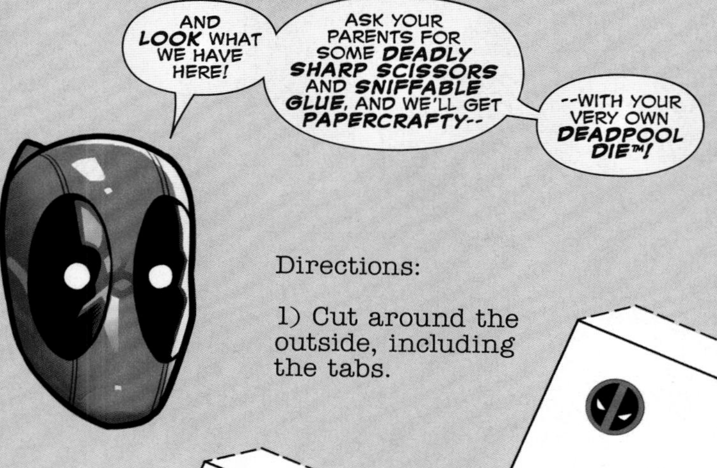
AND LOOK WHAT WE HAVE HERE!
ASK YOUR PARENTS FOR SOME DEADLY SHARP SCISSORS AND SNIFFABLE GLUE, AND WE'LL GET PAPERCRAFTY--
--WITH YOUR VERY OWN DEADPOOL DIE™!

Directions:

1) Cut around the outside, including the tabs.

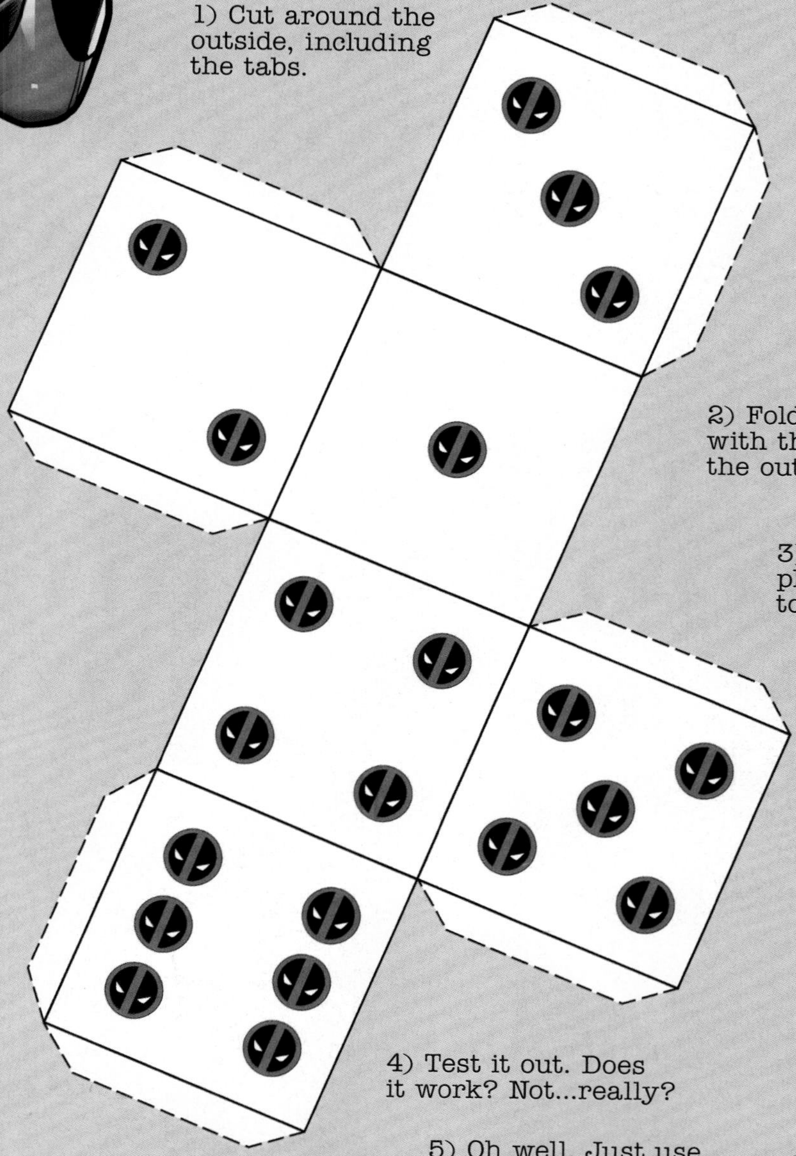

2) Fold into a cube with the spots on the outside.

3) Glue tabs in place. Leave to dry.

4) Test it out. Does it work? Not...really?

5) Oh well. Just use the die from an old board game instead.

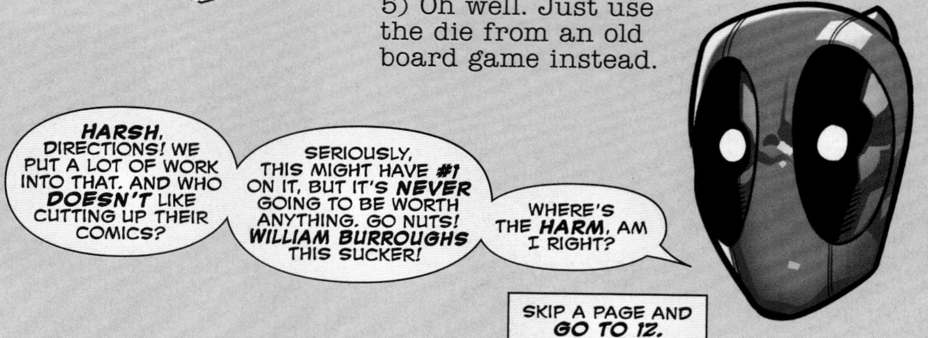
HARSH, DIRECTIONS! WE PUT A LOT OF WORK INTO THAT. AND WHO DOESN'T LIKE CUTTING UP THEIR COMICS?
SERIOUSLY, THIS MIGHT HAVE #1 ON IT, BUT IT'S NEVER GOING TO BE WORTH ANYTHING. GO NUTS! WILLIAM BURROUGHS THIS SUCKER!
WHERE'S THE HARM, AM I RIGHT?

SKIP A PAGE AND GO TO 12.

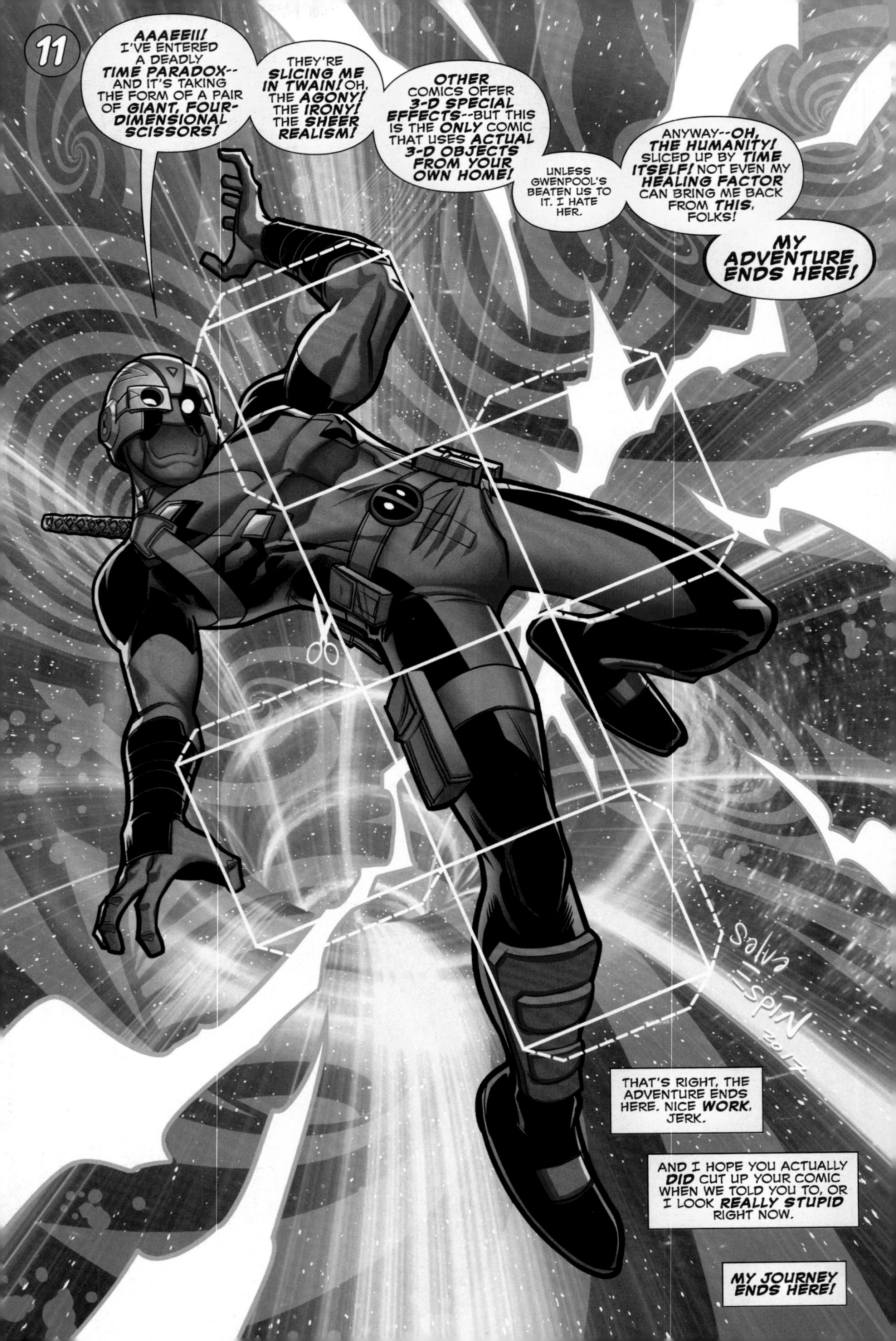
11
AAAEEII! I'VE ENTERED A DEADLY TIME PARADOX--AND IT'S TAKING THE FORM OF A PAIR OF GIANT, FOUR-DIMENSIONAL SCISSORS!
THEY'RE SLICING ME IN TWAIN! OH, THE AGONY! THE IRONY! THE SHEER REALISM!
OTHER COMICS OFFER 3-D SPECIAL EFFECTS--BUT THIS IS THE ONLY COMIC THAT USES ACTUAL 3-D OBJECTS FROM YOUR OWN HOME!
UNLESS GWENPOOL'S BEATEN US TO IT. I HATE HER.
ANYWAY--OH, THE HUMANITY! SLICED UP BY TIME ITSELF! NOT EVEN MY HEALING FACTOR CAN BRING ME BACK FROM THIS, FOLKS!
MY ADVENTURE ENDS HERE!
THAT'S RIGHT, THE ADVENTURE ENDS HERE. NICE WORK, JERK.
AND I HOPE YOU ACTUALLY DID CUT UP YOUR COMIC WHEN WE TOLD YOU TO, OR I LOOK REALLY STUPID RIGHT NOW.
MY JOURNEY ENDS HERE!

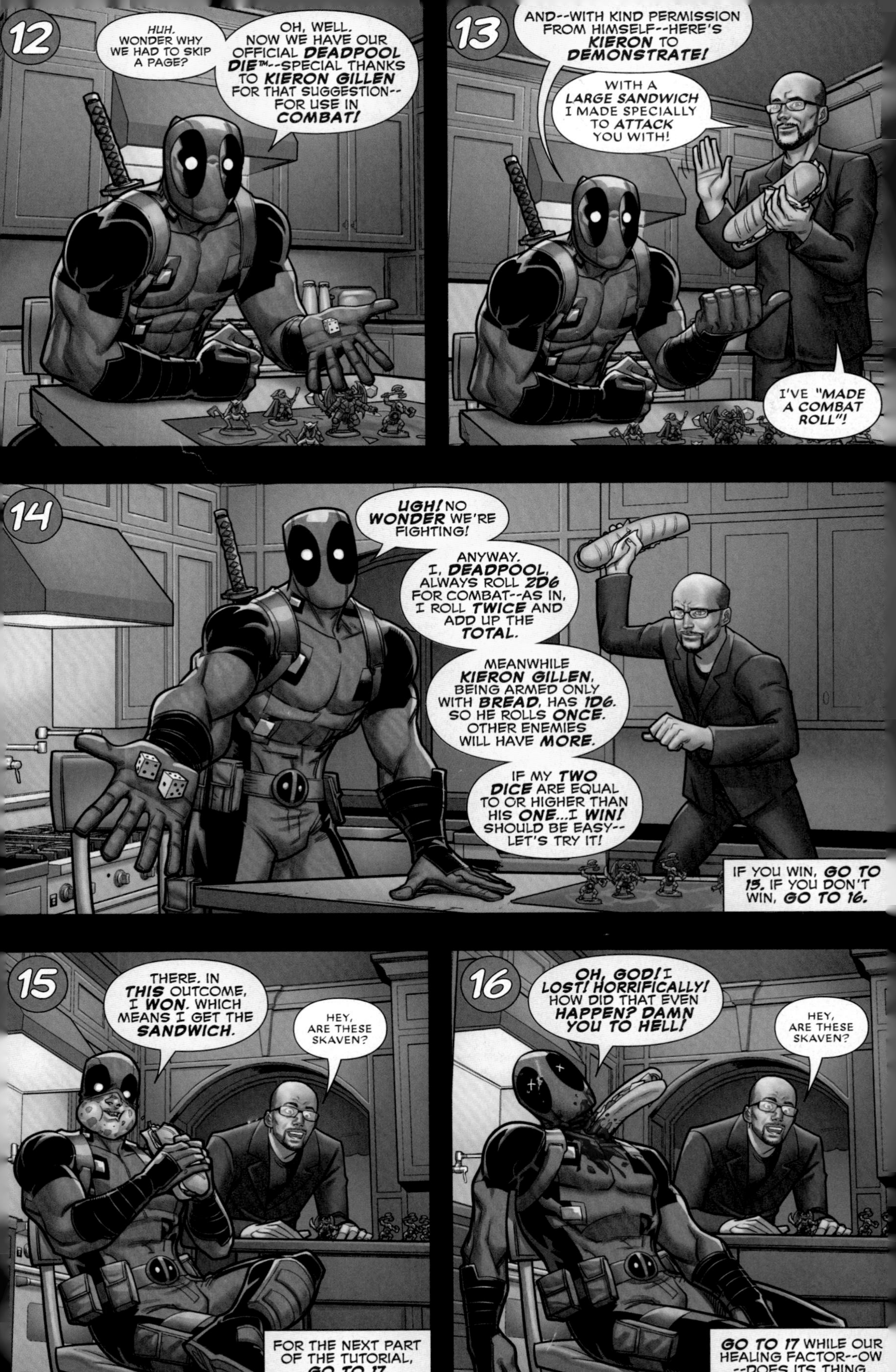
12
HUH. WONDER WHY WE HAD TO SKIP A PAGE?
OH, WELL. NOW WE HAVE OUR OFFICIAL DEADPOOL DIE™--SPECIAL THANKS TO KIERON GILLEN FOR THAT SUGGESTION--FOR USE IN COMBAT!
13
AND--WITH KIND PERMISSION FROM HIMSELF--HERE'S KIERON TO DEMONSTRATE!
WITH A LARGE SANDWICH I MADE SPECIALLY TO ATTACK YOU WITH!
I'VE "MADE A COMBAT ROLL"!
14
UGH! NO WONDER WE'RE FIGHTING!
ANYWAY. I, DEADPOOL, ALWAYS ROLL 2D6 FOR COMBAT--AS IN, I ROLL TWICE AND ADD UP THE TOTAL.
MEANWHILE KIERON GILLEN, BEING ARMED ONLY WITH BREAD, HAS 1D6. SO HE ROLLS ONCE. OTHER ENEMIES WILL HAVE MORE.
IF MY TWO DICE ARE EQUAL TO OR HIGHER THAN HIS ONE...I WIN! SHOULD BE EASY--LET'S TRY IT!
IF YOU WIN, GO TO 15. IF YOU DON'T WIN, GO TO 16.
15
THERE. IN THIS OUTCOME, I WON. WHICH MEANS I GET THE SANDWICH.
HEY, ARE THESE SKAVEN?
FOR THE NEXT PART OF THE TUTORIAL, GO TO 17.
16
OH, GOD! I LOST! HORRIFICALLY! HOW DID THAT EVEN HAPPEN? DAMN YOU TO HELL!
HEY, ARE THESE SKAVEN?
GO TO 17 WHILE OUR HEALING FACTOR--OW--DOES ITS THING.

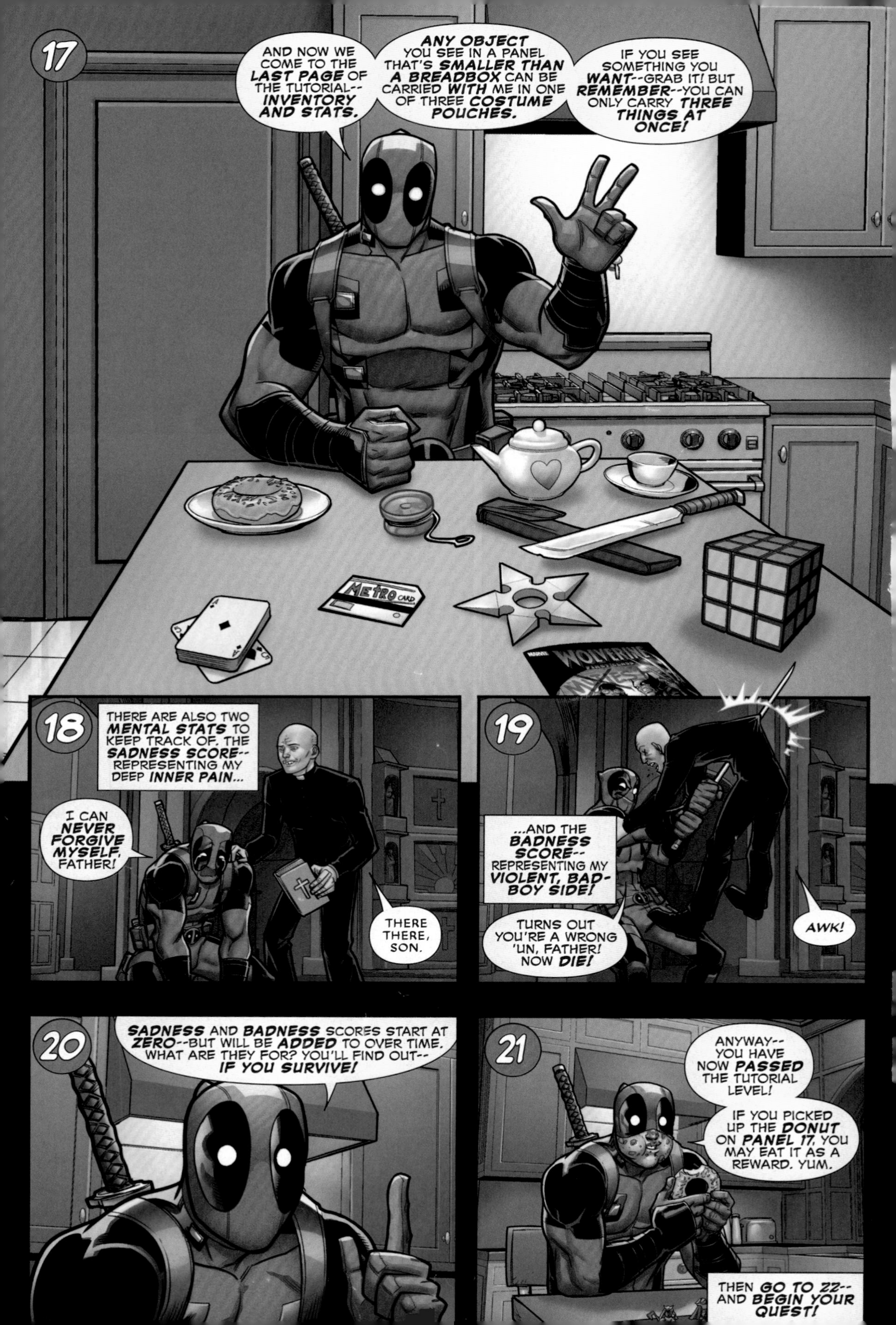
17
AND NOW WE COME TO THE LAST PAGE OF THE TUTORIAL-- INVENTORY AND STATS.
ANY OBJECT YOU SEE IN A PANEL THAT'S SMALLER THAN A BREADBOX CAN BE CARRIED WITH ME IN ONE OF THREE COSTUME POUCHES.
IF YOU SEE SOMETHING YOU WANT--GRAB IT! BUT REMEMBER--YOU CAN ONLY CARRY THREE THINGS AT ONCE!
METRO CARD
WOLVERINE
18
THERE ARE ALSO TWO MENTAL STATS TO KEEP TRACK OF. THE SADNESS SCORE-- REPRESENTING MY DEEP INNER PAIN...
I CAN NEVER FORGIVE MYSELF, FATHER!
THERE THERE, SON.
19
...AND THE BADNESS SCORE-- REPRESENTING MY VIOLENT, BAD-BOY SIDE!
TURNS OUT YOU'RE A WRONG 'UN, FATHER! NOW DIE!
AWK!
20
SADNESS AND BADNESS SCORES START AT ZERO--BUT WILL BE ADDED TO OVER TIME. WHAT ARE THEY FOR? YOU'LL FIND OUT-- IF YOU SURVIVE!
21
ANYWAY-- YOU HAVE NOW PASSED THE TUTORIAL LEVEL!
IF YOU PICKED UP THE DONUT ON PANEL 17, YOU MAY EAT IT AS A REWARD. YUM.
THEN GO TO 22-- AND BEGIN YOUR QUEST!

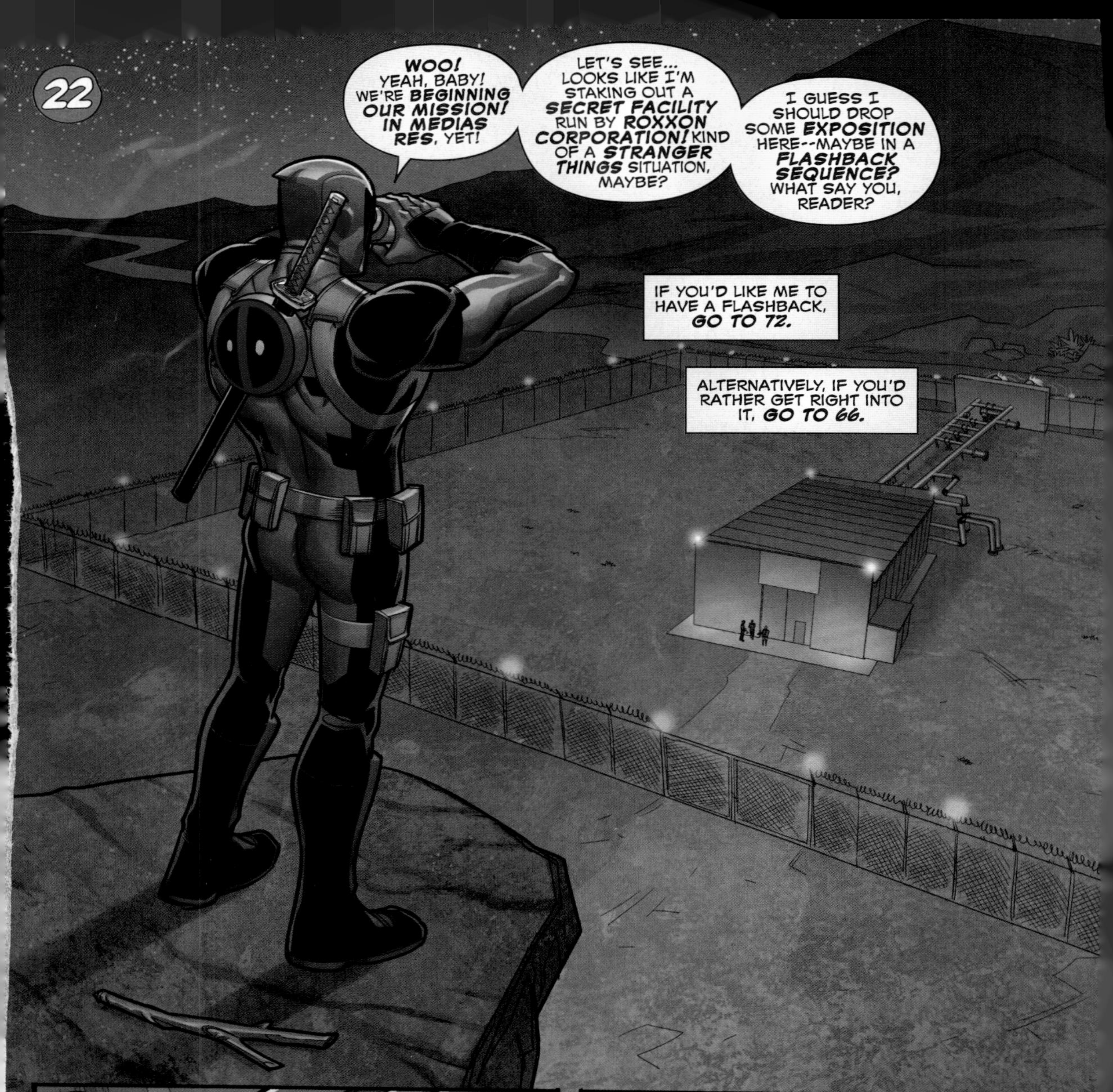
22
WOO! YEAH, BABY! WE'RE BEGINNING OUR MISSION! IN MEDIAS RES, YET!
LET'S SEE... LOOKS LIKE I'M STAKING OUT A SECRET FACILITY RUN BY ROXXON CORPORATION! KIND OF A STRANGER THINGS SITUATION, MAYBE?
I GUESS I SHOULD DROP SOME EXPOSITION HERE--MAYBE IN A FLASHBACK SEQUENCE? WHAT SAY YOU, READER?
IF YOU'D LIKE ME TO HAVE A FLASHBACK, GO TO 72.
ALTERNATIVELY, IF YOU'D RATHER GET RIGHT INTO IT, GO TO 66.

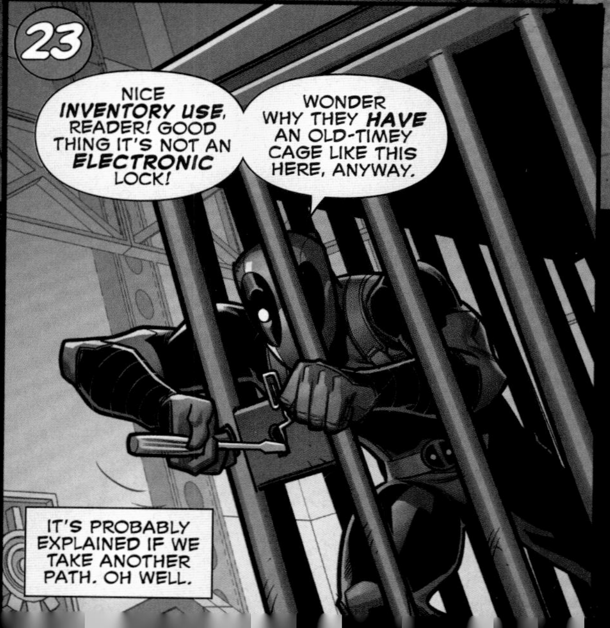
23
NICE INVENTORY USE, READER! GOOD THING IT'S NOT AN ELECTRONIC LOCK!
WONDER WHY THEY HAVE AN OLD-TIMEY CAGE LIKE THIS HERE, ANYWAY.
IT'S PROBABLY EXPLAINED IF WE TAKE ANOTHER PATH. OH WELL.

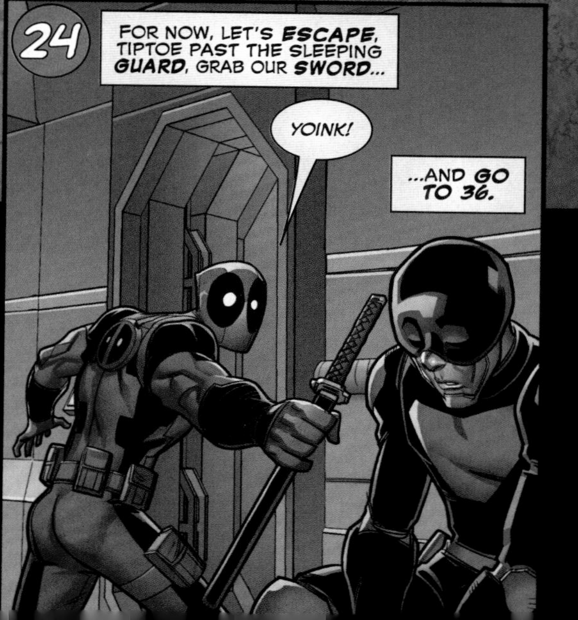
24
FOR NOW, LET'S ESCAPE, TIPTOE PAST THE SLEEPING GUARD, GRAB OUR SWORD...
YOINK!
...AND GO TO 36.

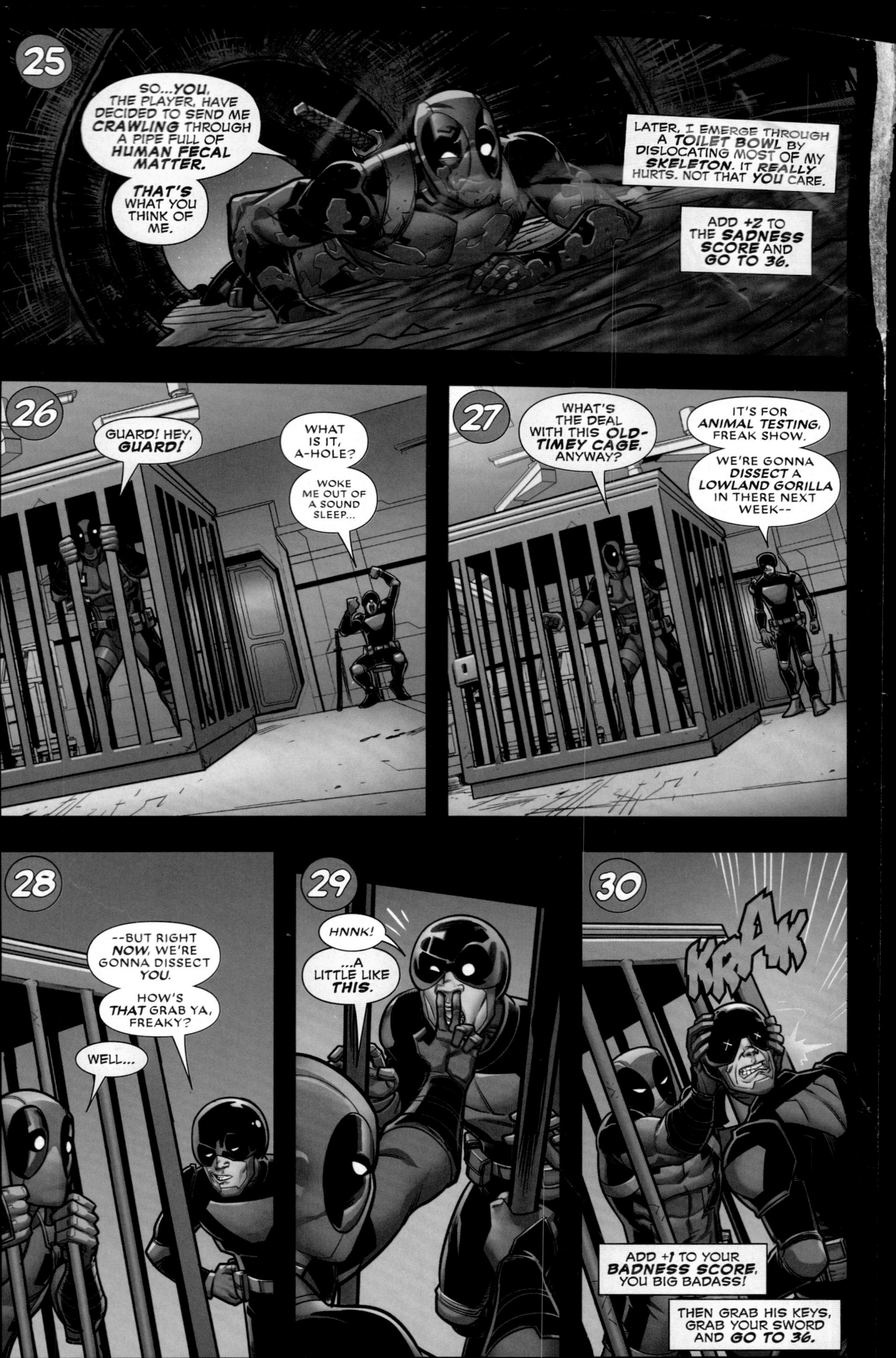
25
SO...YOU, THE PLAYER, HAVE DECIDED TO SEND ME CRAWLING THROUGH A PIPE FULL OF HUMAN FECAL MATTER.
THAT'S WHAT YOU THINK OF ME.
LATER, I EMERGE THROUGH A TOILET BOWL BY DISLOCATING MOST OF MY SKELETON. IT REALLY HURTS. NOT THAT YOU CARE.
ADD +2 TO THE SADNESS SCORE AND GO TO 36.
26
GUARD! HEY, GUARD!
WHAT IS IT, A-HOLE?
WOKE ME OUT OF A SOUND SLEEP...
27
WHAT'S THE DEAL WITH THIS OLD-TIMEY CAGE, ANYWAY?
IT'S FOR ANIMAL TESTING, FREAK SHOW.
WE'RE GONNA DISSECT A LOWLAND GORILLA IN THERE NEXT WEEK--
28
--BUT RIGHT NOW, WE'RE GONNA DISSECT YOU.
HOW'S THAT GRAB YA, FREAKY?
WELL...
29
HNNK!
...A LITTLE LIKE THIS.
30
KRAK
ADD +1 TO YOUR BADNESS SCORE, YOU BIG BADASS!
THEN GRAB HIS KEYS, GRAB YOUR SWORD AND GO TO 36.

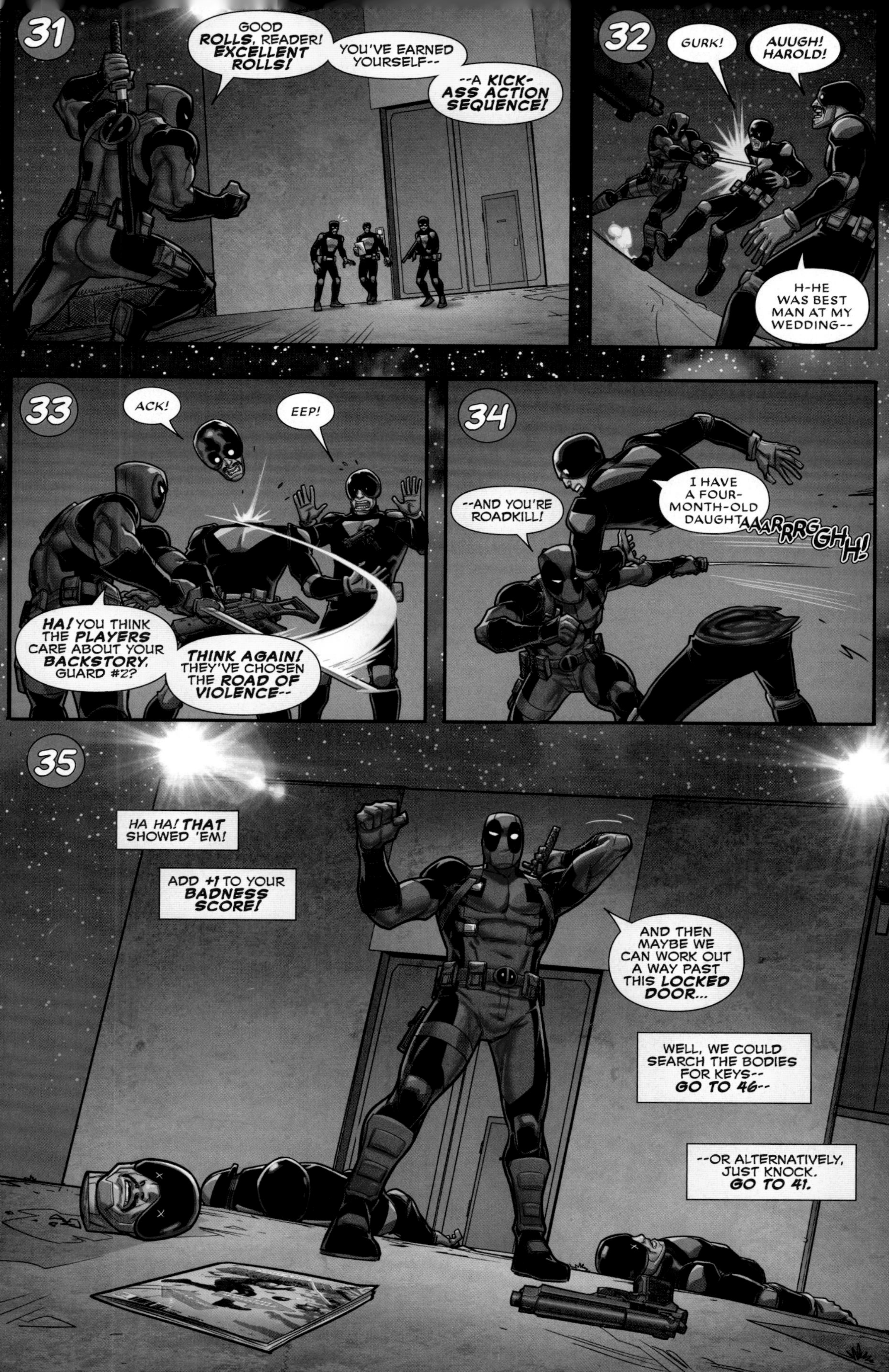
31
GOOD ROLLS, READER! EXCELLENT ROLLS!
YOU'VE EARNED YOURSELF--
--A KICK-ASS ACTION SEQUENCE!
32
GURK!
AUUGH! HAROLD!
H-HE WAS BEST MAN AT MY WEDDING--
33
ACK!
EEP!
HA! YOU THINK THE PLAYERS CARE ABOUT YOUR BACKSTORY, GUARD #2?
THINK AGAIN! THEY'VE CHOSEN THE ROAD OF VIOLENCE--
34
--AND YOU'RE ROADKILL!
I HAVE A FOUR-MONTH-OLD DAUGHTAAARRRGGHH!
35
HA HA! THAT SHOWED 'EM!
ADD +1 TO YOUR BADNESS SCORE!
AND THEN MAYBE WE CAN WORK OUT A WAY PAST THIS LOCKED DOOR...
WELL, WE COULD SEARCH THE BODIES FOR KEYS-- GO TO 46--
--OR ALTERNATIVELY, JUST KNOCK. GO TO 41.

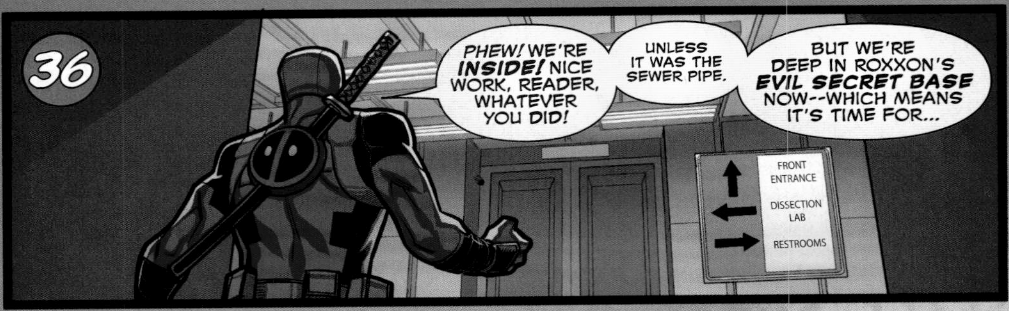
36
PHEW! WE'RE INSIDE! NICE WORK, READER, WHATEVER YOU DID!
UNLESS IT WAS THE SEWER PIPE.
BUT WE'RE DEEP IN ROXXON'S EVIL SECRET BASE NOW--WHICH MEANS IT'S TIME FOR...
FRONT ENTRANCE
DISSECTION LAB
RESTROOMS

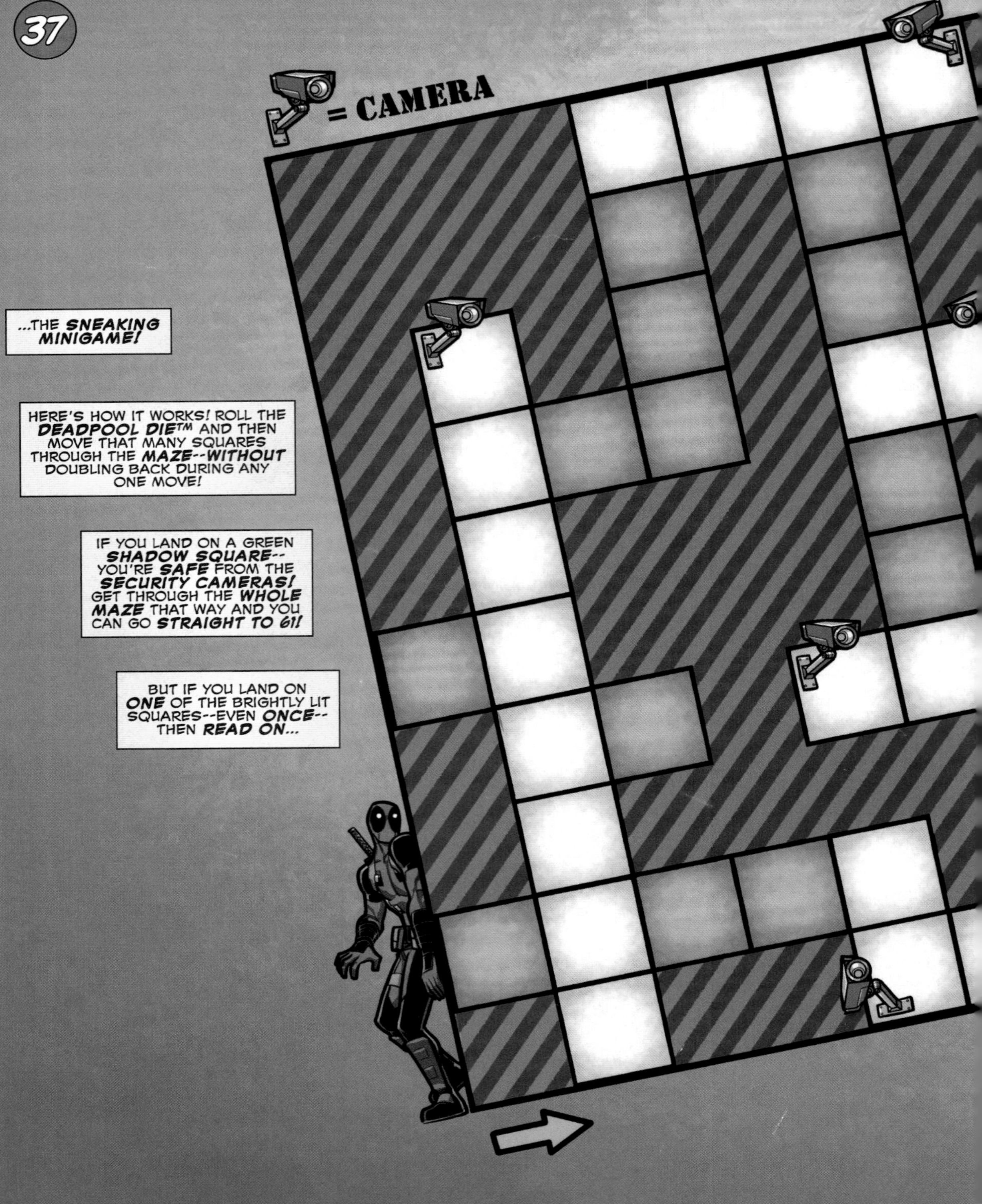
37
= CAMERA
...THE SNEAKING MINIGAME!
HERE'S HOW IT WORKS! ROLL THE DEADPOOL DIE™ AND THEN MOVE THAT MANY SQUARES THROUGH THE MAZE--WITHOUT DOUBLING BACK DURING ANY ONE MOVE!
IF YOU LAND ON A GREEN SHADOW SQUARE--YOU'RE SAFE FROM THE SECURITY CAMERAS! GET THROUGH THE WHOLE MAZE THAT WAY AND YOU CAN GO STRAIGHT TO 61!
BUT IF YOU LAND ON ONE OF THE BRIGHTLY LIT SQUARES--EVEN ONCE--THEN READ ON...

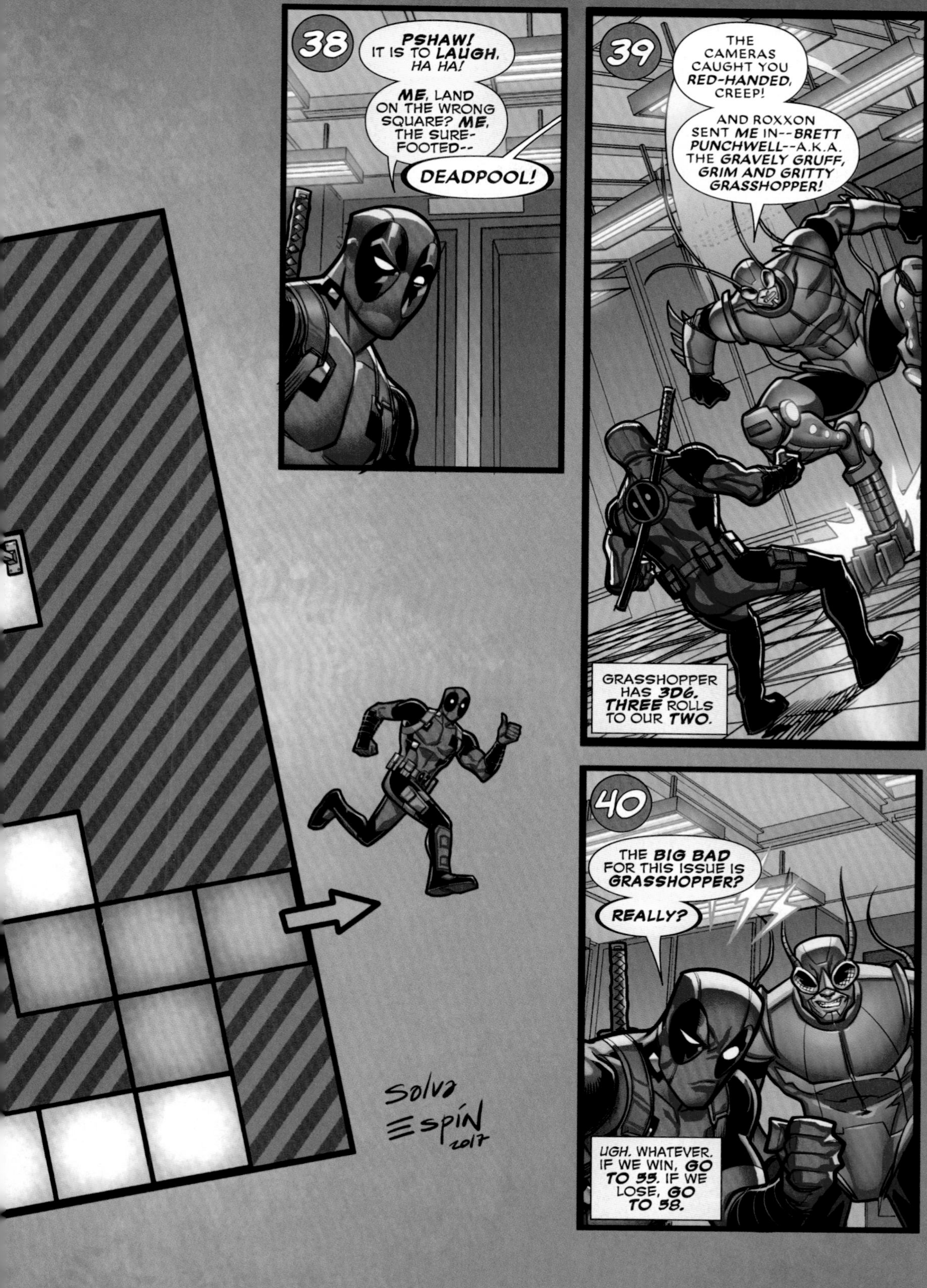
38
PSHAW! IT IS TO LAUGH, HA HA!
ME, LAND ON THE WRONG SQUARE? ME, THE SURE-FOOTED--
DEADPOOL!
39
THE CAMERAS CAUGHT YOU RED-HANDED, CREEP!
AND ROXXON SENT ME IN--BRETT PUNCHWELL--A.K.A. THE GRAVELY GRUFF, GRIM AND GRITTY GRASSHOPPER!
GRASSHOPPER HAS 3D6. THREE ROLLS TO OUR TWO.
40
THE BIG BAD FOR THIS ISSUE IS GRASSHOPPER?
REALLY?
UGH. WHATEVER. IF WE WIN, GO TO 35. IF WE LOSE, GO TO 38.
Solva
Espín
2017

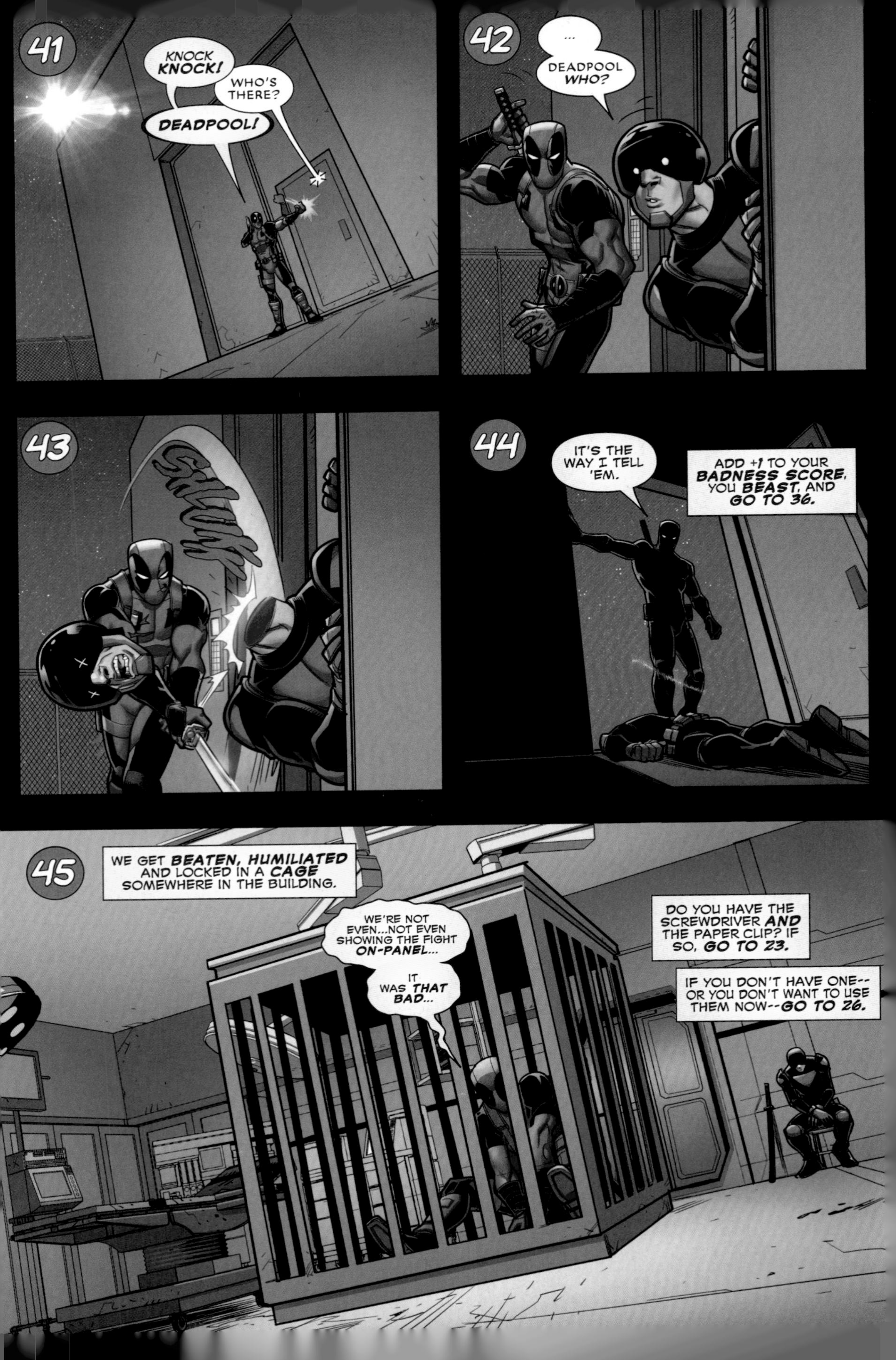
41
KNOCK KNOCK!
WHO'S THERE?
DEADPOOL!
42
...
DEADPOOL WHO?
43
44
IT'S THE WAY I TELL 'EM.
ADD +1 TO YOUR BADNESS SCORE, YOU BEAST, AND GO TO 36.
45
WE GET BEATEN, HUMILIATED AND LOCKED IN A CAGE SOMEWHERE IN THE BUILDING.
WE'RE NOT EVEN...NOT EVEN SHOWING THE FIGHT ON-PANEL...
IT WAS THAT BAD...
DO YOU HAVE THE SCREWDRIVER AND THE PAPER CLIP? IF SO, GO TO 23.
IF YOU DON'T HAVE ONE--OR YOU DON'T WANT TO USE THEM NOW--GO TO 26.

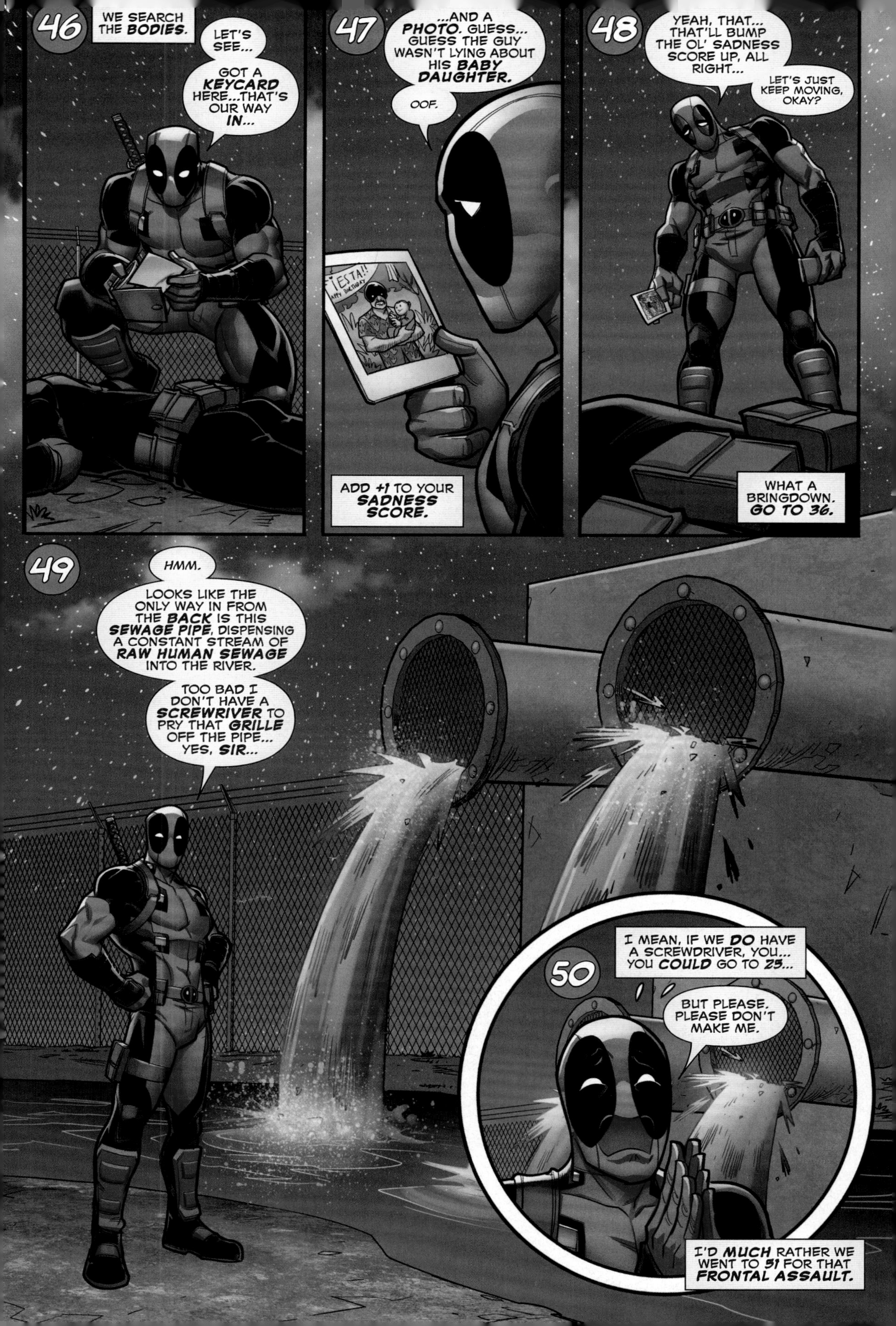
46
WE SEARCH THE BODIES.
LET'S SEE...
GOT A KEYCARD HERE...THAT'S OUR WAY IN...
47
...AND A PHOTO. GUESS... GUESS THE GUY WASN'T LYING ABOUT HIS BABY DAUGHTER.
OOF.
FIESTA!!
ADD +1 TO YOUR SADNESS SCORE.
48
YEAH, THAT... THAT'LL BUMP THE OL' SADNESS SCORE UP, ALL RIGHT...
LET'S JUST KEEP MOVING, OKAY?
WHAT A BRINGDOWN. GO TO 36.
49
HMM.
LOOKS LIKE THE ONLY WAY IN FROM THE BACK IS THIS SEWAGE PIPE, DISPENSING A CONSTANT STREAM OF RAW HUMAN SEWAGE INTO THE RIVER.
TOO BAD I DON'T HAVE A SCREWRIVER TO PRY THAT GRILLE OFF THE PIPE... YES, SIR...
50
I MEAN, IF WE DO HAVE A SCREWDRIVER, YOU... YOU COULD GO TO 25...
BUT PLEASE. PLEASE DON'T MAKE ME.
I'D MUCH RATHER WE WENT TO 51 FOR THAT FRONTAL ASSAULT.

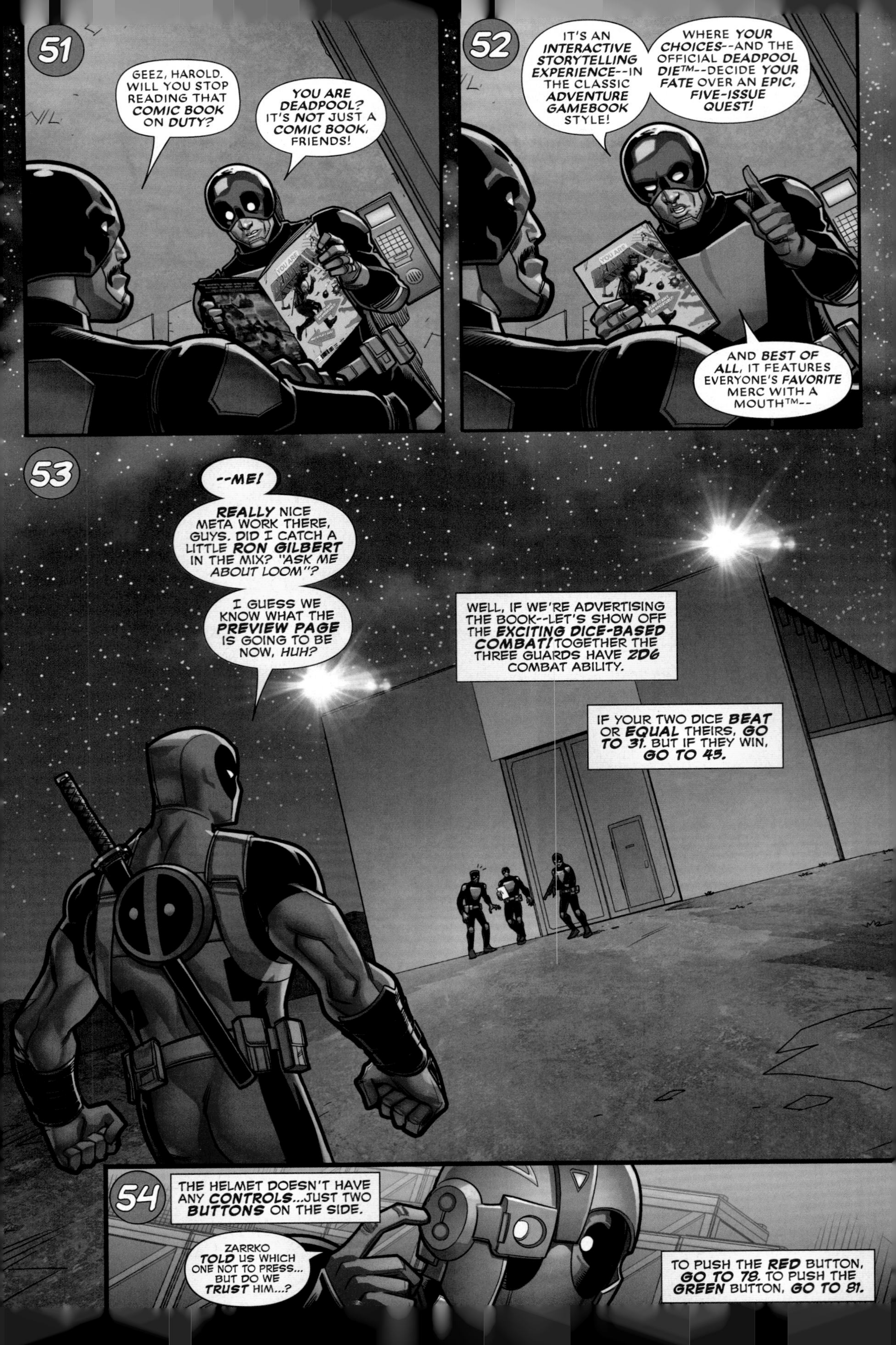
51
GEEZ, HAROLD. WILL YOU STOP READING THAT COMIC BOOK ON DUTY?
YOU ARE DEADPOOL? IT'S NOT JUST A COMIC BOOK, FRIENDS!
52
IT'S AN INTERACTIVE STORYTELLING EXPERIENCE--IN THE CLASSIC ADVENTURE GAMEBOOK STYLE!
WHERE YOUR CHOICES--AND THE OFFICIAL DEADPOOL DIE™--DECIDE YOUR FATE OVER AN EPIC, FIVE-ISSUE QUEST!
AND BEST OF ALL, IT FEATURES EVERYONE'S FAVORITE MERC WITH A MOUTH™--
53
--ME!
REALLY NICE META WORK THERE, GUYS. DID I CATCH A LITTLE RON GILBERT IN THE MIX? "ASK ME ABOUT LOOM"?
I GUESS WE KNOW WHAT THE PREVIEW PAGE IS GOING TO BE NOW, HUH?
WELL, IF WE'RE ADVERTISING THE BOOK--LET'S SHOW OFF THE EXCITING DICE-BASED COMBAT! TOGETHER THE THREE GUARDS HAVE 2D6 COMBAT ABILITY.
IF YOUR TWO DICE BEAT OR EQUAL THEIRS, GO TO 31. BUT IF THEY WIN, GO TO 45.
54
THE HELMET DOESN'T HAVE ANY CONTROLS...JUST TWO BUTTONS ON THE SIDE.
ZARRKO TOLD US WHICH ONE NOT TO PRESS... BUT DO WE TRUST HIM...?
TO PUSH THE RED BUTTON, GO TO 78. TO PUSH THE GREEN BUTTON, GO TO 81.

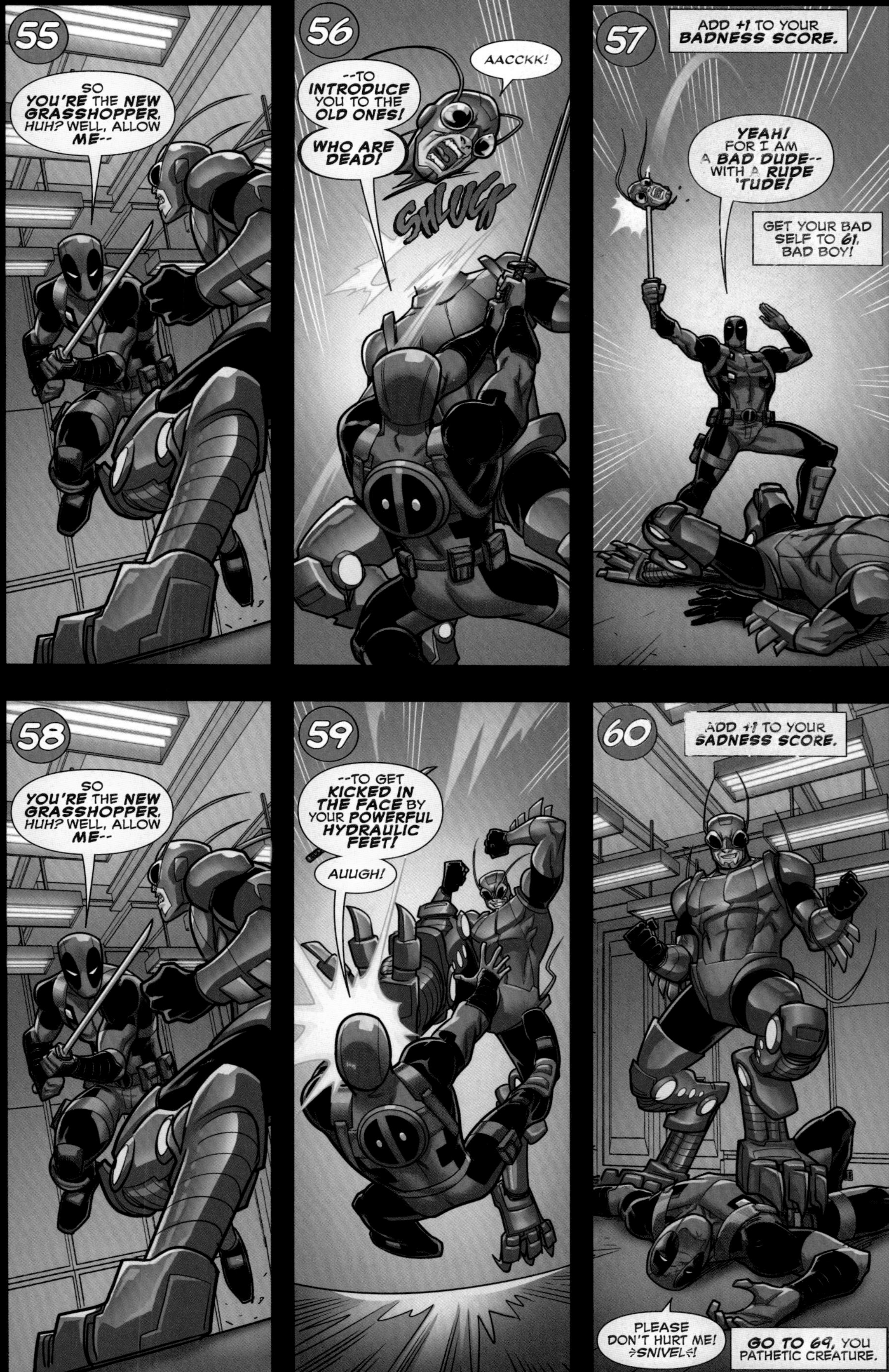
55
SO YOU'RE THE NEW GRASSHOPPER, HUH? WELL, ALLOW ME--
56
--TO INTRODUCE YOU TO THE OLD ONES!
WHO ARE DEAD!
AACCKK!
SHLUCK
57
ADD +1 TO YOUR BADNESS SCORE.
YEAH! FOR I AM A BAD DUDE-- WITH A RUDE 'TUDE!
GET YOUR BAD SELF TO 61, BAD BOY!
58
SO YOU'RE THE NEW GRASSHOPPER, HUH? WELL, ALLOW ME--
59
--TO GET KICKED IN THE FACE BY YOUR POWERFUL HYDRAULIC FEET!
AUUGH!
60
ADD +1 TO YOUR SADNESS SCORE.
PLEASE DON'T HURT ME! »SNIVEL«!
GO TO 69, YOU PATHETIC CREATURE.

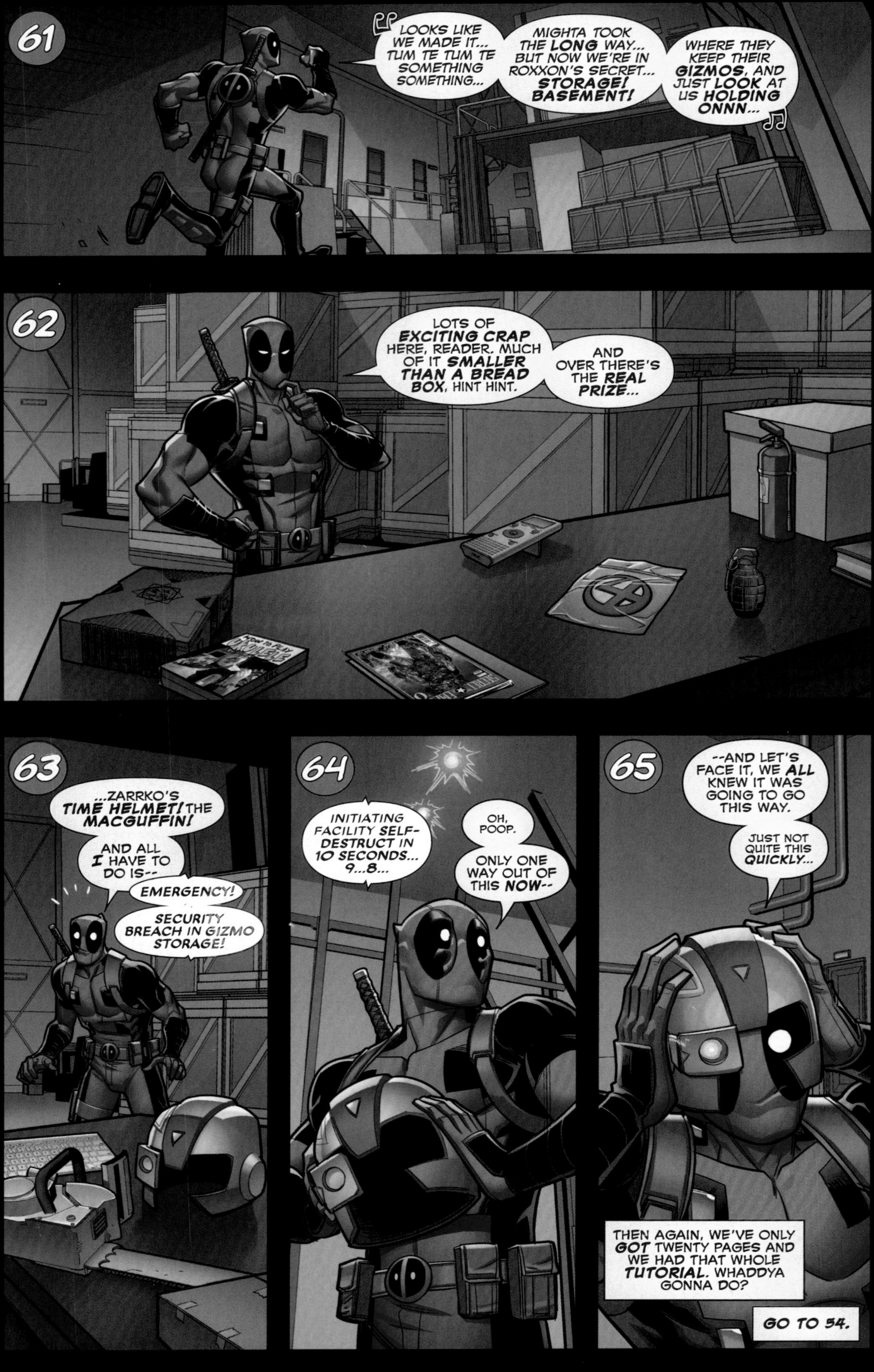
61
LOOKS LIKE WE MADE IT... TUM TE TUM TE SOMETHING SOMETHING...
MIGHTA TOOK THE LONG WAY... BUT NOW WE'RE IN ROXXON'S SECRET... STORAGE! BASEMENT!
WHERE THEY KEEP THEIR GIZMOS, AND JUST LOOK AT US HOLDING ONNN...
62
LOTS OF EXCITING CRAP HERE, READER. MUCH OF IT SMALLER THAN A BREAD BOX, HINT HINT.
AND OVER THERE'S THE REAL PRIZE...
63
...ZARRKO'S TIME HELMET! THE MACGUFFIN!
AND ALL I HAVE TO DO IS--
EMERGENCY!
SECURITY BREACH IN GIZMO STORAGE!
64
INITIATING FACILITY SELF-DESTRUCT IN 10 SECONDS... 9...8...
OH, POOP.
ONLY ONE WAY OUT OF THIS NOW--
65
--AND LET'S FACE IT, WE ALL KNEW IT WAS GOING TO GO THIS WAY.
JUST NOT QUITE THIS QUICKLY...
THEN AGAIN, WE'VE ONLY GOT TWENTY PAGES AND WE HAD THAT WHOLE TUTORIAL. WHADDYA GONNA DO?
GO TO 54.

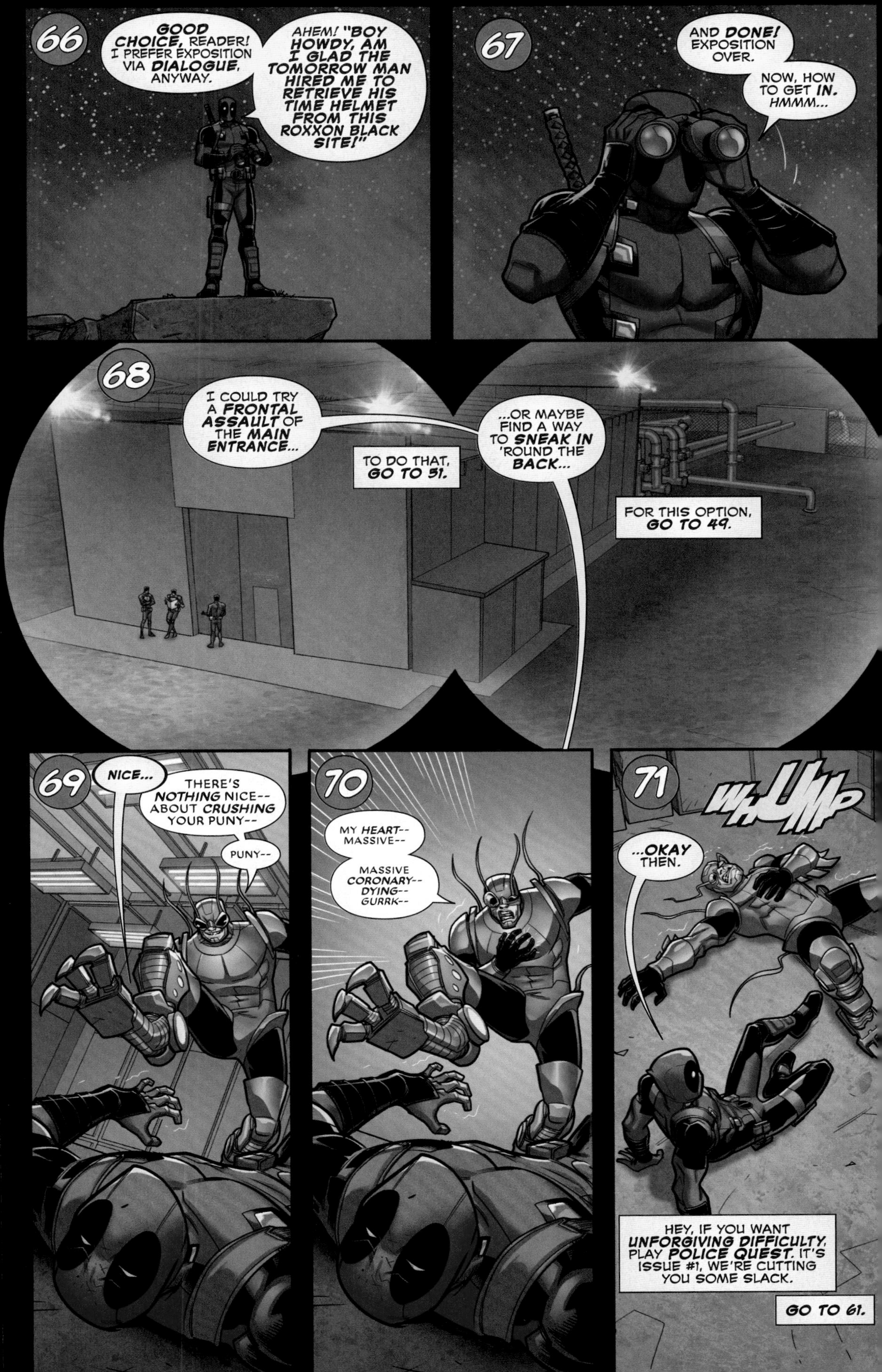
66
GOOD CHOICE, READER! I PREFER EXPOSITION VIA DIALOGUE, ANYWAY.
AHEM! "BOY HOWDY, AM I GLAD THE TOMORROW MAN HIRED ME TO RETRIEVE HIS TIME HELMET FROM THIS ROXXON BLACK SITE!"
67
AND DONE! EXPOSITION OVER.
NOW, HOW TO GET IN. HMMM...
68
I COULD TRY A FRONTAL ASSAULT OF THE MAIN ENTRANCE...
TO DO THAT, GO TO 51.
...OR MAYBE FIND A WAY TO SNEAK IN 'ROUND THE BACK...
FOR THIS OPTION, GO TO 49.
69
NICE...
THERE'S NOTHING NICE-- ABOUT CRUSHING YOUR PUNY--
PUNY--
70
MY HEART-- MASSIVE--
MASSIVE CORONARY-- DYING-- GURRK--
71
WHUMP
...OKAY THEN.
HEY, IF YOU WANT UNFORGIVING DIFFICULTY, PLAY POLICE QUEST. IT'S ISSUE #1, WE'RE CUTTING YOU SOME SLACK.
GO TO 61.

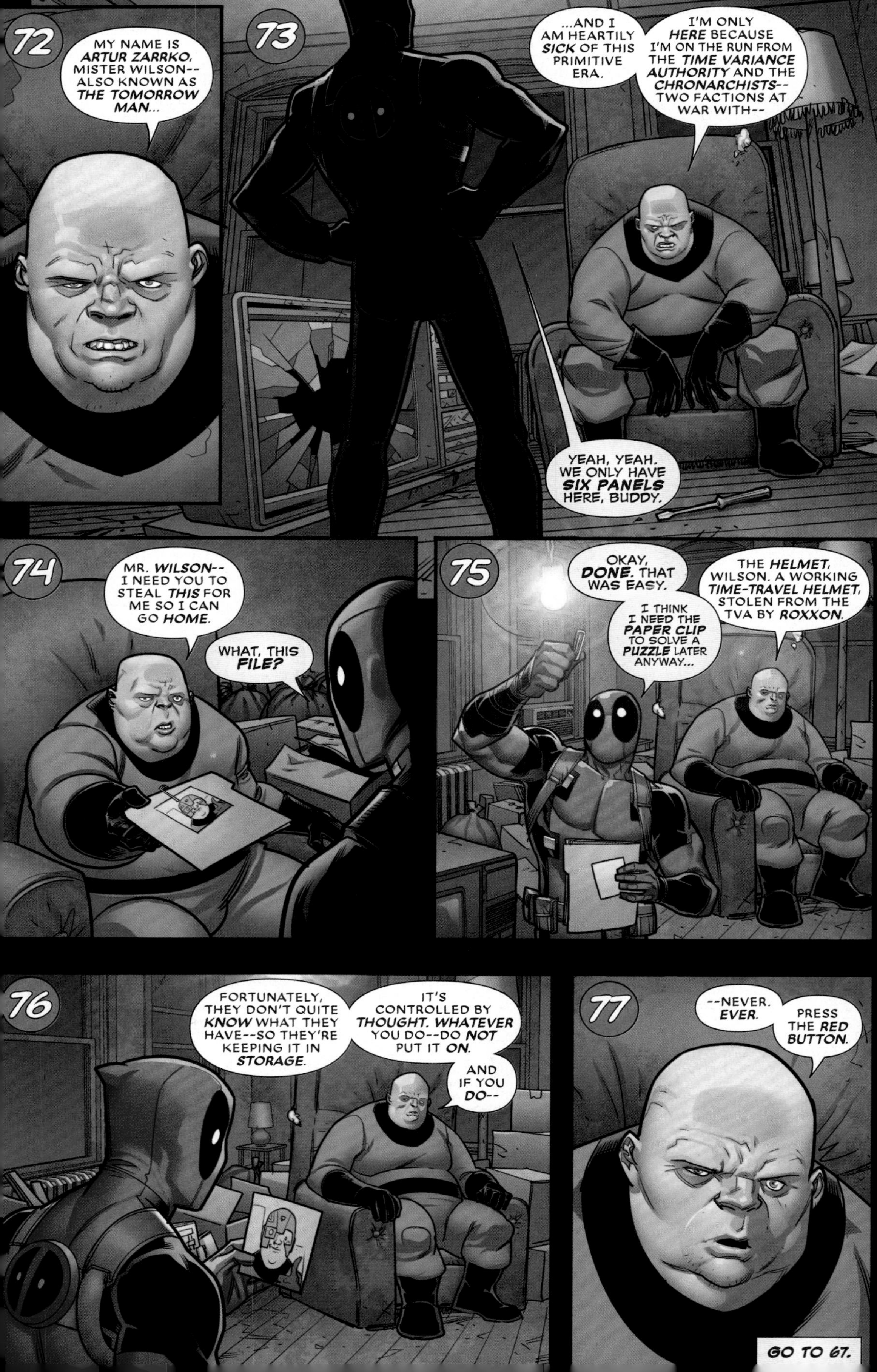
72
MY NAME IS ARTUR ZARRKO, MISTER WILSON-- ALSO KNOWN AS THE TOMORROW MAN...
73
...AND I AM HEARTILY SICK OF THIS PRIMITIVE ERA.
I'M ONLY HERE BECAUSE I'M ON THE RUN FROM THE TIME VARIANCE AUTHORITY AND THE CHRONARCHISTS-- TWO FACTIONS AT WAR WITH--
YEAH, YEAH. WE ONLY HAVE SIX PANELS HERE, BUDDY.
74
MR. WILSON-- I NEED YOU TO STEAL THIS FOR ME SO I CAN GO HOME.
WHAT, THIS FILE?
75
OKAY, DONE. THAT WAS EASY.
I THINK I NEED THE PAPER CLIP TO SOLVE A PUZZLE LATER ANYWAY...
THE HELMET, WILSON. A WORKING TIME-TRAVEL HELMET, STOLEN FROM THE TVA BY ROXXON.
76
FORTUNATELY, THEY DON'T QUITE KNOW WHAT THEY HAVE--SO THEY'RE KEEPING IT IN STORAGE.
IT'S CONTROLLED BY THOUGHT. WHATEVER YOU DO--DO NOT PUT IT ON.
AND IF YOU DO--
77
--NEVER. EVER.
PRESS THE RED BUTTON.
GO TO 67.

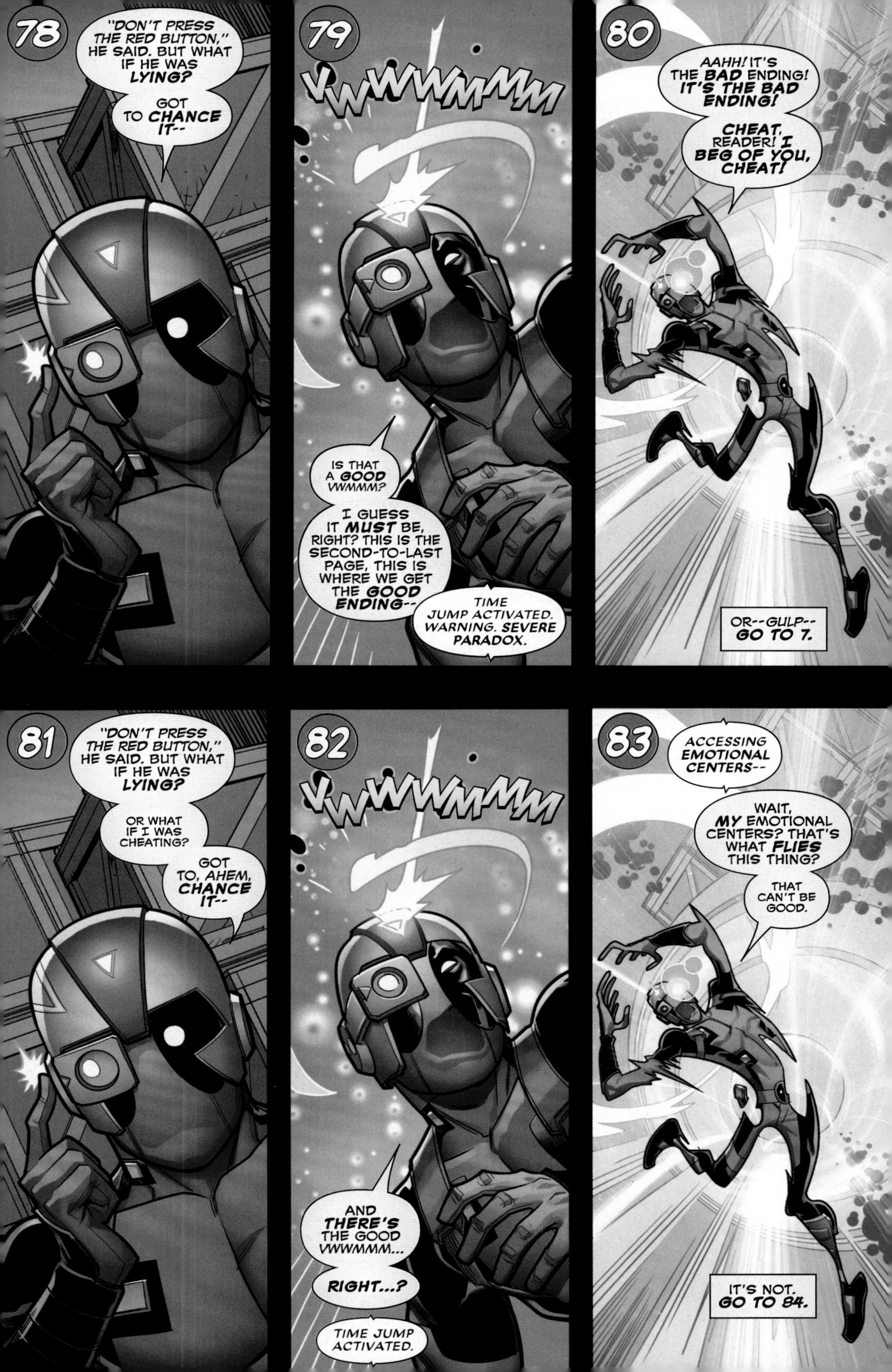
78
"DON'T PRESS THE RED BUTTON," HE SAID. BUT WHAT IF HE WAS LYING?
GOT TO CHANCE IT--
79
VWWWMMM
IS THAT A GOOD VWMMM?
I GUESS IT MUST BE, RIGHT? THIS IS THE SECOND-TO-LAST PAGE, THIS IS WHERE WE GET THE GOOD ENDING--
TIME JUMP ACTIVATED. WARNING. SEVERE PARADOX.
80
AAHH! IT'S THE BAD ENDING! IT'S THE BAD ENDING!
CHEAT, READER! I BEG OF YOU, CHEAT!
OR--GULP-- GO TO 7.
81
"DON'T PRESS THE RED BUTTON," HE SAID. BUT WHAT IF HE WAS LYING?
OR WHAT IF I WAS CHEATING?
GOT TO, AHEM, CHANCE IT--
82
VWWWMMM
AND THERE'S THE GOOD VWWMMM...
RIGHT...?
TIME JUMP ACTIVATED.
83
ACCESSING EMOTIONAL CENTERS--
WAIT, MY EMOTIONAL CENTERS? THAT'S WHAT FLIES THIS THING?
THAT CAN'T BE GOOD.
IT'S NOT. GO TO 84.

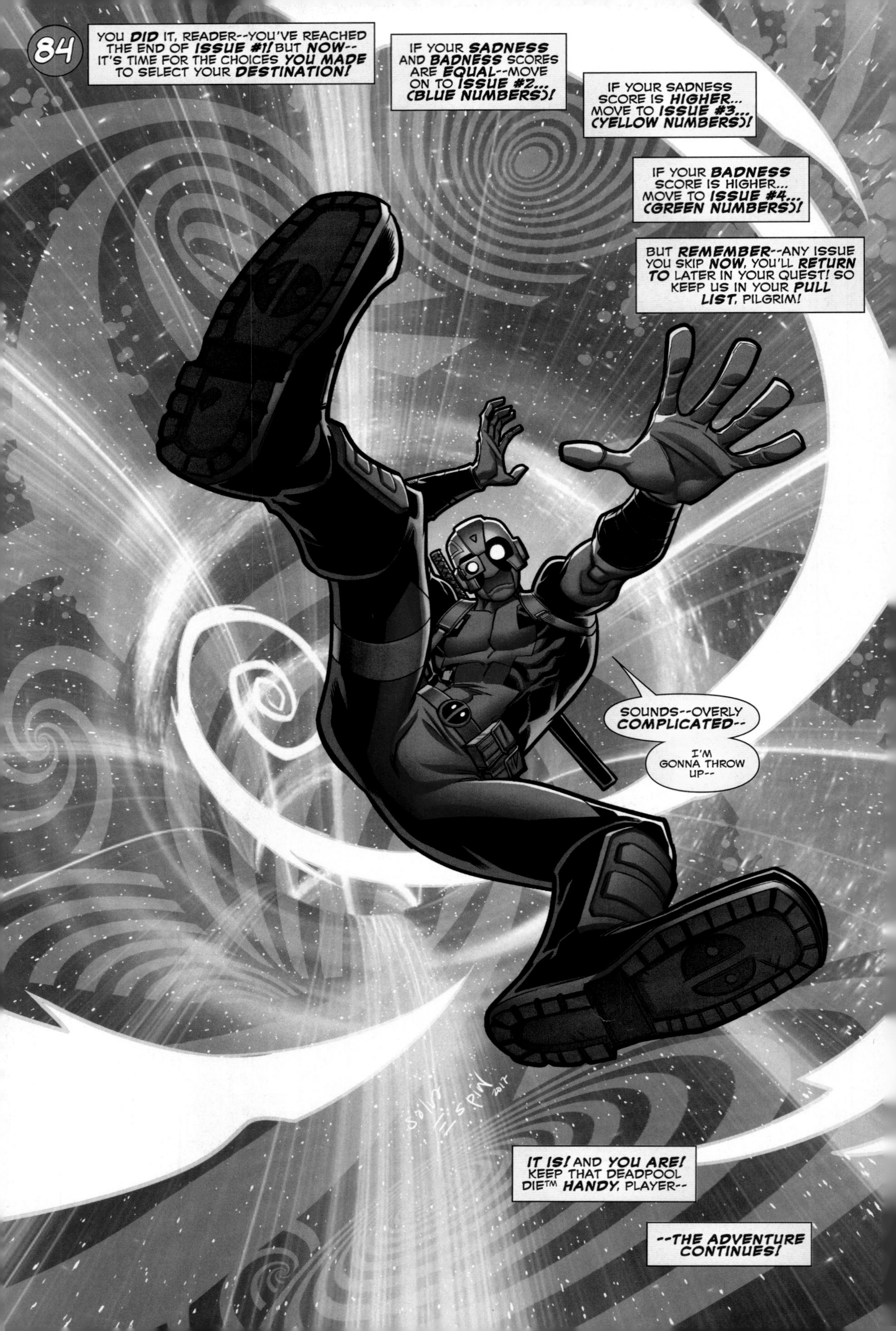
84
YOU DID IT, READER--YOU'VE REACHED THE END OF ISSUE #1! BUT NOW--IT'S TIME FOR THE CHOICES YOU MADE TO SELECT YOUR DESTINATION!
IF YOUR SADNESS AND BADNESS SCORES ARE EQUAL--MOVE ON TO ISSUE #2... (BLUE NUMBERS)!
IF YOUR SADNESS SCORE IS HIGHER... MOVE TO ISSUE #3... (YELLOW NUMBERS)!
IF YOUR BADNESS SCORE IS HIGHER... MOVE TO ISSUE #4... (GREEN NUMBERS)!
BUT REMEMBER--ANY ISSUE YOU SKIP NOW, YOU'LL RETURN TO LATER IN YOUR QUEST! SO KEEP US IN YOUR PULL LIST, PILGRIM!
SOUNDS--OVERLY COMPLICATED--
I'M GONNA THROW UP--
IT IS! AND YOU ARE! KEEP THAT DEADPOOL DIE™ HANDY, PLAYER--
--THE ADVENTURE CONTINUES!

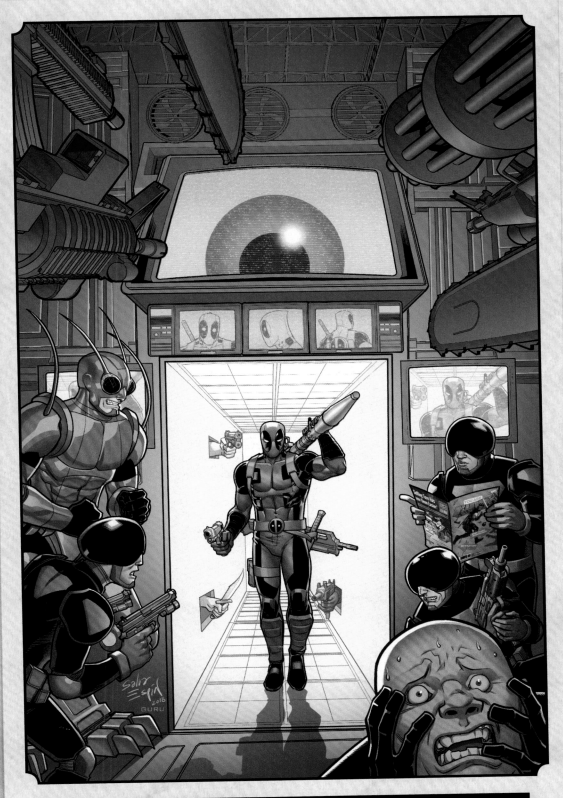

1 VARIANT BY **SALVA ESPIN** & **GURU**-ᴇFX

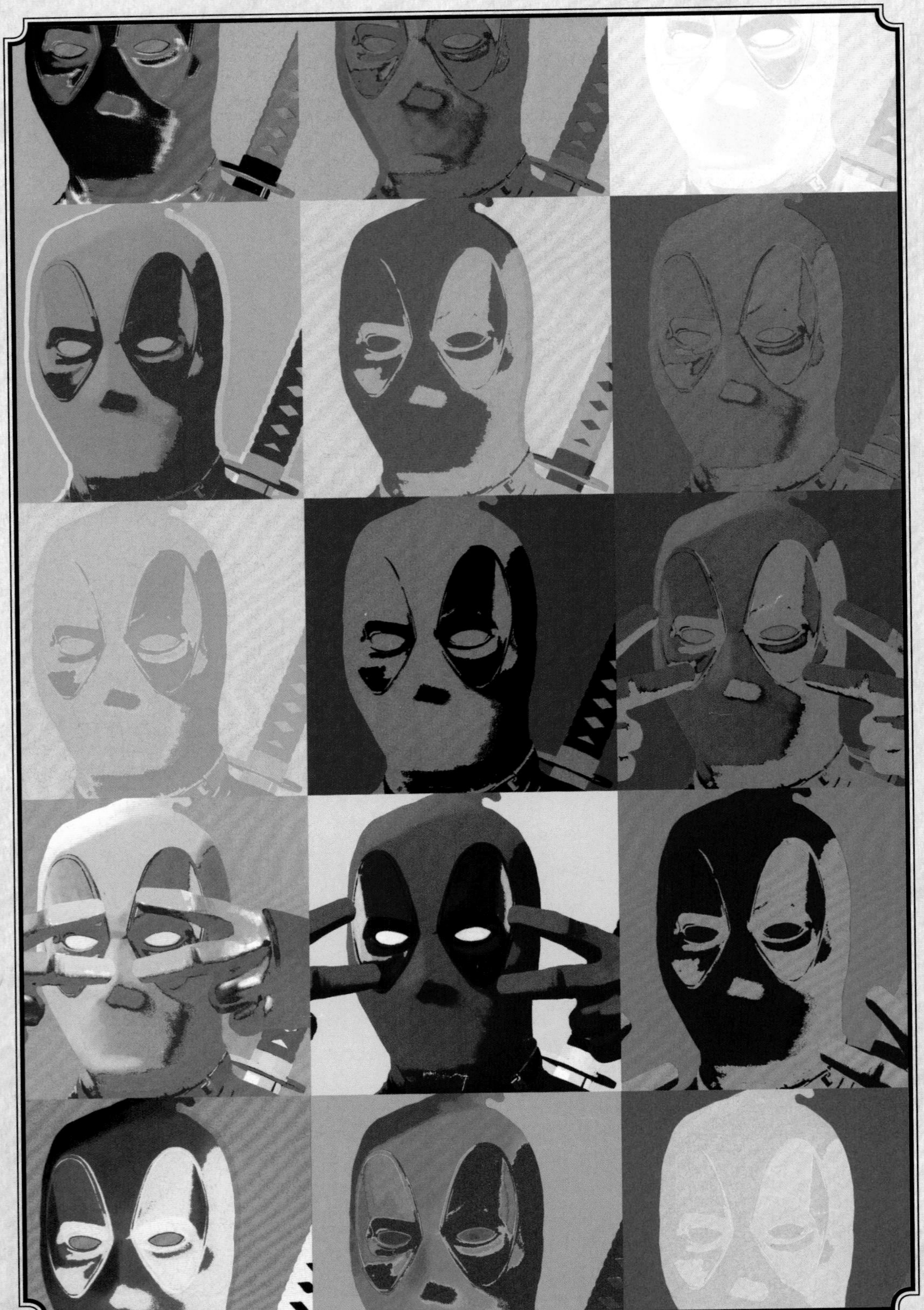

two

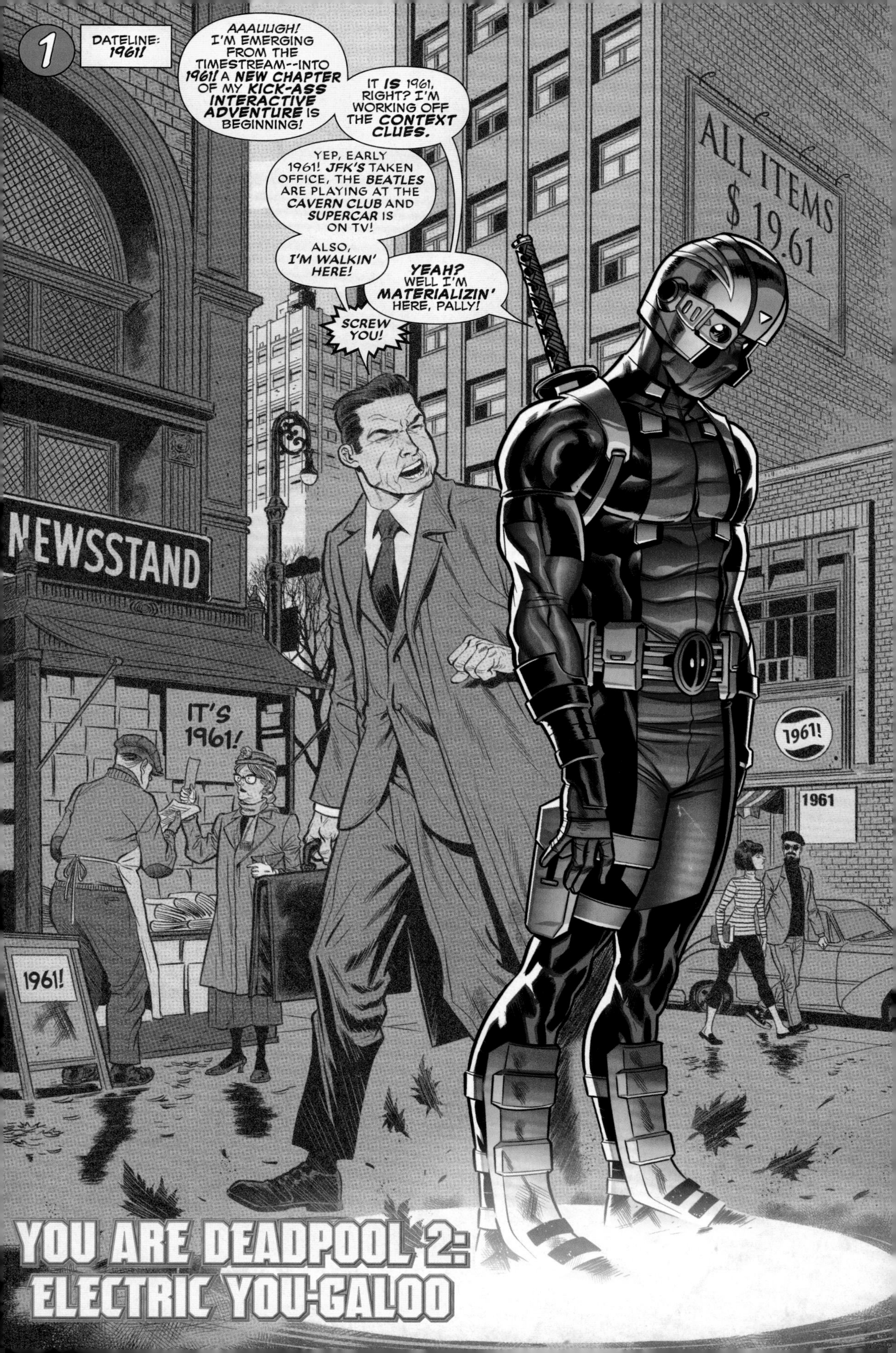
1
DATELINE: 1961!
AAAUUGH! I'M EMERGING FROM THE TIMESTREAM--INTO 1961! A NEW CHAPTER OF MY KICK-ASS INTERACTIVE ADVENTURE IS BEGINNING!
IT IS 1961, RIGHT? I'M WORKING OFF THE CONTEXT CLUES.
YEP, EARLY 1961! JFK'S TAKEN OFFICE, THE BEATLES ARE PLAYING AT THE CAVERN CLUB AND SUPERCAR IS ON TV!
ALSO, I'M WALKIN' HERE!
YEAH? WELL I'M MATERIALIZIN' HERE, PALLY!
SCREW YOU!
ALL ITEMS $ 19.61
NEWSSTAND
IT'S 1961!
1961!
1961
1961!
YOU ARE DEADPOOL 2: ELECTRIC YOU-GALOO

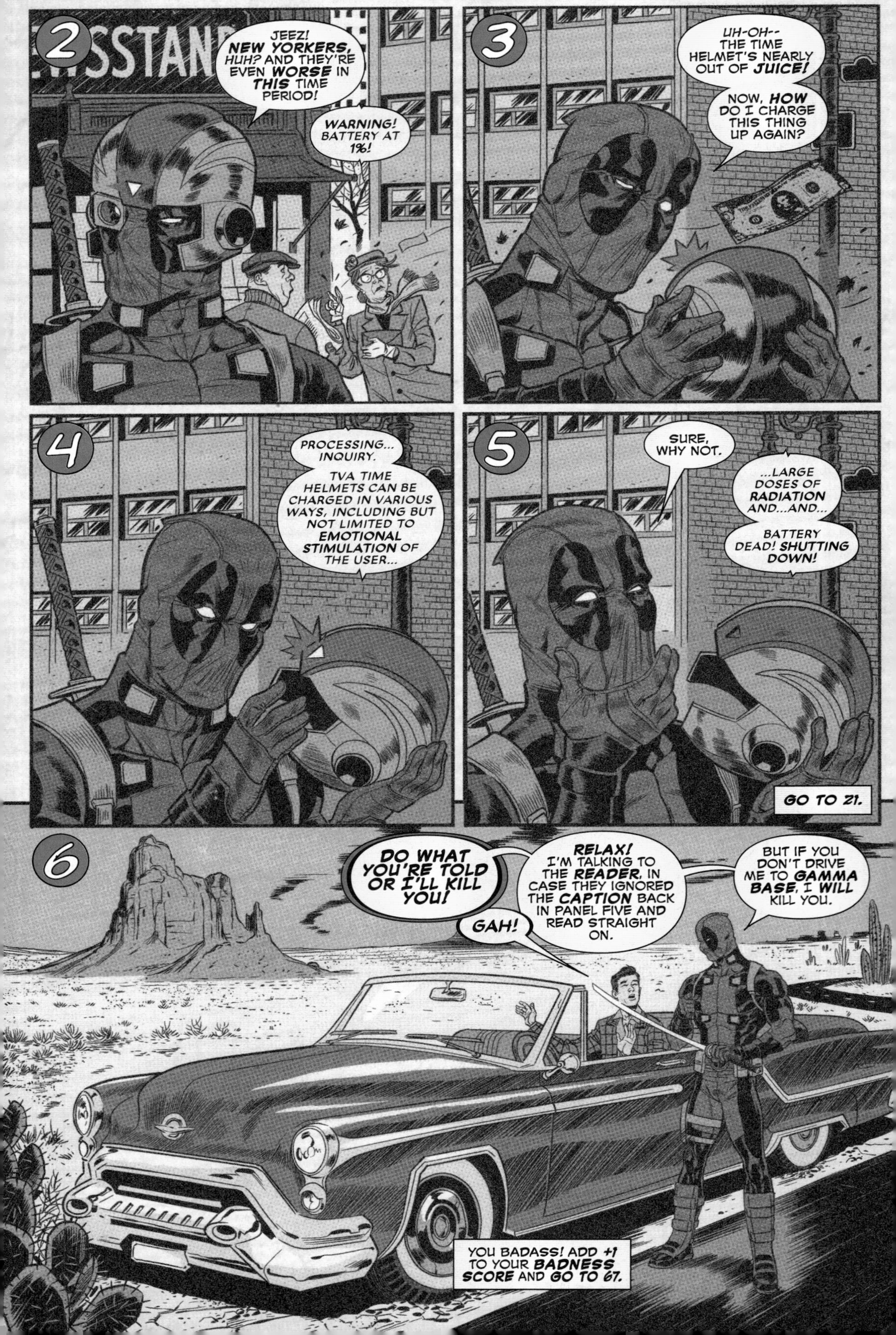
2
SSTAN
JEEZ! NEW YORKERS, HUH? AND THEY'RE EVEN WORSE IN THIS TIME PERIOD!
WARNING! BATTERY AT 1%!
3
UH-OH-- THE TIME HELMET'S NEARLY OUT OF JUICE!
NOW, HOW DO I CHARGE THIS THING UP AGAIN?
4
PROCESSING... INQUIRY.
TVA TIME HELMETS CAN BE CHARGED IN VARIOUS WAYS, INCLUDING BUT NOT LIMITED TO EMOTIONAL STIMULATION OF THE USER...
5
SURE, WHY NOT.
...LARGE DOSES OF RADIATION AND...AND...
BATTERY DEAD! SHUTTING DOWN!
GO TO 21.
6
DO WHAT YOU'RE TOLD OR I'LL KILL YOU!
GAH!
RELAX! I'M TALKING TO THE READER, IN CASE THEY IGNORED THE CAPTION BACK IN PANEL FIVE AND READ STRAIGHT ON.
BUT IF YOU DON'T DRIVE ME TO GAMMA BASE, I WILL KILL YOU.
YOU BADASS! ADD +1 TO YOUR BADNESS SCORE AND GO TO 67.

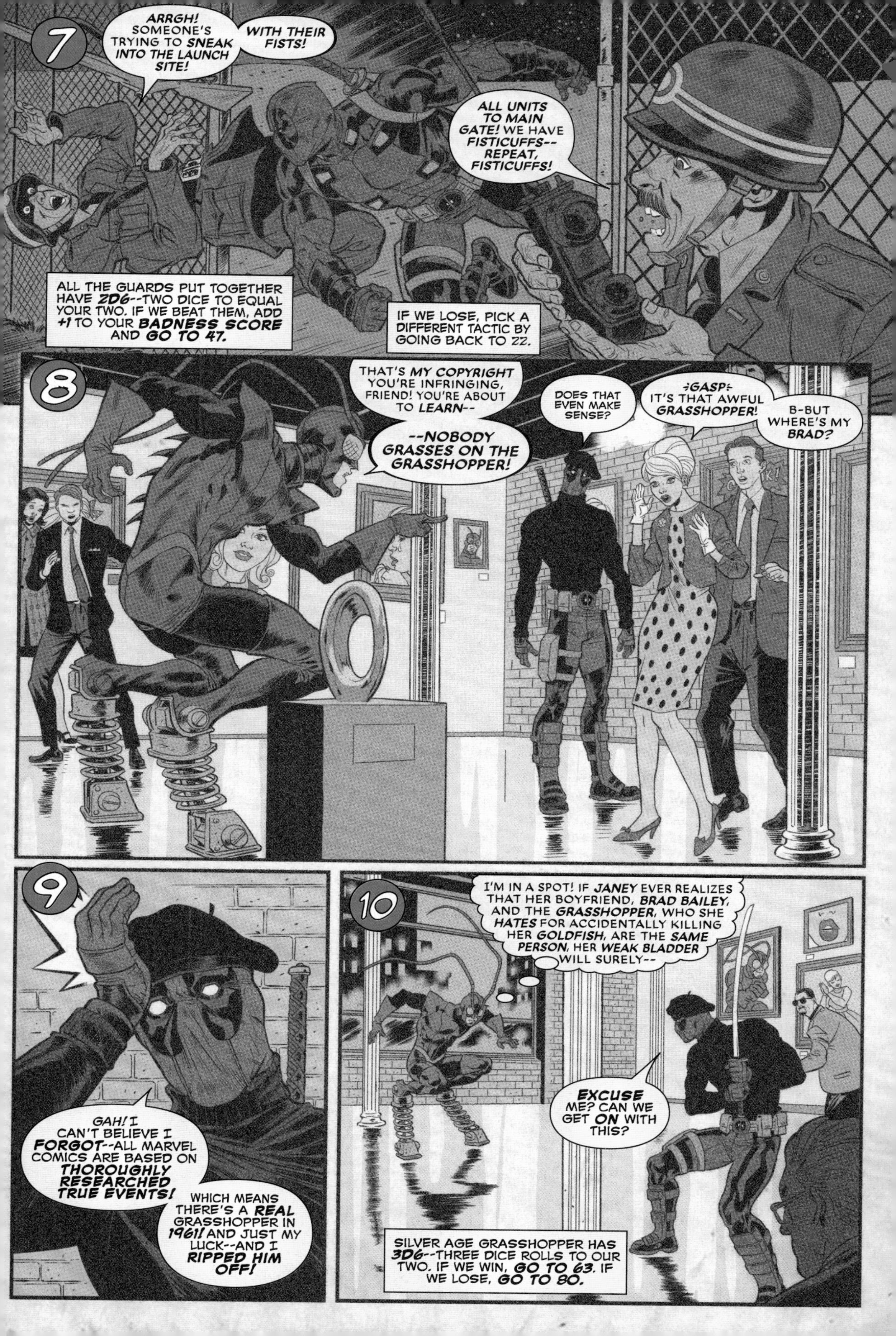
7
ARRGH! SOMEONE'S TRYING TO SNEAK INTO THE LAUNCH SITE!
WITH THEIR FISTS!
ALL UNITS TO MAIN GATE! WE HAVE FISTICUFFS-- REPEAT, FISTICUFFS!
ALL THE GUARDS PUT TOGETHER HAVE 2D6--TWO DICE TO EQUAL YOUR TWO. IF WE BEAT THEM, ADD +1 TO YOUR BADNESS SCORE AND GO TO 47.
IF WE LOSE, PICK A DIFFERENT TACTIC BY GOING BACK TO 22.
8
THAT'S MY COPYRIGHT YOU'RE INFRINGING, FRIEND! YOU'RE ABOUT TO LEARN--
--NOBODY GRASSES ON THE GRASSHOPPER!
DOES THAT EVEN MAKE SENSE?
GASP IT'S THAT AWFUL GRASSHOPPER!
B-BUT WHERE'S MY BRAD?
9
GAH! I CAN'T BELIEVE I FORGOT--ALL MARVEL COMICS ARE BASED ON THOROUGHLY RESEARCHED TRUE EVENTS!
WHICH MEANS THERE'S A REAL GRASSHOPPER IN 1961! AND JUST MY LUCK--AND I RIPPED HIM OFF!
10
I'M IN A SPOT! IF JANEY EVER REALIZES THAT HER BOYFRIEND, BRAD BAILEY, AND THE GRASSHOPPER, WHO SHE HATES FOR ACCIDENTALLY KILLING HER GOLDFISH, ARE THE SAME PERSON, HER WEAK BLADDER WILL SURELY--
EXCUSE ME? CAN WE GET ON WITH THIS?
SILVER AGE GRASSHOPPER HAS 3D6--THREE DICE ROLLS TO OUR TWO. IF WE WIN, GO TO 63. IF WE LOSE, GO TO 80.

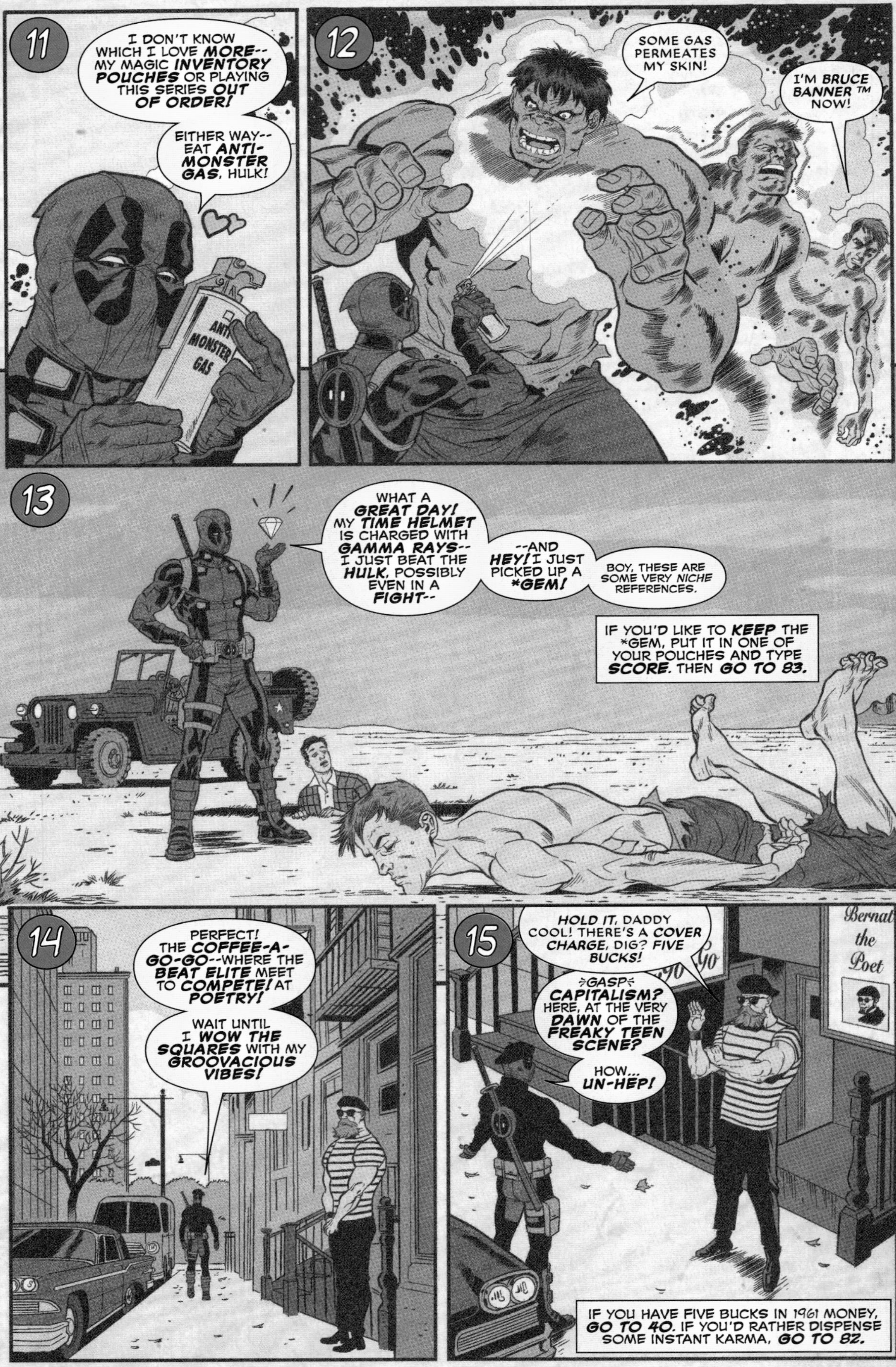
11
I DON'T KNOW WHICH I LOVE MORE-- MY MAGIC INVENTORY POUCHES OR PLAYING THIS SERIES OUT OF ORDER!
EITHER WAY-- EAT ANTI-MONSTER GAS, HULK!
ANTI MONSTER GAS
12
SOME GAS PERMEATES MY SKIN!
I'M BRUCE BANNER ™ NOW!
13
WHAT A GREAT DAY! MY TIME HELMET IS CHARGED WITH GAMMA RAYS-- I JUST BEAT THE HULK, POSSIBLY EVEN IN A FIGHT--
--AND HEY! I JUST PICKED UP A *GEM!
BOY, THESE ARE SOME VERY NICHE REFERENCES.
IF YOU'D LIKE TO KEEP THE *GEM, PUT IT IN ONE OF YOUR POUCHES AND TYPE SCORE. THEN GO TO 83.
14
PERFECT! THE COFFEE-A-GO-GO--WHERE THE BEAT ELITE MEET TO COMPETE! AT POETRY!
WAIT UNTIL I WOW THE SQUARES WITH MY GROOVACIOUS VIBES!
15
HOLD IT, DADDY COOL! THERE'S A COVER CHARGE, DIG? FIVE BUCKS!
GASP CAPITALISM? HERE, AT THE VERY DAWN OF THE FREAKY TEEN SCENE?
HOW... UN-HEP!
Bernat the Poet
IF YOU HAVE FIVE BUCKS IN 1961 MONEY, GO TO 40. IF YOU'D RATHER DISPENSE SOME INSTANT KARMA, GO TO 82.

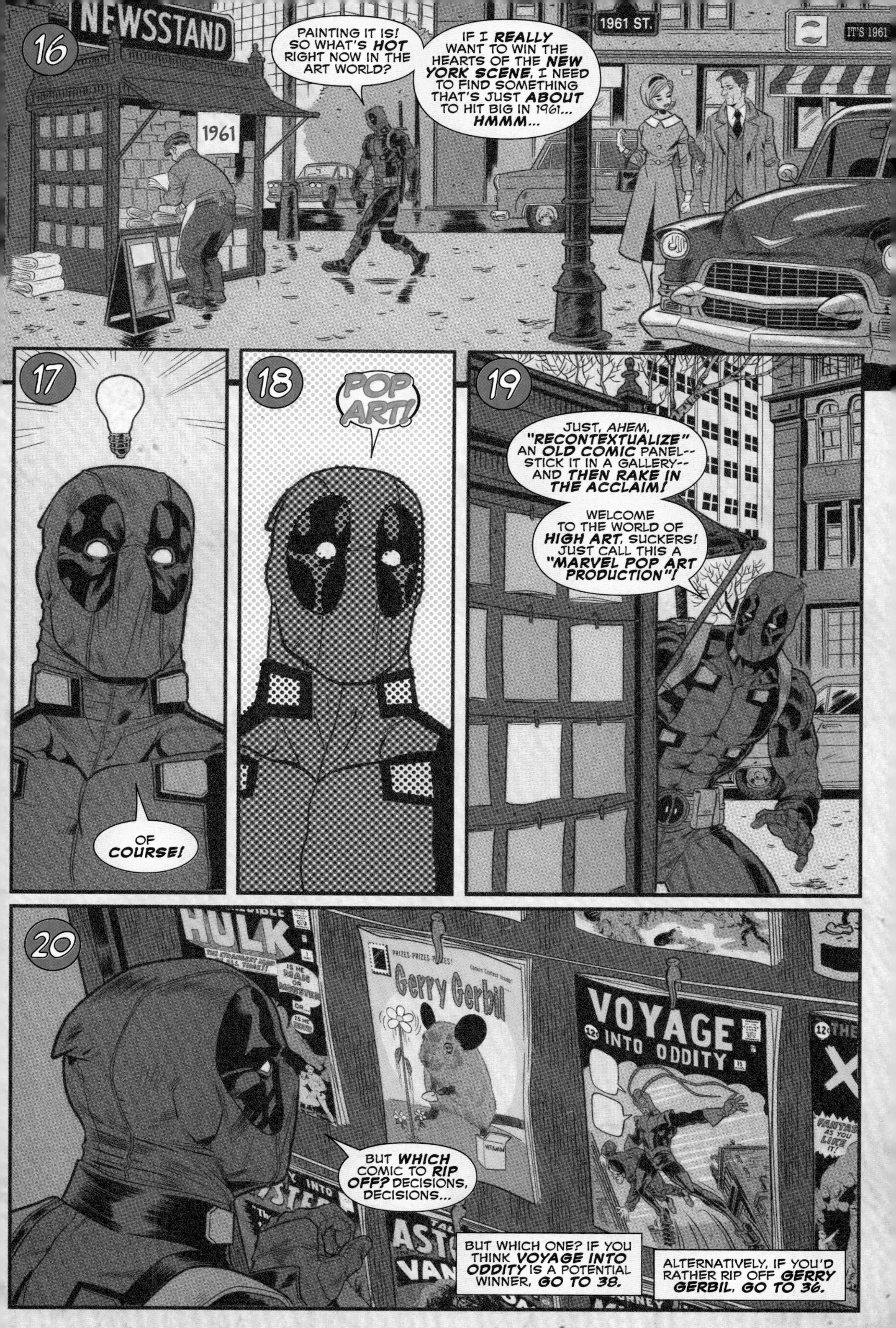
16
NEWSSTAND
1961
1961 ST.
IT'S 1961
PAINTING IT IS! SO WHAT'S HOT RIGHT NOW IN THE ART WORLD?
IF I REALLY WANT TO WIN THE HEARTS OF THE NEW YORK SCENE, I NEED TO FIND SOMETHING THAT'S JUST ABOUT TO HIT BIG IN 1961... HMMM...
17
OF COURSE!
18
POP ART!
19
JUST, AHEM, "RECONTEXTUALIZE" AN OLD COMIC PANEL--STICK IT IN A GALLERY--AND THEN RAKE IN THE ACCLAIM!
WELCOME TO THE WORLD OF HIGH ART, SUCKERS! JUST CALL THIS A "MARVEL POP ART PRODUCTION"!
20
HULK
PRIZES-PRIZES-PRIZES!
Gerry Gerbil
VITAMIN
VOYAGE INTO ODDITY
12¢
BUT WHICH COMIC TO RIP OFF? DECISIONS, DECISIONS...
BUT WHICH ONE? IF YOU THINK VOYAGE INTO ODDITY IS A POTENTIAL WINNER, GO TO 38.
ALTERNATIVELY, IF YOU'D RATHER RIP OFF GERRY GERBIL, GO TO 36.

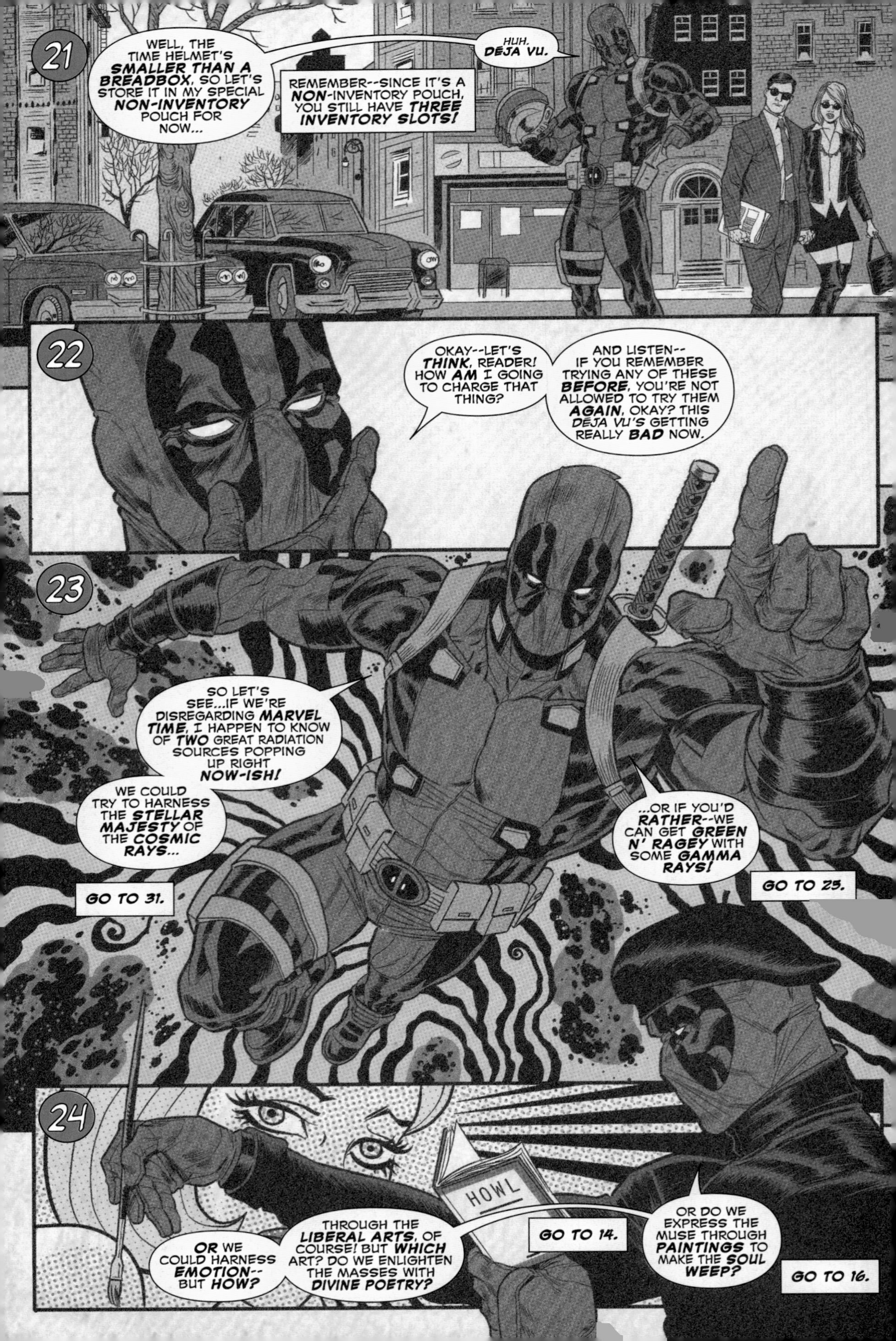
21
WELL, THE TIME HELMET'S SMALLER THAN A BREADBOX, SO LET'S STORE IT IN MY SPECIAL NON-INVENTORY POUCH FOR NOW...
HUH. DEJA VU.
REMEMBER--SINCE IT'S A NON-INVENTORY POUCH, YOU STILL HAVE THREE INVENTORY SLOTS!
22
OKAY--LET'S THINK, READER! HOW AM I GOING TO CHARGE THAT THING?
AND LISTEN-- IF YOU REMEMBER TRYING ANY OF THESE BEFORE, YOU'RE NOT ALLOWED TO TRY THEM AGAIN, OKAY? THIS DEJA VU'S GETTING REALLY BAD NOW.
23
SO LET'S SEE...IF WE'RE DISREGARDING MARVEL TIME, I HAPPEN TO KNOW OF TWO GREAT RADIATION SOURCES POPPING UP RIGHT NOW-ISH!
WE COULD TRY TO HARNESS THE STELLAR MAJESTY OF THE COSMIC RAYS...
GO TO 31.
...OR IF YOU'D RATHER--WE CAN GET GREEN N' RAGEY WITH SOME GAMMA RAYS!
GO TO 25.
24
HOWL
OR WE COULD HARNESS EMOTION-- BUT HOW?
THROUGH THE LIBERAL ARTS, OF COURSE! BUT WHICH ART? DO WE ENLIGHTEN THE MASSES WITH DIVINE POETRY?
GO TO 14.
OR DO WE EXPRESS THE MUSE THROUGH PAINTINGS TO MAKE THE SOUL WEEP?
GO TO 16.

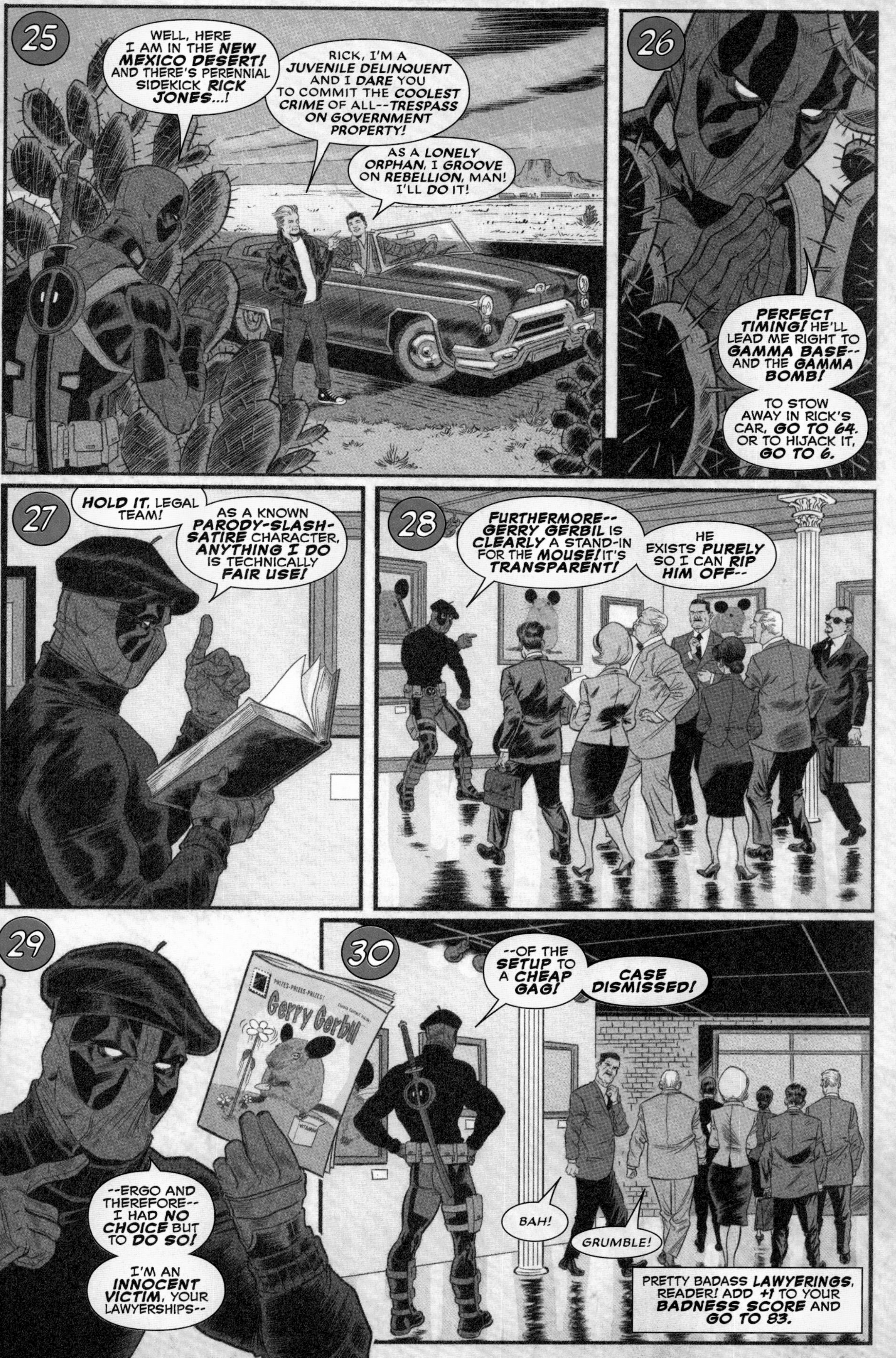
25
WELL, HERE I AM IN THE NEW MEXICO DESERT! AND THERE'S PERENNIAL SIDEKICK RICK JONES...!
RICK, I'M A JUVENILE DELINQUENT AND I DARE YOU TO COMMIT THE COOLEST CRIME OF ALL--TRESPASS ON GOVERNMENT PROPERTY!
AS A LONELY ORPHAN, I GROOVE ON REBELLION, MAN! I'LL DO IT!
26
PERFECT TIMING! HE'LL LEAD ME RIGHT TO GAMMA BASE-- AND THE GAMMA BOMB!
TO STOW AWAY IN RICK'S CAR, GO TO 64. OR TO HIJACK IT, GO TO 6.
27
HOLD IT, LEGAL TEAM!
AS A KNOWN PARODY-SLASH-SATIRE CHARACTER, ANYTHING I DO IS TECHNICALLY FAIR USE!
28
FURTHERMORE-- GERRY GERBIL IS CLEARLY A STAND-IN FOR THE MOUSE! IT'S TRANSPARENT!
HE EXISTS PURELY SO I CAN RIP HIM OFF--
29
Gerry Gerbil
--ERGO AND THEREFORE-- I HAD NO CHOICE BUT TO DO SO!
I'M AN INNOCENT VICTIM, YOUR LAWYERSHIPS--
30
--OF THE SETUP TO A CHEAP GAG!
CASE DISMISSED!
BAH!
GRUMBLE!
PRETTY BADASS LAWYERINGS, READER! ADD +1 TO YOUR BADNESS SCORE AND GO TO 83.

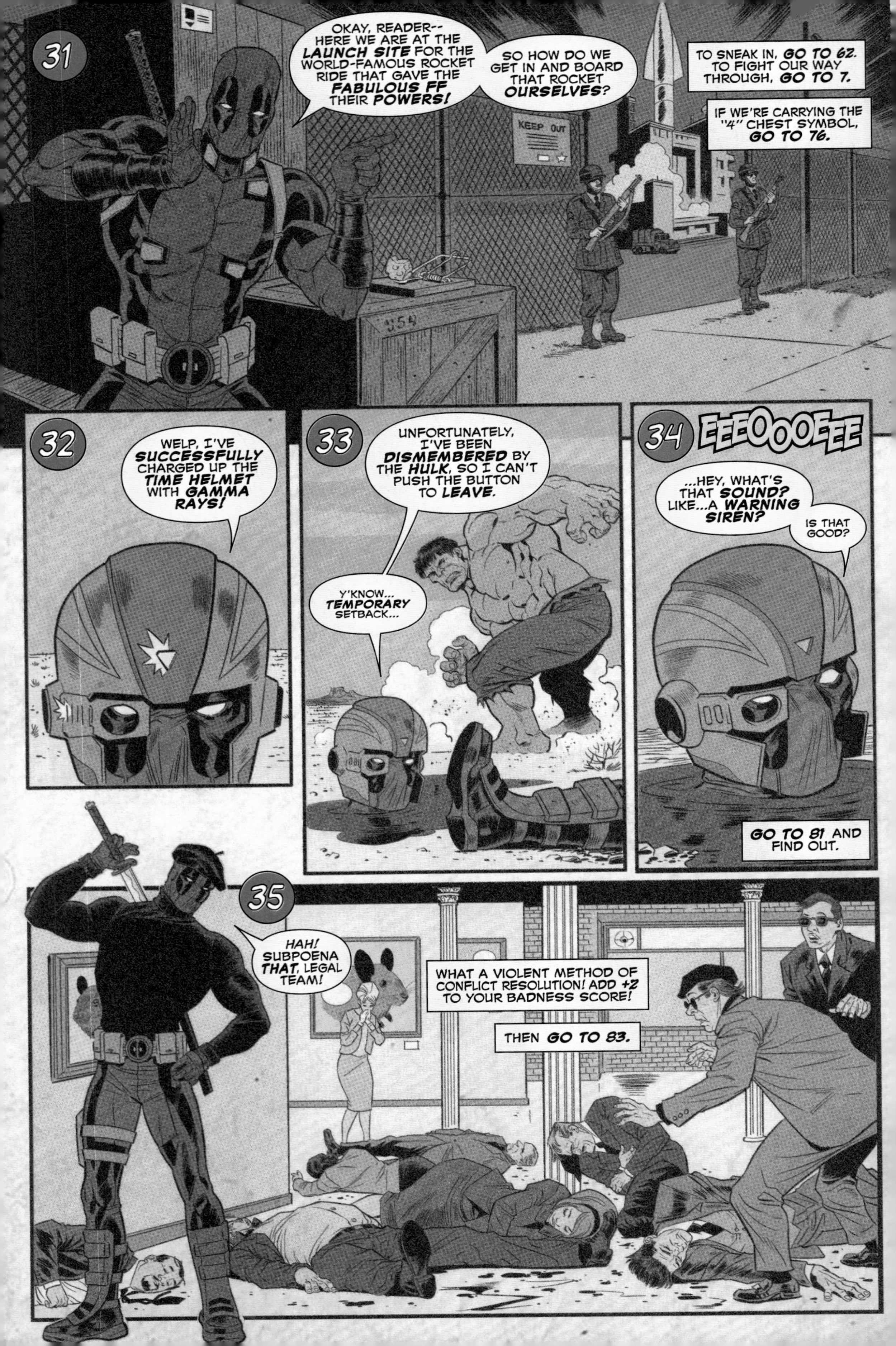
31
OKAY, READER-- HERE WE ARE AT THE LAUNCH SITE FOR THE WORLD-FAMOUS ROCKET RIDE THAT GAVE THE FABULOUS FF THEIR POWERS!
SO HOW DO WE GET IN AND BOARD THAT ROCKET OURSELVES?
TO SNEAK IN, GO TO 62. TO FIGHT OUR WAY THROUGH, GO TO 7.
IF WE'RE CARRYING THE "4" CHEST SYMBOL, GO TO 76.
KEEP OUT
354
32
WELP, I'VE SUCCESSFULLY CHARGED UP THE TIME HELMET WITH GAMMA RAYS!
33
UNFORTUNATELY, I'VE BEEN DISMEMBERED BY THE HULK, SO I CAN'T PUSH THE BUTTON TO LEAVE.
Y'KNOW... TEMPORARY SETBACK...
34
EEEOOOOEEE
...HEY, WHAT'S THAT SOUND? LIKE...A WARNING SIREN?
IS THAT GOOD?
GO TO 81 AND FIND OUT.
35
HAH! SUBPOENA THAT, LEGAL TEAM!
WHAT A VIOLENT METHOD OF CONFLICT RESOLUTION! ADD +2 TO YOUR BADNESS SCORE!
THEN GO TO 83.

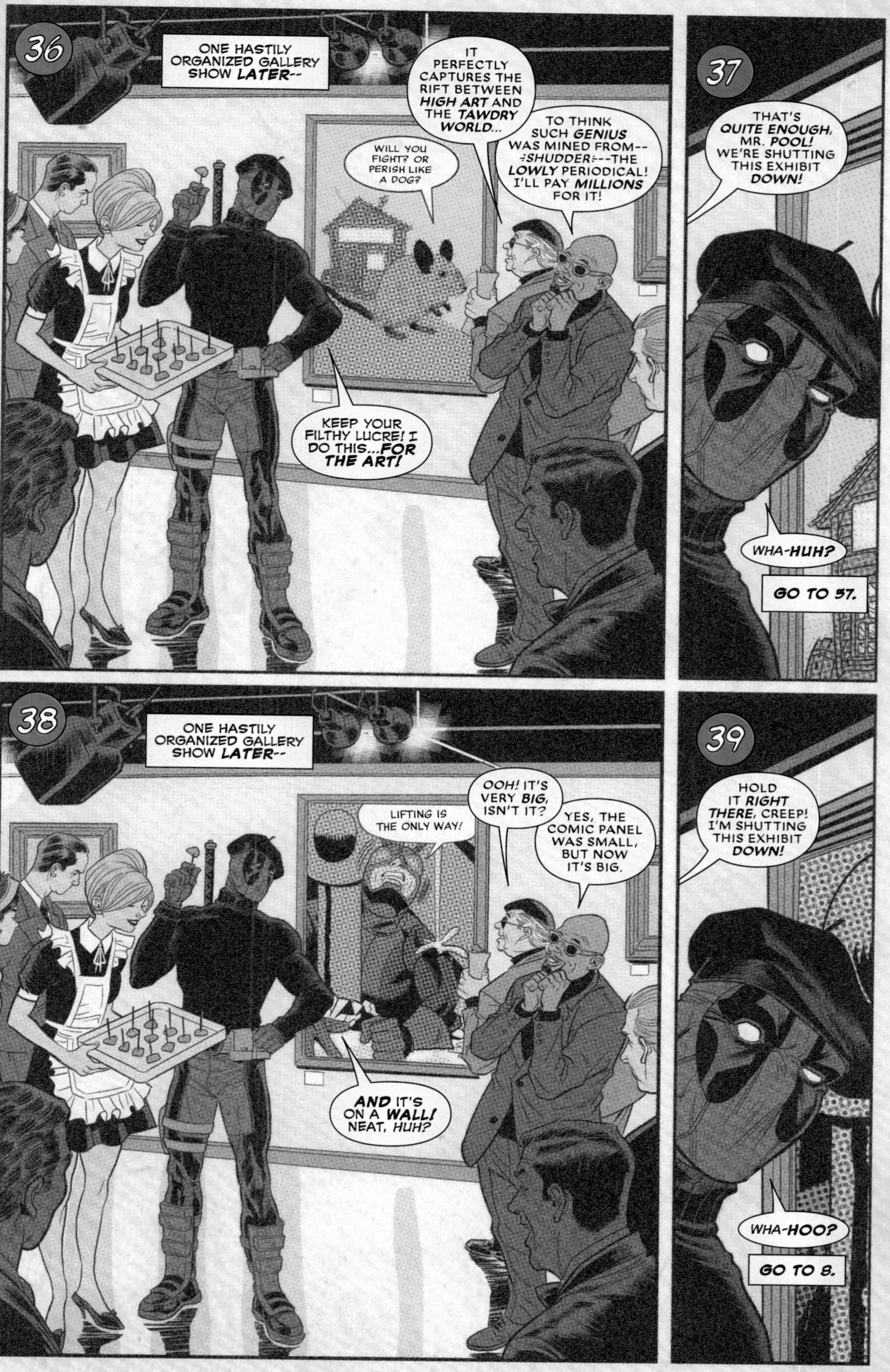
36
ONE HASTILY ORGANIZED GALLERY SHOW LATER--
IT PERFECTLY CAPTURES THE RIFT BETWEEN HIGH ART AND THE TAWDRY WORLD...
TO THINK SUCH GENIUS WAS MINED FROM-- ÷SHUDDER÷ --THE LOWLY PERIODICAL! I'LL PAY MILLIONS FOR IT!
WILL YOU FIGHT? OR PERISH LIKE A DOG?
KEEP YOUR FILTHY LUCRE! I DO THIS...FOR THE ART!
37
THAT'S QUITE ENOUGH, MR. POOL! WE'RE SHUTTING THIS EXHIBIT DOWN!
WHA-HUH?
GO TO 57.
38
ONE HASTILY ORGANIZED GALLERY SHOW LATER--
OOH! IT'S VERY BIG, ISN'T IT?
YES, THE COMIC PANEL WAS SMALL, BUT NOW IT'S BIG.
LIFTING IS THE ONLY WAY!
AND IT'S ON A WALL! NEAT, HUH?
39
HOLD IT RIGHT THERE, CREEP! I'M SHUTTING THIS EXHIBIT DOWN!
WHA-HOO?
GO TO 8.

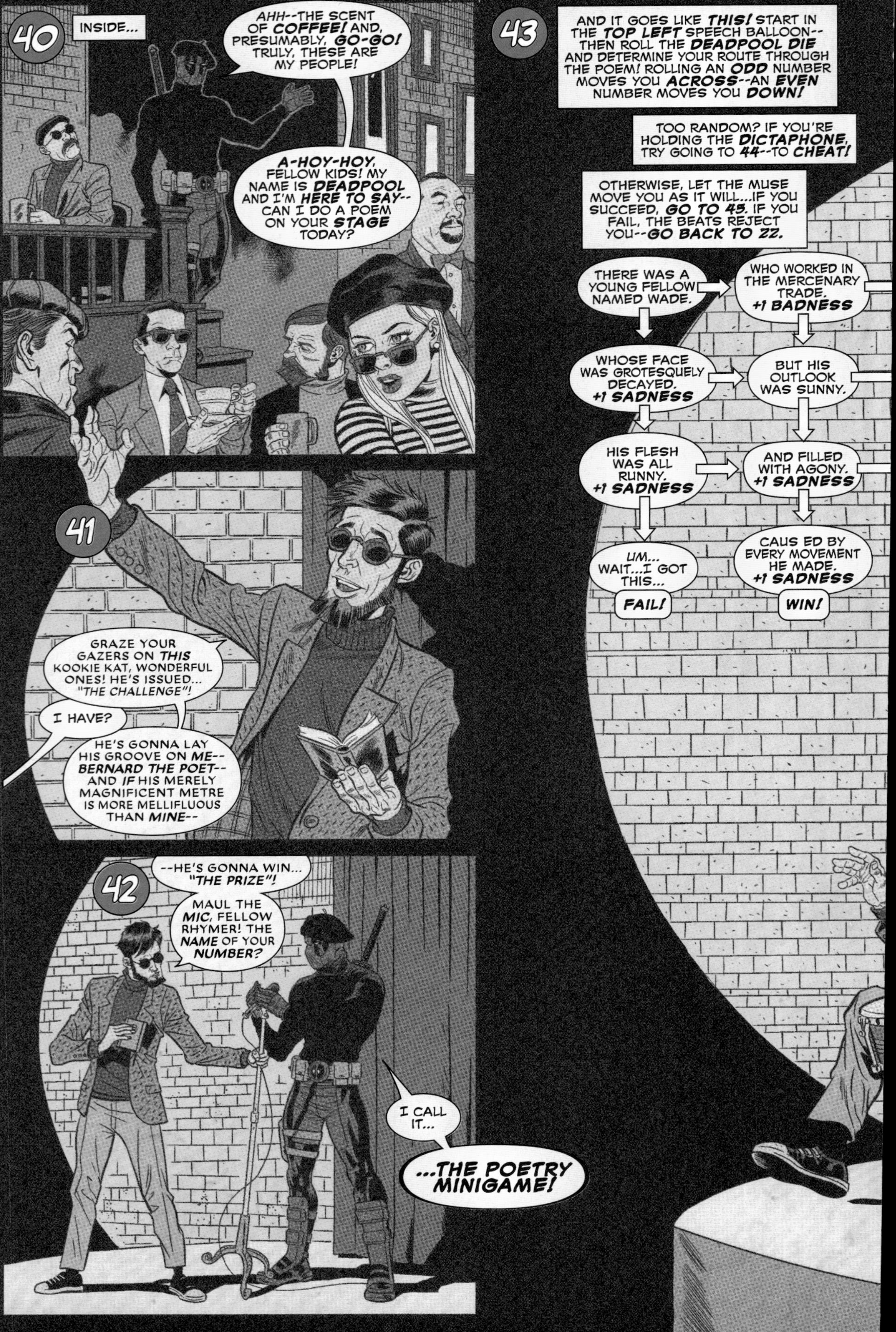
40
INSIDE...
AHH--THE SCENT OF COFFEE! AND, PRESUMABLY, GO-GO! TRULY, THESE ARE MY PEOPLE!
A-HOY-HOY, FELLOW KIDS! MY NAME IS DEADPOOL AND I'M HERE TO SAY-- CAN I DO A POEM ON YOUR STAGE TODAY?
41
GRAZE YOUR GAZERS ON THIS KOOKIE KAT, WONDERFUL ONES! HE'S ISSUED... "THE CHALLENGE"!
I HAVE?
HE'S GONNA LAY HIS GROOVE ON ME-- BERNARD THE POET-- AND IF HIS MERELY MAGNIFICENT METRE IS MORE MELLIFLUOUS THAN MINE--
42
--HE'S GONNA WIN... "THE PRIZE"!
MAUL THE MIC, FELLOW RHYMER! THE NAME OF YOUR NUMBER?
I CALL IT...
...THE POETRY MINIGAME!
43
AND IT GOES LIKE THIS! START IN THE TOP LEFT SPEECH BALLOON-- THEN ROLL THE DEADPOOL DIE AND DETERMINE YOUR ROUTE THROUGH THE POEM! ROLLING AN ODD NUMBER MOVES YOU ACROSS--AN EVEN NUMBER MOVES YOU DOWN!
TOO RANDOM? IF YOU'RE HOLDING THE DICTAPHONE, TRY GOING TO 44--TO CHEAT!
OTHERWISE, LET THE MUSE MOVE YOU AS IT WILL...IF YOU SUCCEED, GO TO 45. IF YOU FAIL, THE BEATS REJECT YOU--GO BACK TO 22.
THERE WAS A YOUNG FELLOW NAMED WADE.
WHO WORKED IN THE MERCENARY TRADE. +1 BADNESS
WHOSE FACE WAS GROTESQUELY DECAYED. +1 SADNESS
BUT HIS OUTLOOK WAS SUNNY.
HIS FLESH WAS ALL RUNNY. +1 SADNESS
AND FILLED WITH AGONY. +1 SADNESS
UM... WAIT...I GOT THIS...
FAIL!
CAUS ED BY EVERY MOVEMENT HE MADE. +1 SADNESS
WIN!

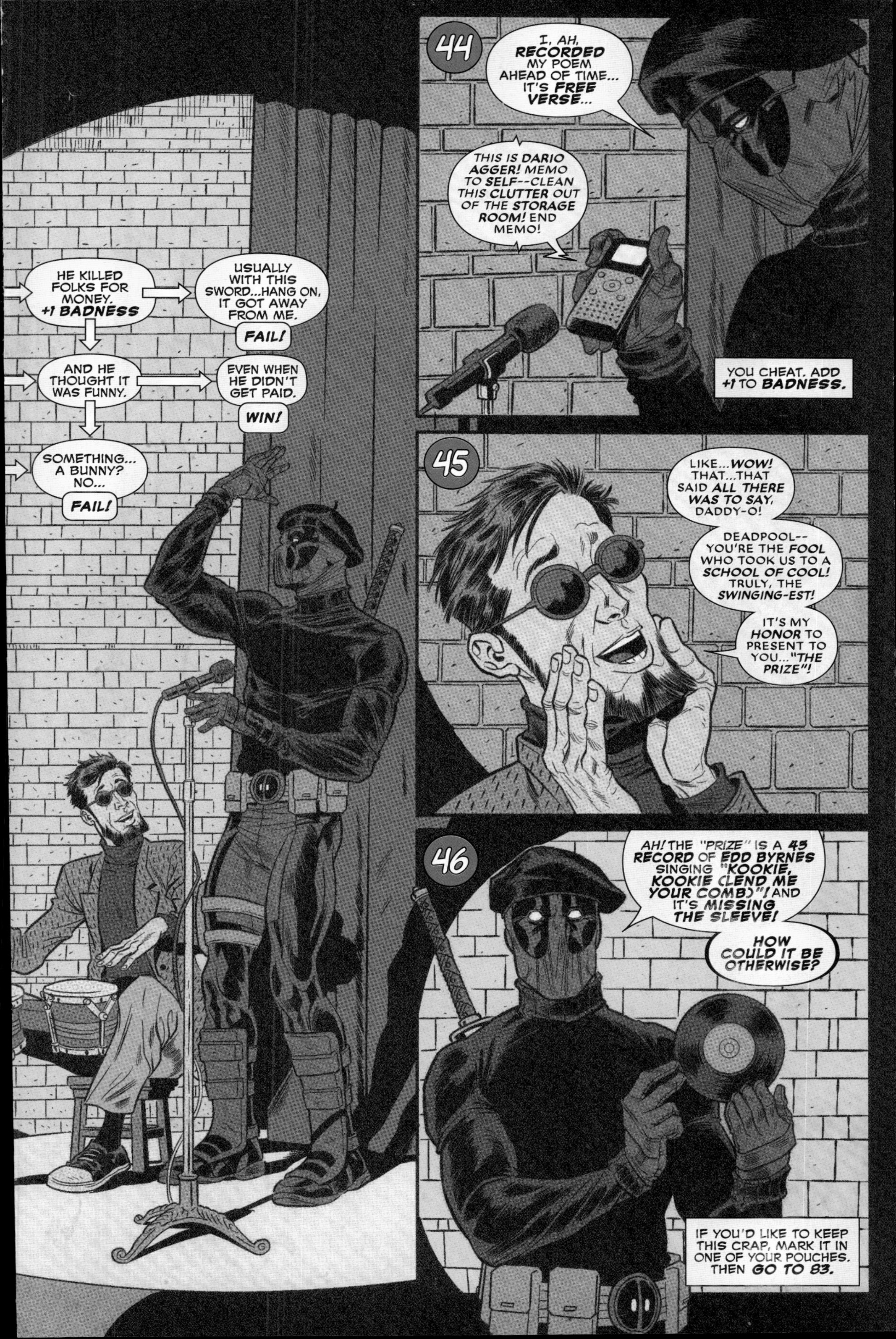

HE KILLED FOLKS FOR MONEY. +1 BADNESS
USUALLY WITH THIS SWORD...HANG ON, IT GOT AWAY FROM ME.
FAIL!
AND HE THOUGHT IT WAS FUNNY.
EVEN WHEN HE DIDN'T GET PAID.
WIN!
SOMETHING... A BUNNY? NO...
FAIL!
44
I, AH, RECORDED MY POEM AHEAD OF TIME... IT'S FREE VERSE...
THIS IS DARIO AGGER! MEMO TO SELF--CLEAN THIS CLUTTER OUT OF THE STORAGE ROOM! END MEMO!
YOU CHEAT. ADD +1 TO BADNESS.
45
LIKE...WOW! THAT...THAT SAID ALL THERE WAS TO SAY, DADDY-O!
DEADPOOL-- YOU'RE THE FOOL WHO TOOK US TO A SCHOOL OF COOL! TRULY, THE SWINGING-EST!
IT'S MY HONOR TO PRESENT TO YOU..."THE PRIZE"!
46
AH! THE "PRIZE" IS A 45 RECORD OF EDD BYRNES SINGING "KOOKIE, KOOKIE (LEND ME YOUR COMB)"! AND IT'S MISSING THE SLEEVE!
HOW COULD IT BE OTHERWISE?
IF YOU'D LIKE TO KEEP THIS CRAP, MARK IT IN ONE OF YOUR POUCHES. THEN GO TO 83.

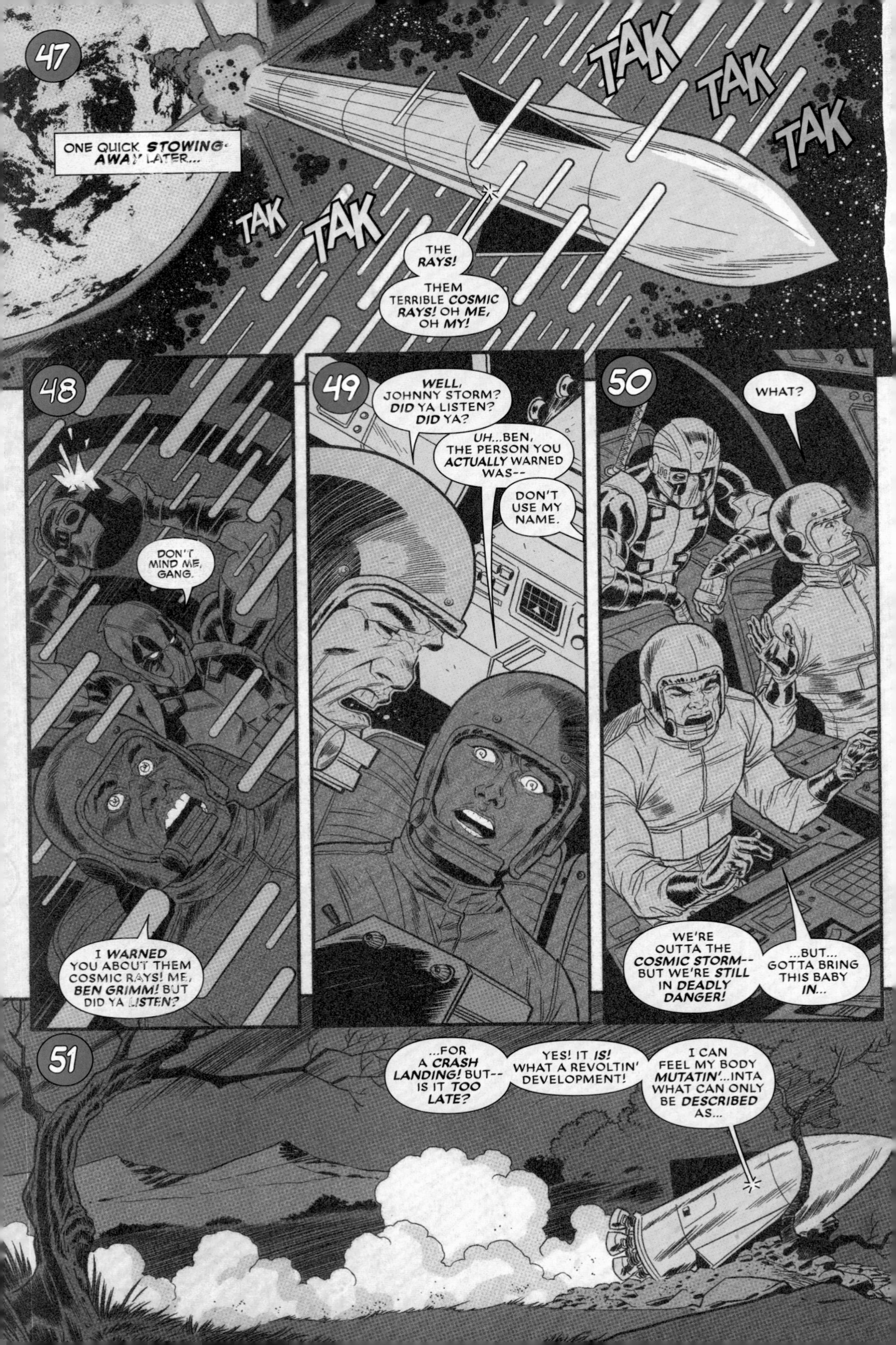
47
ONE QUICK STOWING-AWAY LATER...
TAK
TAK
TAK
TAK
TAK
THE RAYS!
THEM TERRIBLE COSMIC RAYS! OH ME, OH MY!
48
DON'T MIND ME, GANG.
I WARNED YOU ABOUT THEM COSMIC RAYS! ME, BEN GRIMM! BUT DID YA LISTEN?
49
WELL, JOHNNY STORM? DID YA LISTEN? DID YA?
UH...BEN, THE PERSON YOU ACTUALLY WARNED WAS--
DON'T USE MY NAME.
50
WHAT?
WE'RE OUTTA THE COSMIC STORM-- BUT WE'RE STILL IN DEADLY DANGER!
...BUT... GOTTA BRING THIS BABY IN...
51
...FOR A CRASH LANDING! BUT-- IS IT TOO LATE?
YES! IT IS! WHAT A REVOLTIN' DEVELOPMENT!
I CAN FEEL MY BODY MUTATIN'...INTA WHAT CAN ONLY BE DESCRIBED AS...

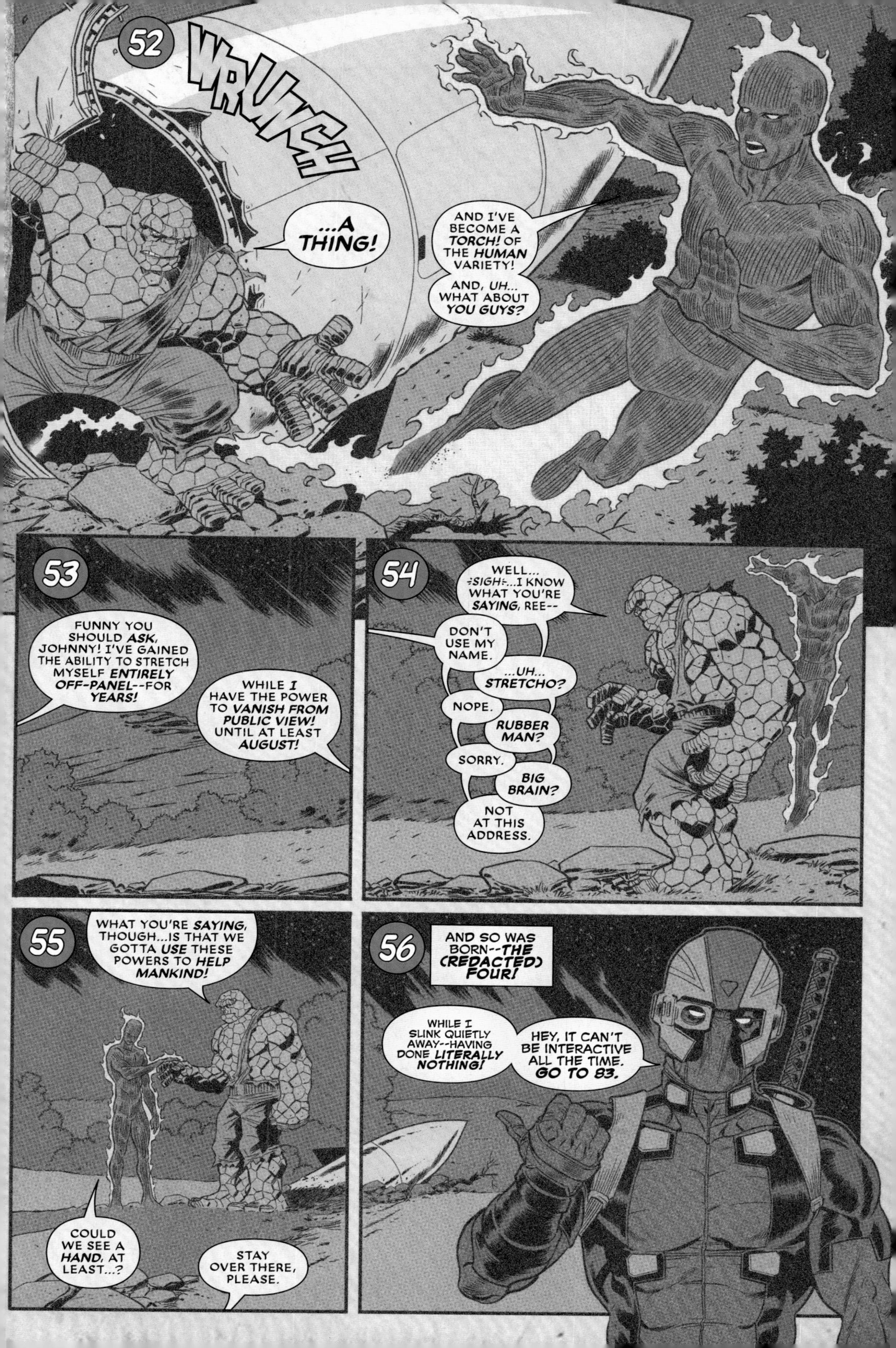
52
WRUNCH
...A THING!
AND I'VE BECOME A TORCH! OF THE HUMAN VARIETY!
AND, UH... WHAT ABOUT YOU GUYS?
53
FUNNY YOU SHOULD ASK, JOHNNY! I'VE GAINED THE ABILITY TO STRETCH MYSELF ENTIRELY OFF-PANEL--FOR YEARS!
WHILE I HAVE THE POWER TO VANISH FROM PUBLIC VIEW! UNTIL AT LEAST AUGUST!
54
WELL... ÷SIGH÷...I KNOW WHAT YOU'RE SAYING, REE--
DON'T USE MY NAME.
...UH... STRETCHO?
NOPE.
RUBBER MAN?
SORRY.
BIG BRAIN?
NOT AT THIS ADDRESS.
55
WHAT YOU'RE SAYING, THOUGH...IS THAT WE GOTTA USE THESE POWERS TO HELP MANKIND!
COULD WE SEE A HAND, AT LEAST...?
STAY OVER THERE, PLEASE.
56
AND SO WAS BORN--THE (REDACTED) FOUR!
WHILE I SLINK QUIETLY AWAY--HAVING DONE LITERALLY NOTHING!
HEY, IT CAN'T BE INTERACTIVE ALL THE TIME. GO TO 83.

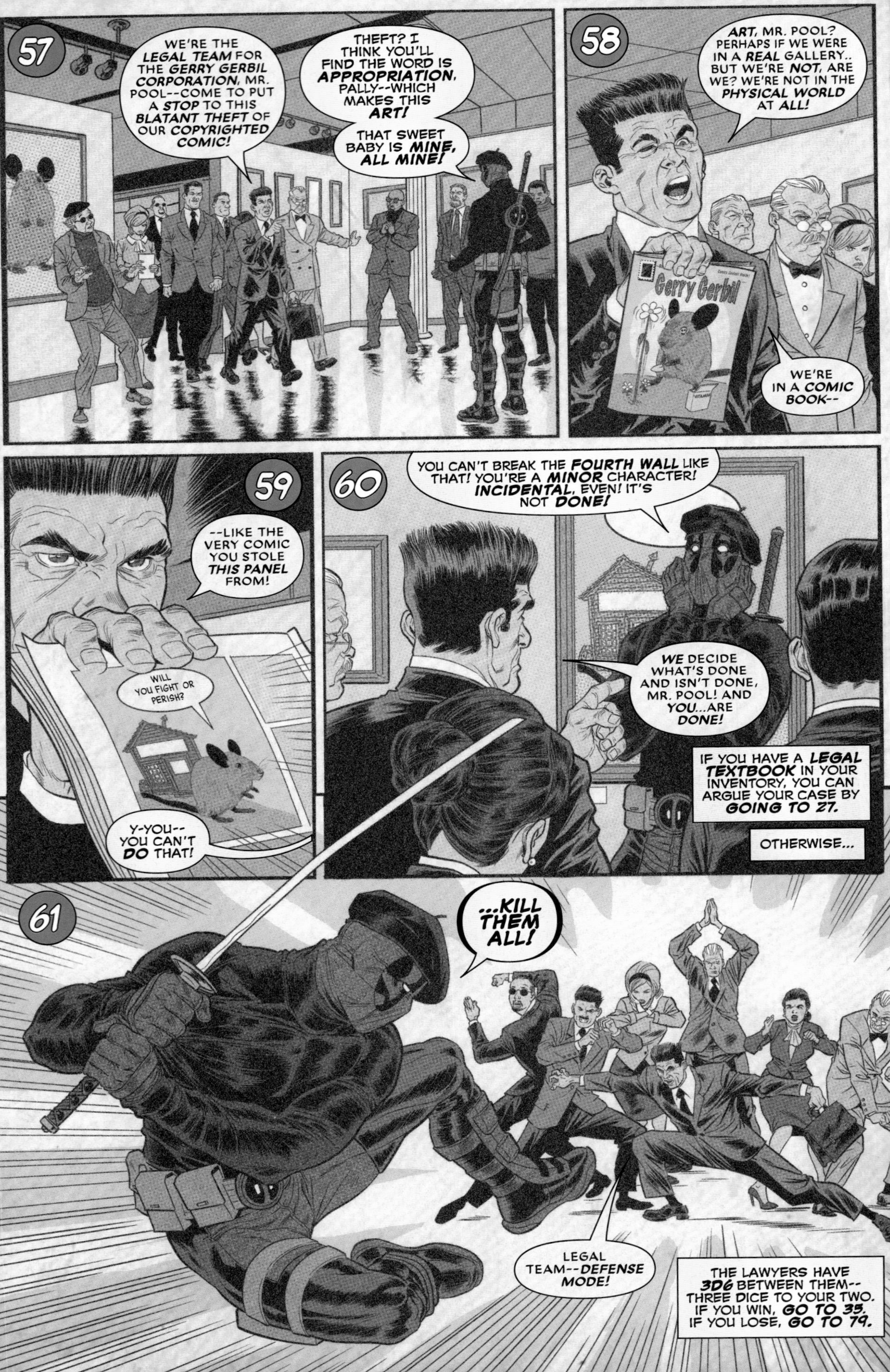
57
WE'RE THE LEGAL TEAM FOR THE GERRY GERBIL CORPORATION, MR. POOL--COME TO PUT A STOP TO THIS BLATANT THEFT OF OUR COPYRIGHTED COMIC!
THEFT? I THINK YOU'LL FIND THE WORD IS APPROPRIATION, PALLY--WHICH MAKES THIS ART!
THAT SWEET BABY IS MINE, ALL MINE!
58
ART, MR. POOL? PERHAPS IF WE WERE IN A REAL GALLERY.. BUT WE'RE NOT, ARE WE? WE'RE NOT IN THE PHYSICAL WORLD AT ALL!
Gerry Gerbil
WE'RE IN A COMIC BOOK--
59
--LIKE THE VERY COMIC YOU STOLE THIS PANEL FROM!
WILL YOU FIGHT OR PERISH?
Y-YOU-- YOU CAN'T DO THAT!
60
YOU CAN'T BREAK THE FOURTH WALL LIKE THAT! YOU'RE A MINOR CHARACTER! INCIDENTAL, EVEN! IT'S NOT DONE!
WE DECIDE WHAT'S DONE AND ISN'T DONE, MR. POOL! AND YOU...ARE DONE!
IF YOU HAVE A LEGAL TEXTBOOK IN YOUR INVENTORY, YOU CAN ARGUE YOUR CASE BY GOING TO 27.
OTHERWISE...
61
...KILL THEM ALL!
LEGAL TEAM--DEFENSE MODE!
THE LAWYERS HAVE 3D6 BETWEEN THEM-- THREE DICE TO YOUR TWO. IF YOU WIN, GO TO 35. IF YOU LOSE, GO TO 79.

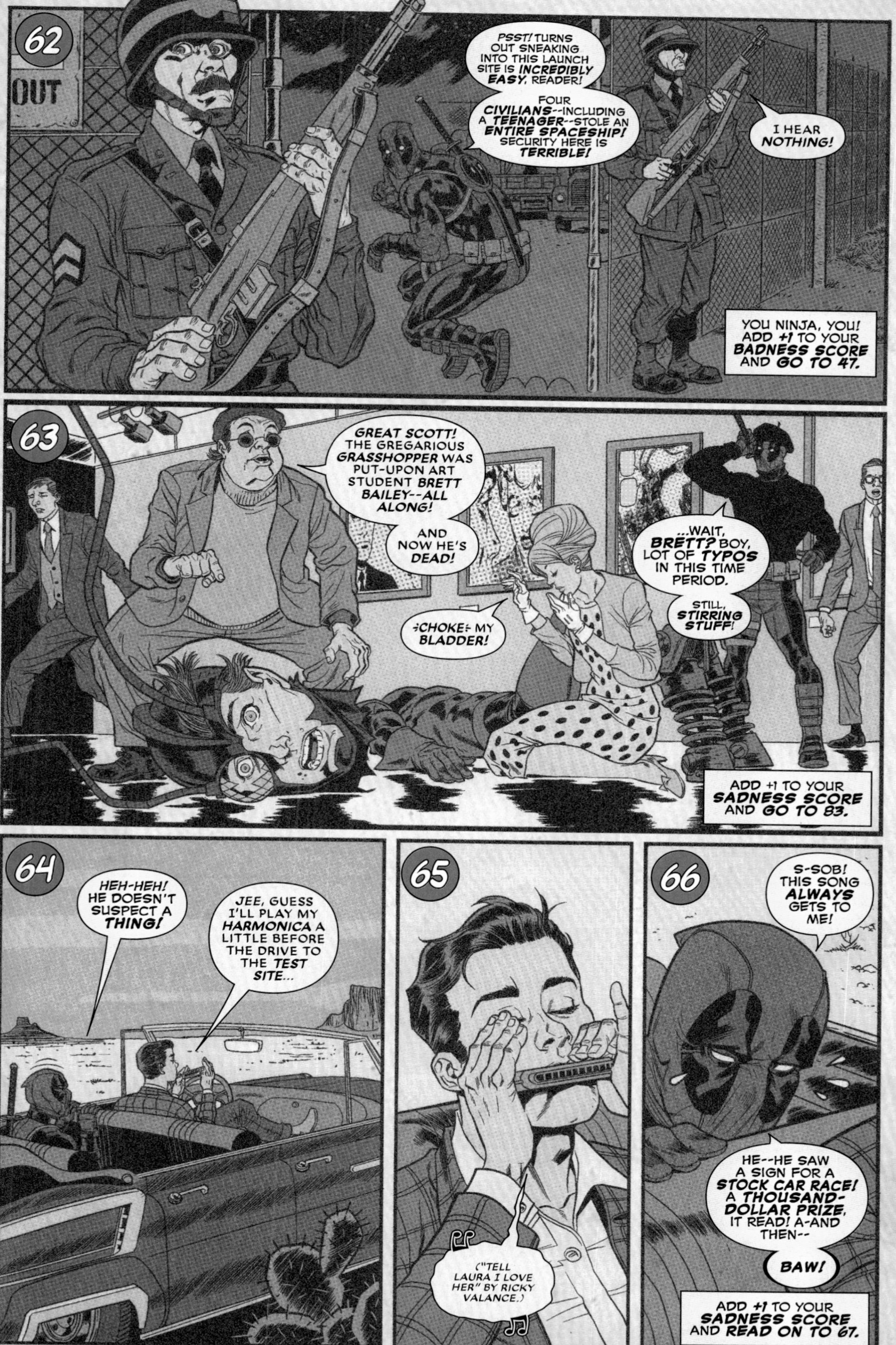
62
OUT
PSST! TURNS OUT SNEAKING INTO THIS LAUNCH SITE IS INCREDIBLY EASY, READER!
FOUR CIVILIANS--INCLUDING A TEENAGER--STOLE AN ENTIRE SPACESHIP! SECURITY HERE IS TERRIBLE!
I HEAR NOTHING!
YOU NINJA, YOU! ADD +1 TO YOUR BADNESS SCORE AND GO TO 47.
63
GREAT SCOTT! THE GREGARIOUS GRASSHOPPER WAS PUT-UPON ART STUDENT BRETT BAILEY--ALL ALONG!
AND NOW HE'S DEAD!
-CHOKE- MY BLADDER!
...WAIT, BRETT? BOY, LOT OF TYPOS IN THIS TIME PERIOD.
STILL, STIRRING STUFF!
ADD +1 TO YOUR SADNESS SCORE AND GO TO 83.
64
HEH-HEH! HE DOESN'T SUSPECT A THING!
JEE, GUESS I'LL PLAY MY HARMONICA A LITTLE BEFORE THE DRIVE TO THE TEST SITE...
65
("TELL LAURA I LOVE HER" BY RICKY VALANCE.)
66
S-SOB! THIS SONG ALWAYS GETS TO ME!
HE--HE SAW A SIGN FOR A STOCK CAR RACE! A THOUSAND-DOLLAR PRIZE, IT READ! A-AND THEN--
BAW!
ADD +1 TO YOUR SADNESS SCORE AND READ ON TO 67.

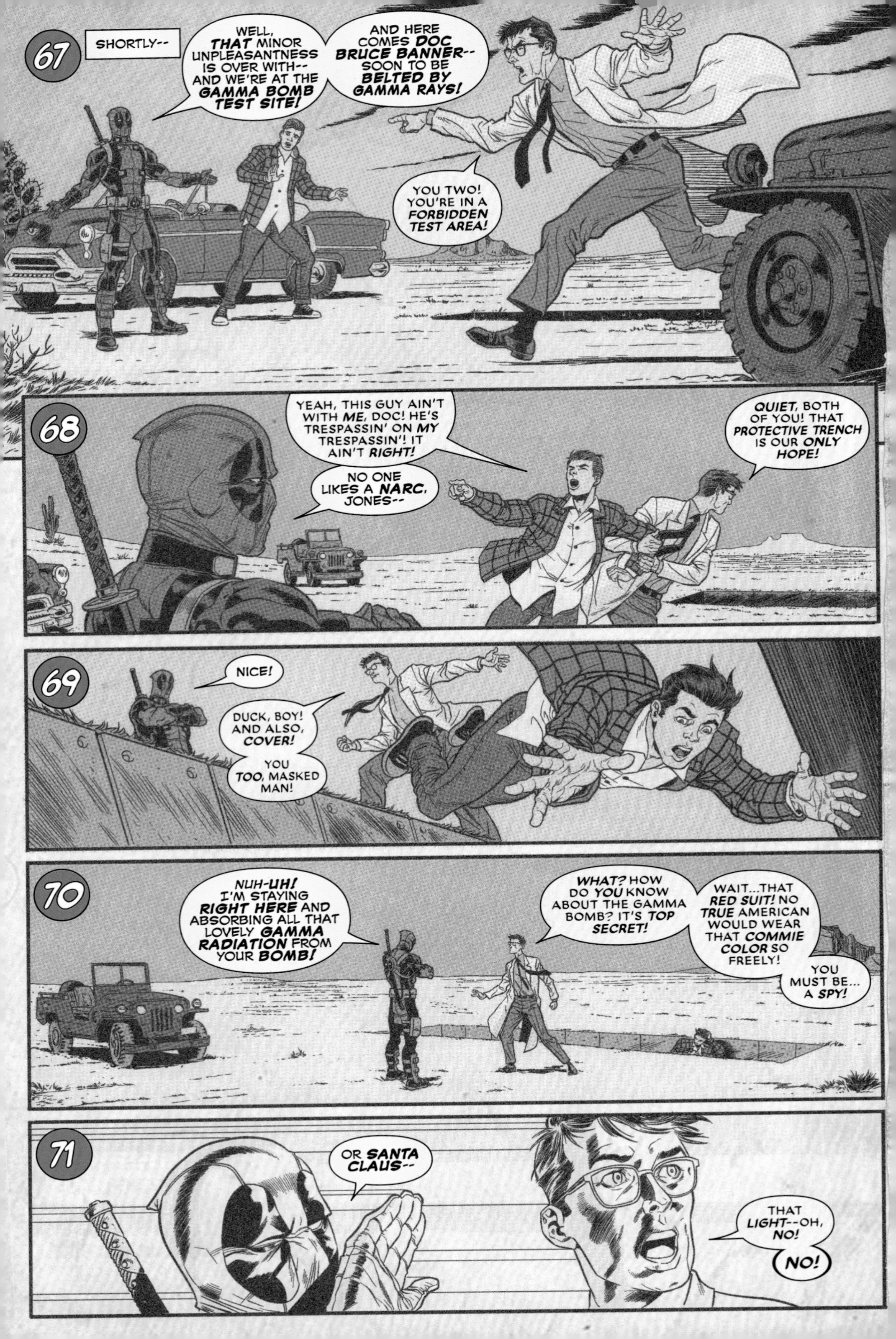
67
SHORTLY--
WELL, THAT MINOR UNPLEASANTNESS IS OVER WITH-- AND WE'RE AT THE GAMMA BOMB TEST SITE!
AND HERE COMES DOC BRUCE BANNER-- SOON TO BE BELTED BY GAMMA RAYS!
YOU TWO! YOU'RE IN A FORBIDDEN TEST AREA!
68
YEAH, THIS GUY AIN'T WITH ME, DOC! HE'S TRESPASSIN' ON MY TRESPASSIN'! IT AIN'T RIGHT!
NO ONE LIKES A NARC, JONES--
QUIET, BOTH OF YOU! THAT PROTECTIVE TRENCH IS OUR ONLY HOPE!
69
NICE!
DUCK, BOY! AND ALSO, COVER!
YOU TOO, MASKED MAN!
70
NUH-UH! I'M STAYING RIGHT HERE AND ABSORBING ALL THAT LOVELY GAMMA RADIATION FROM YOUR BOMB!
WHAT? HOW DO YOU KNOW ABOUT THE GAMMA BOMB? IT'S TOP SECRET!
WAIT...THAT RED SUIT! NO TRUE AMERICAN WOULD WEAR THAT COMMIE COLOR SO FREELY!
YOU MUST BE... A SPY!
71
OR SANTA CLAUS--
THAT LIGHT--OH, NO!
NO!

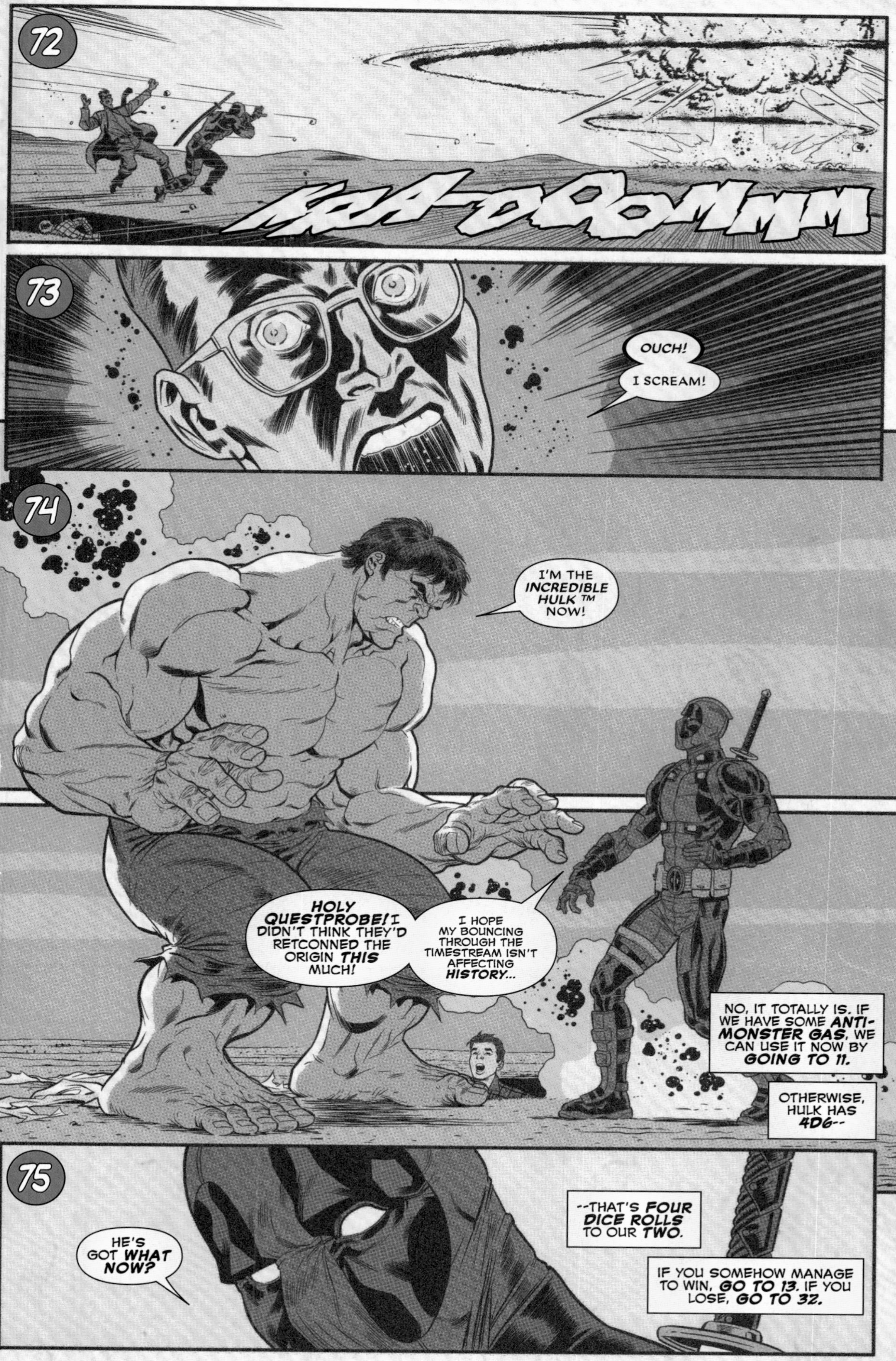
72
KRA-DOOMMM
73
OUCH!
I SCREAM!
74
I'M THE *INCREDIBLE HULK™* NOW!
HOLY QUESTPROBE! I DIDN'T THINK THEY'D RETCONNED THE ORIGIN ***THIS*** MUCH!
I HOPE MY BOUNCING THROUGH THE TIMESTREAM ISN'T AFFECTING ***HISTORY...***
NO, IT TOTALLY IS. IF WE HAVE SOME ***ANTI-MONSTER GAS***, WE CAN USE IT NOW BY ***GOING TO 11.***
OTHERWISE, HULK HAS ***4D6--***
75
HE'S GOT ***WHAT NOW?***
--THAT'S ***FOUR DICE ROLLS*** TO OUR ***TWO.***
IF YOU SOMEHOW MANAGE TO WIN, ***GO TO 13.*** IF YOU LOSE, ***GO TO 32.***

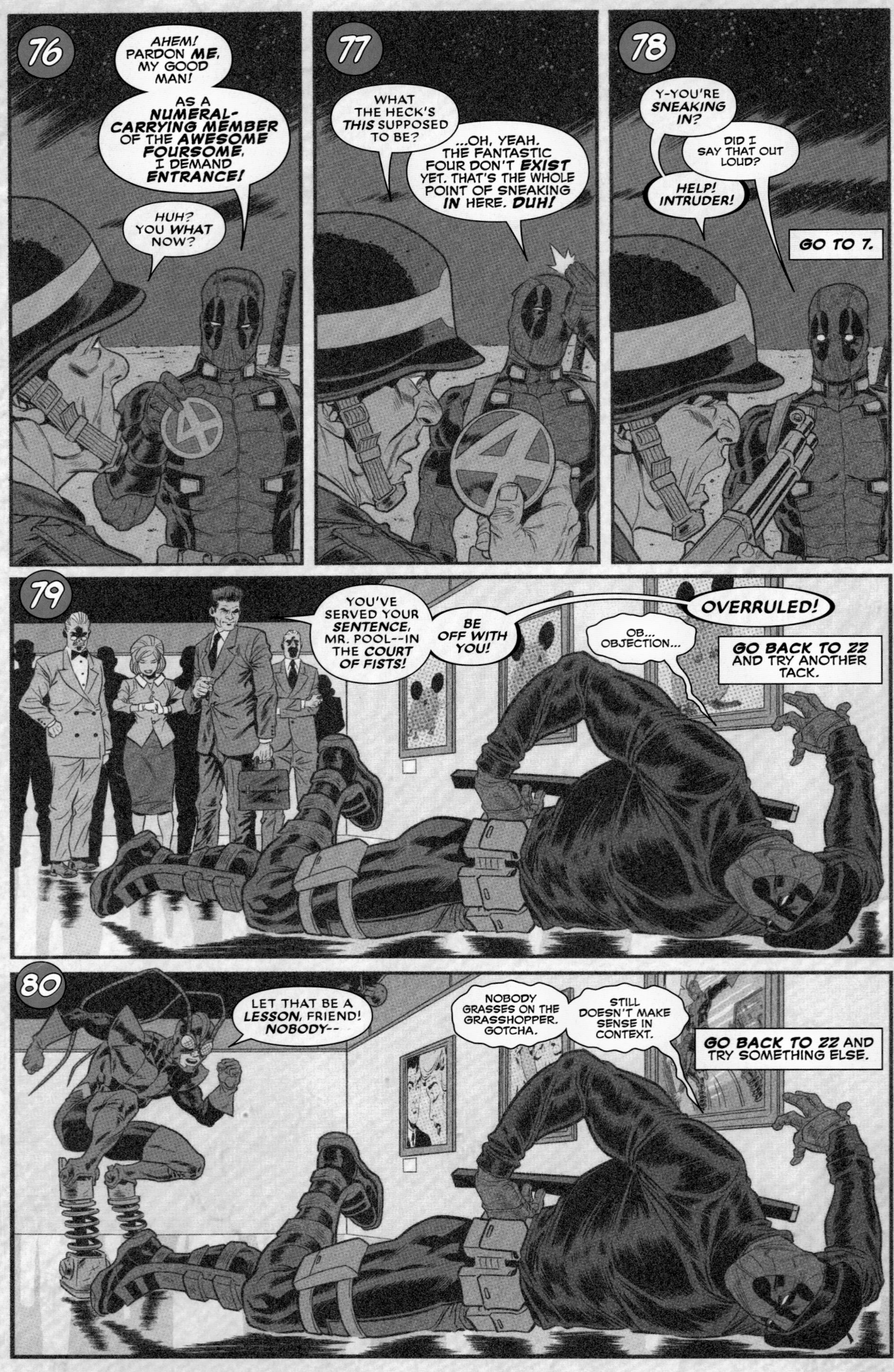

76
AHEM! PARDON ME, MY GOOD MAN!
AS A NUMERAL-CARRYING MEMBER OF THE AWESOME FOURSOME, I DEMAND ENTRANCE!
HUH? YOU WHAT NOW?
77
WHAT THE HECK'S THIS SUPPOSED TO BE?
...OH, YEAH. THE FANTASTIC FOUR DON'T EXIST YET. THAT'S THE WHOLE POINT OF SNEAKING IN HERE. DUH!
78
Y-YOU'RE SNEAKING IN?
DID I SAY THAT OUT LOUD?
HELP! INTRUDER!
GO TO 7.
79
YOU'VE SERVED YOUR SENTENCE, MR. POOL--IN THE COURT OF FISTS!
BE OFF WITH YOU!
OVERRULED!
OB... OBJECTION...
GO BACK TO 22 AND TRY ANOTHER TACK.
80
LET THAT BE A LESSON, FRIEND! NOBODY--
NOBODY GRASSES ON THE GRASSHOPPER. GOTCHA.
STILL DOESN'T MAKE SENSE IN CONTEXT.
GO BACK TO 22 AND TRY SOMETHING ELSE.

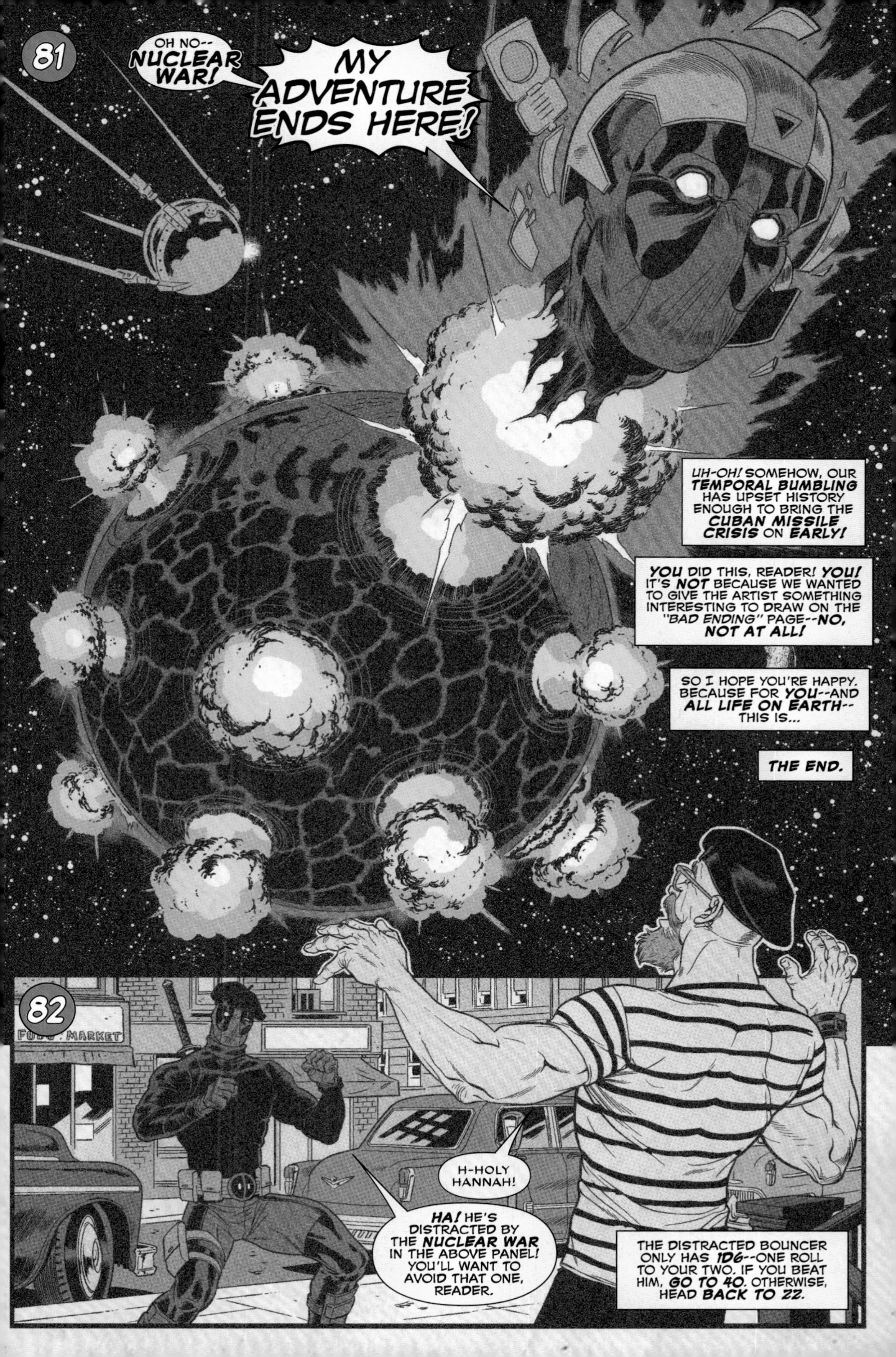
81
OH NO--NUCLEAR WAR!
MY ADVENTURE ENDS HERE!
UH-OH! SOMEHOW, OUR TEMPORAL BUMBLING HAS UPSET HISTORY ENOUGH TO BRING THE CUBAN MISSILE CRISIS ON EARLY!
YOU DID THIS, READER! YOU! IT'S NOT BECAUSE WE WANTED TO GIVE THE ARTIST SOMETHING INTERESTING TO DRAW ON THE "BAD ENDING" PAGE--NO, NOT AT ALL!
SO I HOPE YOU'RE HAPPY. BECAUSE FOR YOU--AND ALL LIFE ON EARTH--THIS IS...
THE END.
82
FOOD MARKET
H-HOLY HANNAH!
HA! HE'S DISTRACTED BY THE NUCLEAR WAR IN THE ABOVE PANEL! YOU'LL WANT TO AVOID THAT ONE, READER.
THE DISTRACTED BOUNCER ONLY HAS 1D6--ONE ROLL TO YOUR TWO. IF YOU BEAT HIM, GO TO 40. OTHERWISE, HEAD BACK TO 22.

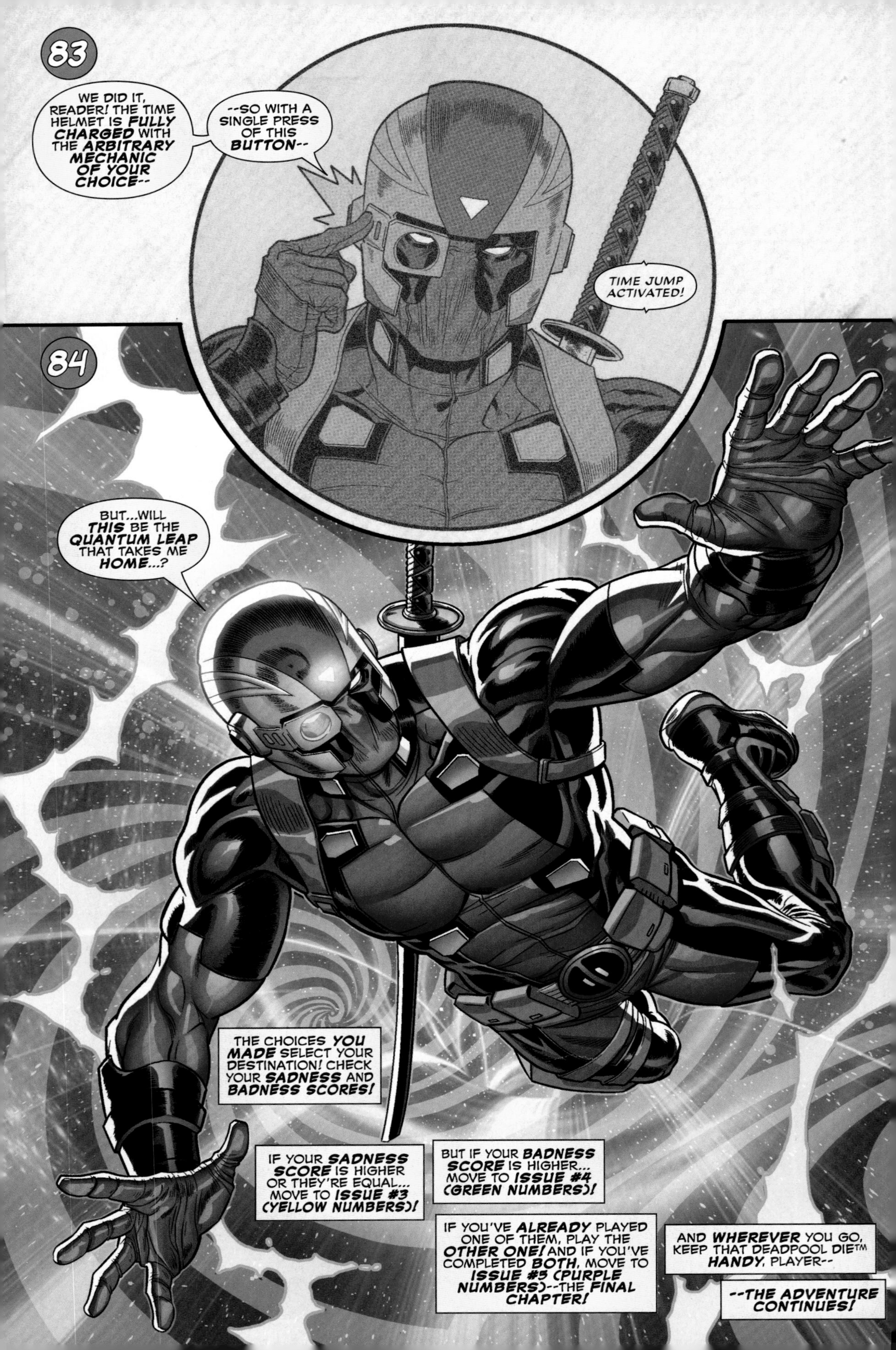
83
WE DID IT, READER! THE TIME HELMET IS FULLY CHARGED WITH THE ARBITRARY MECHANIC OF YOUR CHOICE--
--SO WITH A SINGLE PRESS OF THIS BUTTON--
TIME JUMP ACTIVATED!
84
BUT...WILL THIS BE THE QUANTUM LEAP THAT TAKES ME HOME...?
THE CHOICES YOU MADE SELECT YOUR DESTINATION! CHECK YOUR SADNESS AND BADNESS SCORES!
IF YOUR SADNESS SCORE IS HIGHER OR THEY'RE EQUAL... MOVE TO ISSUE #3 (YELLOW NUMBERS)!
BUT IF YOUR BADNESS SCORE IS HIGHER... MOVE TO ISSUE #4 (GREEN NUMBERS)!
IF YOU'VE ALREADY PLAYED ONE OF THEM, PLAY THE OTHER ONE! AND IF YOU'VE COMPLETED BOTH, MOVE TO ISSUE #5 (PURPLE NUMBERS)--THE FINAL CHAPTER!
AND WHEREVER YOU GO, KEEP THAT DEADPOOL DIE™ HANDY, PLAYER--
--THE ADVENTURE CONTINUES!

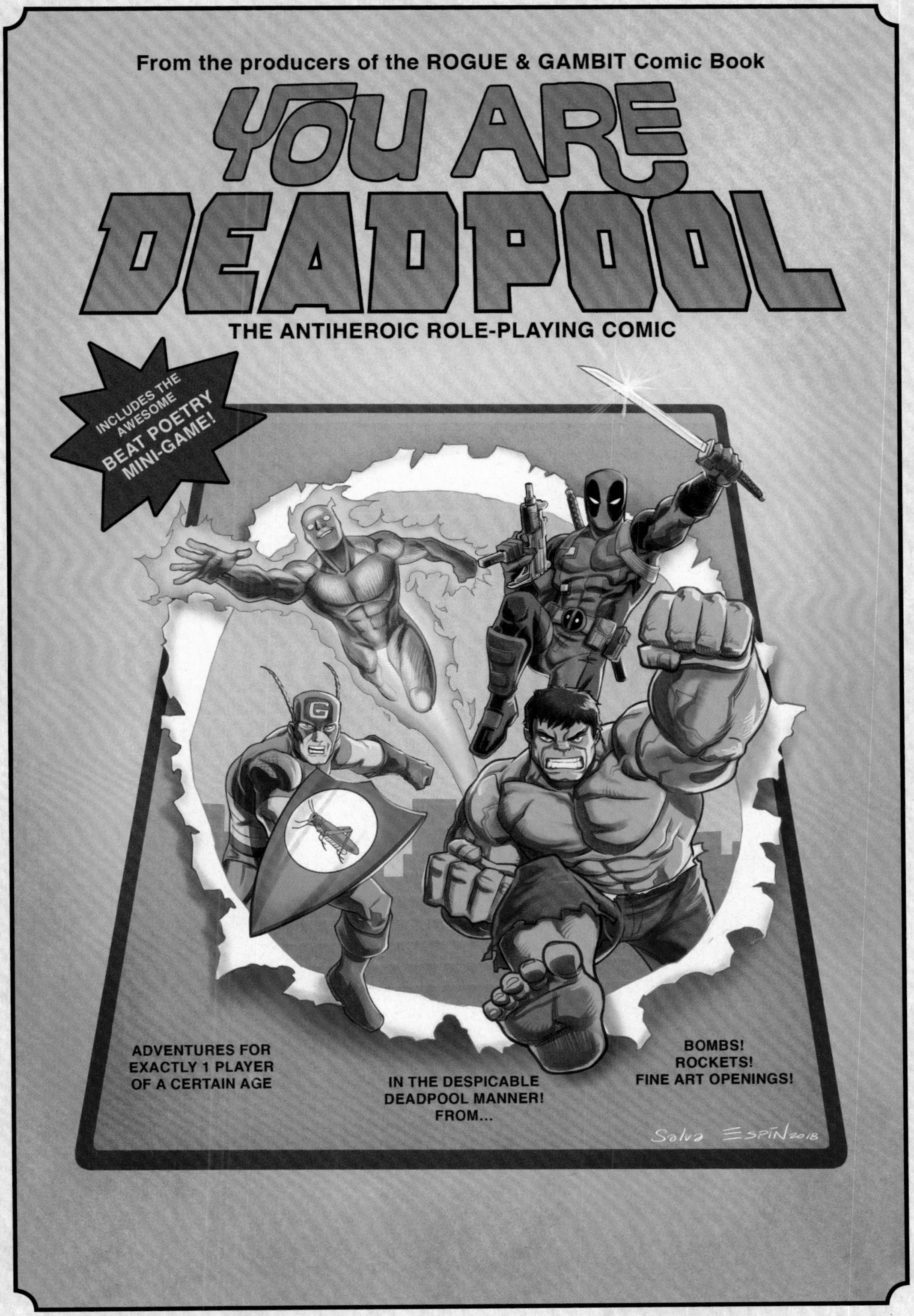
From the producers of the ROGUE & GAMBIT Comic Book
YOU ARE DEADPOOL
THE ANTIHEROIC ROLE-PLAYING COMIC
INCLUDES THE AWESOME BEAT POETRY MINI-GAME!
ADVENTURES FOR EXACTLY 1 PLAYER OF A CERTAIN AGE
IN THE DESPICABLE DEADPOOL MANNER! FROM...
BOMBS! ROCKETS! FINE ART OPENINGS!
Salva Espin 2018

2 VARIANT BY **SALVA ESPIN**

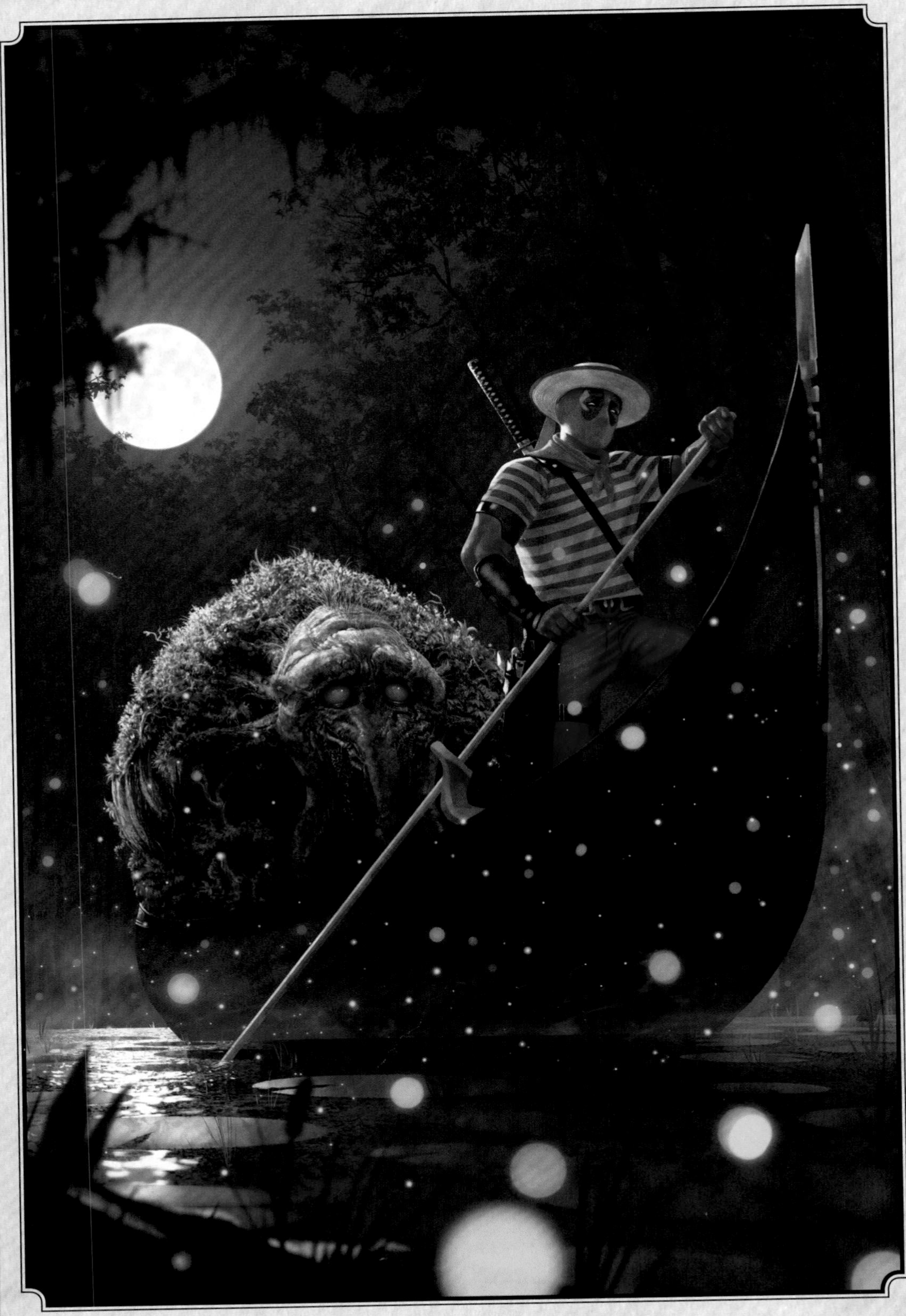

three

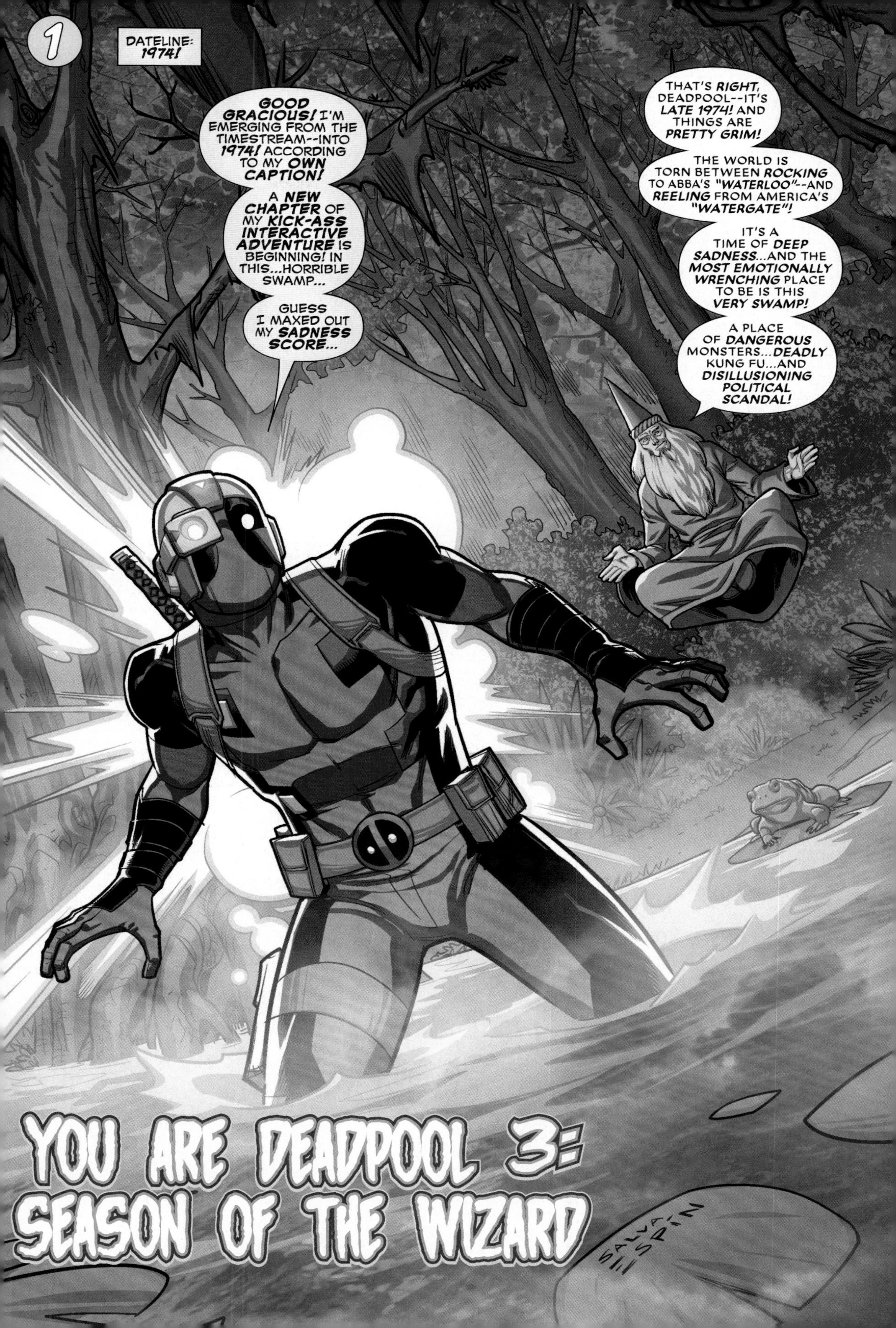
1
DATELINE: 1974!
GOOD GRACIOUS! I'M EMERGING FROM THE TIMESTREAM--INTO 1974! ACCORDING TO MY OWN CAPTION!
A NEW CHAPTER OF MY KICK-ASS INTERACTIVE ADVENTURE IS BEGINNING! IN THIS...HORRIBLE SWAMP...
GUESS I MAXED OUT MY SADNESS SCORE...
THAT'S RIGHT, DEADPOOL--IT'S LATE 1974! AND THINGS ARE PRETTY GRIM!
THE WORLD IS TORN BETWEEN ROCKING TO ABBA'S "WATERLOO"--AND REELING FROM AMERICA'S "WATERGATE"!
IT'S A TIME OF DEEP SADNESS...AND THE MOST EMOTIONALLY WRENCHING PLACE TO BE IS THIS VERY SWAMP!
A PLACE OF DANGEROUS MONSTERS...DEADLY KUNG FU...AND DISILLUSIONING POLITICAL SCANDAL!
YOU ARE DEADPOOL 3: SEASON OF THE WIZARD
SALVA ESPIN

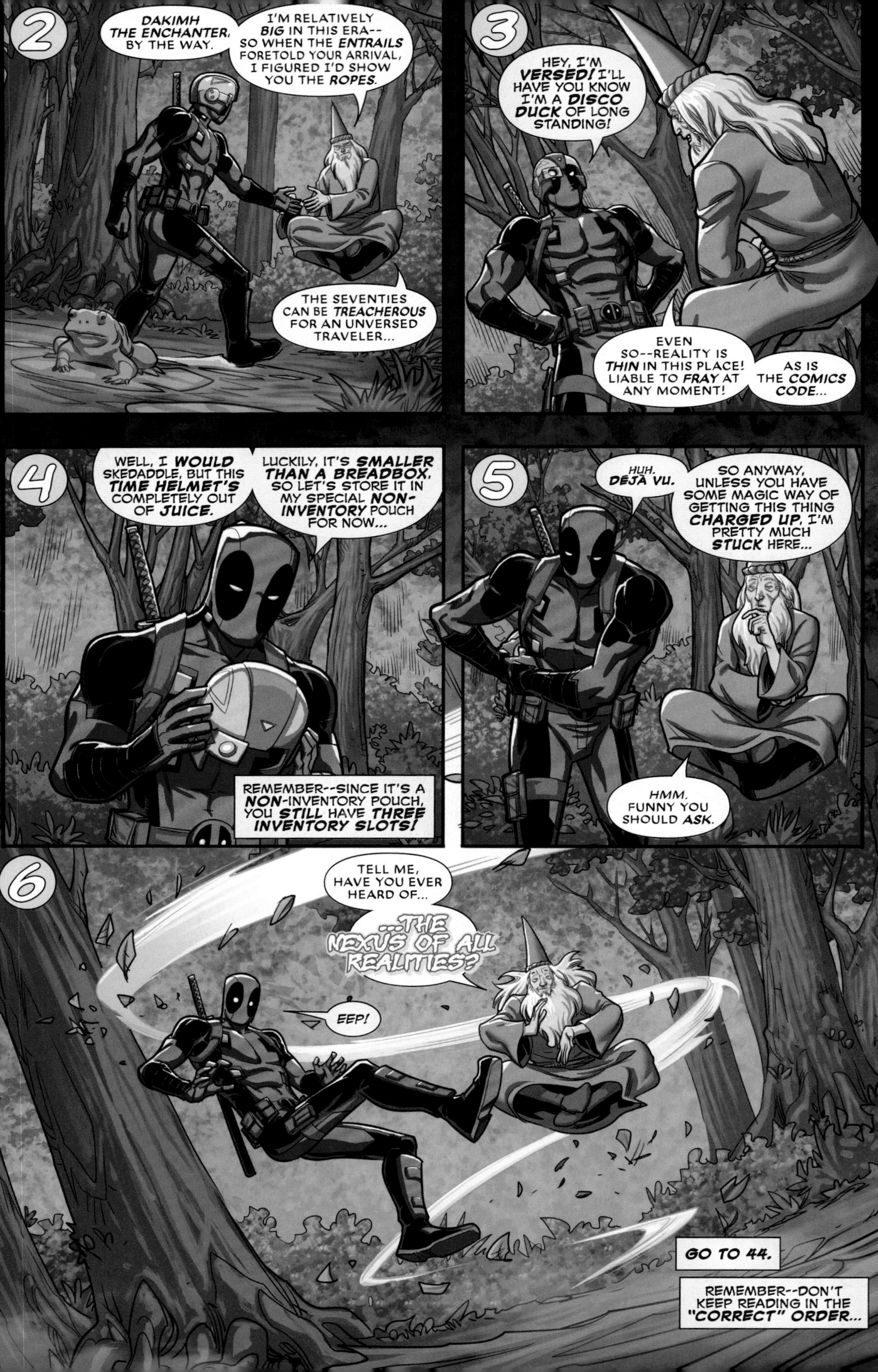
2
DAKIMH THE ENCHANTER, BY THE WAY.
I'M RELATIVELY BIG IN THIS ERA-- SO WHEN THE ENTRAILS FORETOLD YOUR ARRIVAL, I FIGURED I'D SHOW YOU THE ROPES.
THE SEVENTIES CAN BE TREACHEROUS FOR AN UNVERSED TRAVELER...
3
HEY, I'M VERSED! I'LL HAVE YOU KNOW I'M A DISCO DUCK OF LONG STANDING!
EVEN SO--REALITY IS THIN IN THIS PLACE! LIABLE TO FRAY AT ANY MOMENT!
AS IS THE COMICS CODE...
4
WELL, I WOULD SKEDADDLE, BUT THIS TIME HELMET'S COMPLETELY OUT OF JUICE.
LUCKILY, IT'S SMALLER THAN A BREADBOX, SO LET'S STORE IT IN MY SPECIAL NON-INVENTORY POUCH FOR NOW...
REMEMBER--SINCE IT'S A NON-INVENTORY POUCH, YOU STILL HAVE THREE INVENTORY SLOTS!
5
HUH. DEJA VU.
SO ANYWAY, UNLESS YOU HAVE SOME MAGIC WAY OF GETTING THIS THING CHARGED UP, I'M PRETTY MUCH STUCK HERE...
HMM. FUNNY YOU SHOULD ASK.
6
TELL ME, HAVE YOU EVER HEARD OF...
...THE NEXUS OF ALL REALITIES?
EEP!
GO TO 44.
REMEMBER--DON'T KEEP READING IN THE "CORRECT" ORDER...

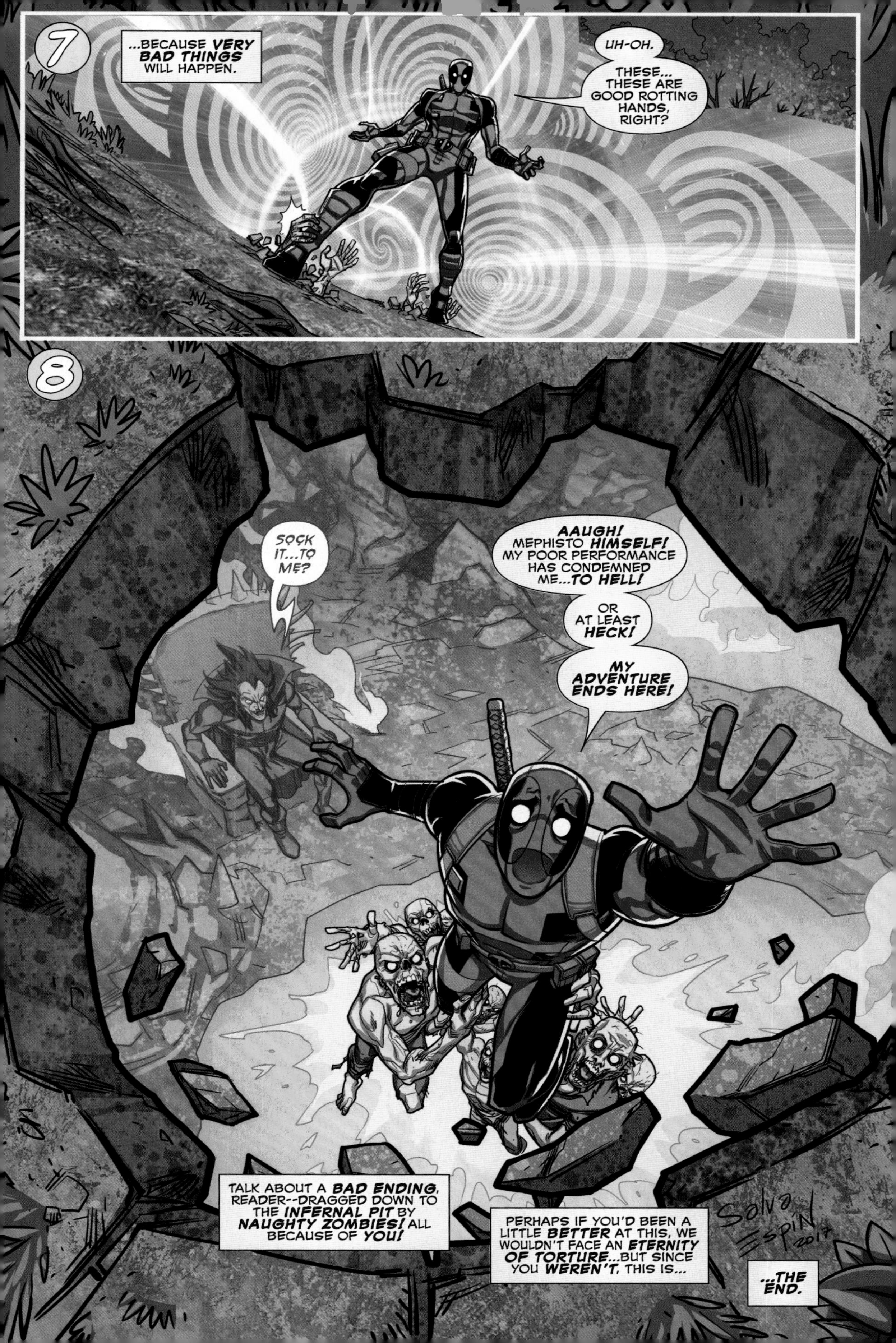
7
...BECAUSE VERY BAD THINGS WILL HAPPEN.
UH-OH.
THESE... THESE ARE GOOD ROTTING HANDS, RIGHT?
8
SOCK IT...TO ME?
AAUGH! MEPHISTO HIMSELF! MY POOR PERFORMANCE HAS CONDEMNED ME...TO HELL!
OR AT LEAST HECK!
MY ADVENTURE ENDS HERE!
TALK ABOUT A BAD ENDING, READER--DRAGGED DOWN TO THE INFERNAL PIT BY NAUGHTY ZOMBIES! ALL BECAUSE OF YOU!
PERHAPS IF YOU'D BEEN A LITTLE BETTER AT THIS, WE WOULDN'T FACE AN ETERNITY OF TORTURE...BUT SINCE YOU WEREN'T, THIS IS...
...THE END.
Salva Espin 2017

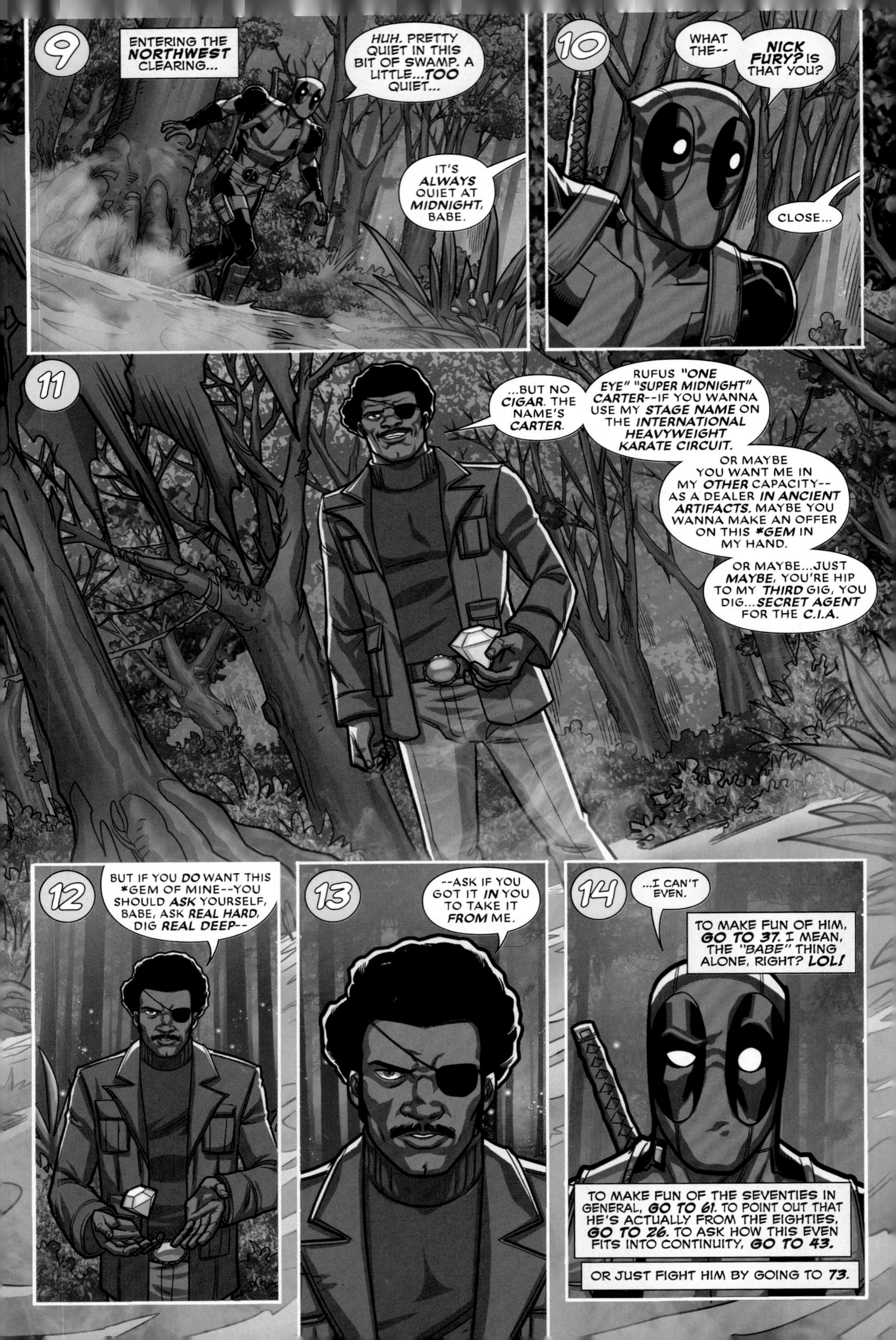
9
ENTERING THE NORTHWEST CLEARING...
HUH. PRETTY QUIET IN THIS BIT OF SWAMP. A LITTLE...TOO QUIET...
IT'S ALWAYS QUIET AT MIDNIGHT, BABE.
10
WHAT THE--
NICK FURY? IS THAT YOU?
CLOSE...
11
...BUT NO CIGAR. THE NAME'S CARTER.
RUFUS "ONE EYE" "SUPER MIDNIGHT" CARTER--IF YOU WANNA USE MY STAGE NAME ON THE INTERNATIONAL HEAVYWEIGHT KARATE CIRCUIT.
OR MAYBE YOU WANT ME IN MY OTHER CAPACITY--AS A DEALER IN ANCIENT ARTIFACTS. MAYBE YOU WANNA MAKE AN OFFER ON THIS *GEM IN MY HAND.
OR MAYBE...JUST MAYBE, YOU'RE HIP TO MY THIRD GIG, YOU DIG...SECRET AGENT FOR THE C.I.A.
12
BUT IF YOU DO WANT THIS *GEM OF MINE--YOU SHOULD ASK YOURSELF, BABE, ASK REAL HARD, DIG REAL DEEP--
13
--ASK IF YOU GOT IT IN YOU TO TAKE IT FROM ME.
14
...I CAN'T EVEN.
TO MAKE FUN OF HIM, GO TO 37. I MEAN, THE "BABE" THING ALONE, RIGHT? LOL!
TO MAKE FUN OF THE SEVENTIES IN GENERAL, GO TO 61. TO POINT OUT THAT HE'S ACTUALLY FROM THE EIGHTIES, GO TO 26. TO ASK HOW THIS EVEN FITS INTO CONTINUITY, GO TO 43.
OR JUST FIGHT HIM BY GOING TO 73.

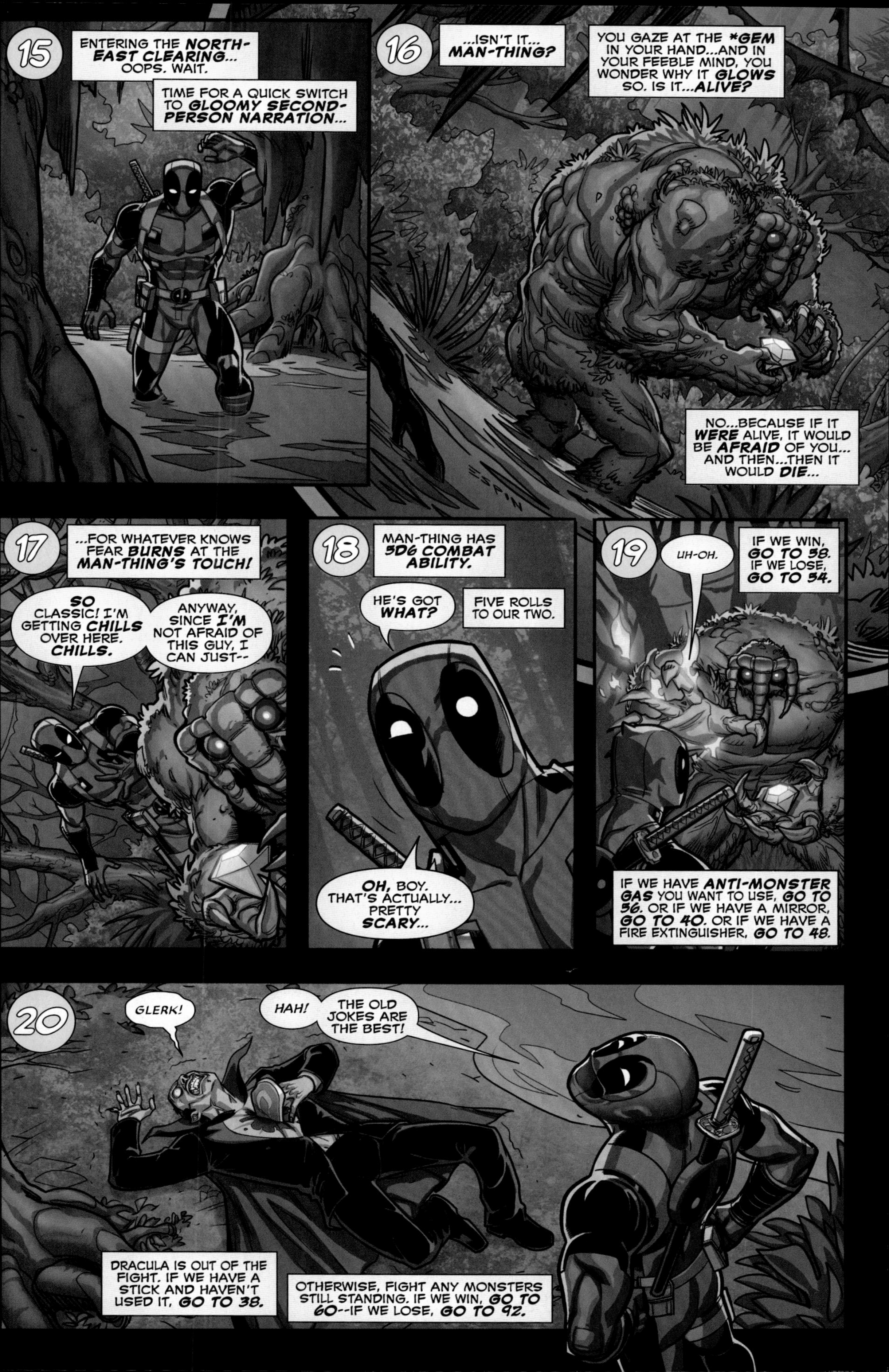
15
ENTERING THE NORTH-EAST CLEARING... OOPS. WAIT.
TIME FOR A QUICK SWITCH TO GLOOMY SECOND-PERSON NARRATION...
16
...ISN'T IT... MAN-THING?
YOU GAZE AT THE *GEM IN YOUR HAND...AND IN YOUR FEEBLE MIND, YOU WONDER WHY IT GLOWS SO. IS IT...ALIVE?
NO...BECAUSE IF IT WERE ALIVE, IT WOULD BE AFRAID OF YOU... AND THEN...THEN IT WOULD DIE...
SPIN
17
...FOR WHATEVER KNOWS FEAR BURNS AT THE MAN-THING'S TOUCH!
SO CLASSIC! I'M GETTING CHILLS OVER HERE. CHILLS.
ANYWAY, SINCE I'M NOT AFRAID OF THIS GUY, I CAN JUST--
18
MAN-THING HAS 5D6 COMBAT ABILITY.
HE'S GOT WHAT?
FIVE ROLLS TO OUR TWO.
OH, BOY. THAT'S ACTUALLY... PRETTY SCARY...
19
UH-OH.
IF WE WIN, GO TO 58. IF WE LOSE, GO TO 54.
IF WE HAVE ANTI-MONSTER GAS YOU WANT TO USE, GO TO 56. OR IF WE HAVE A MIRROR, GO TO 40. OR IF WE HAVE A FIRE EXTINGUISHER, GO TO 48.
20
GLERK!
HAH!
THE OLD JOKES ARE THE BEST!
DRACULA IS OUT OF THE FIGHT. IF WE HAVE A STICK AND HAVEN'T USED IT, GO TO 38.
OTHERWISE, FIGHT ANY MONSTERS STILL STANDING. IF WE WIN, GO TO 60--IF WE LOSE, GO TO 92.

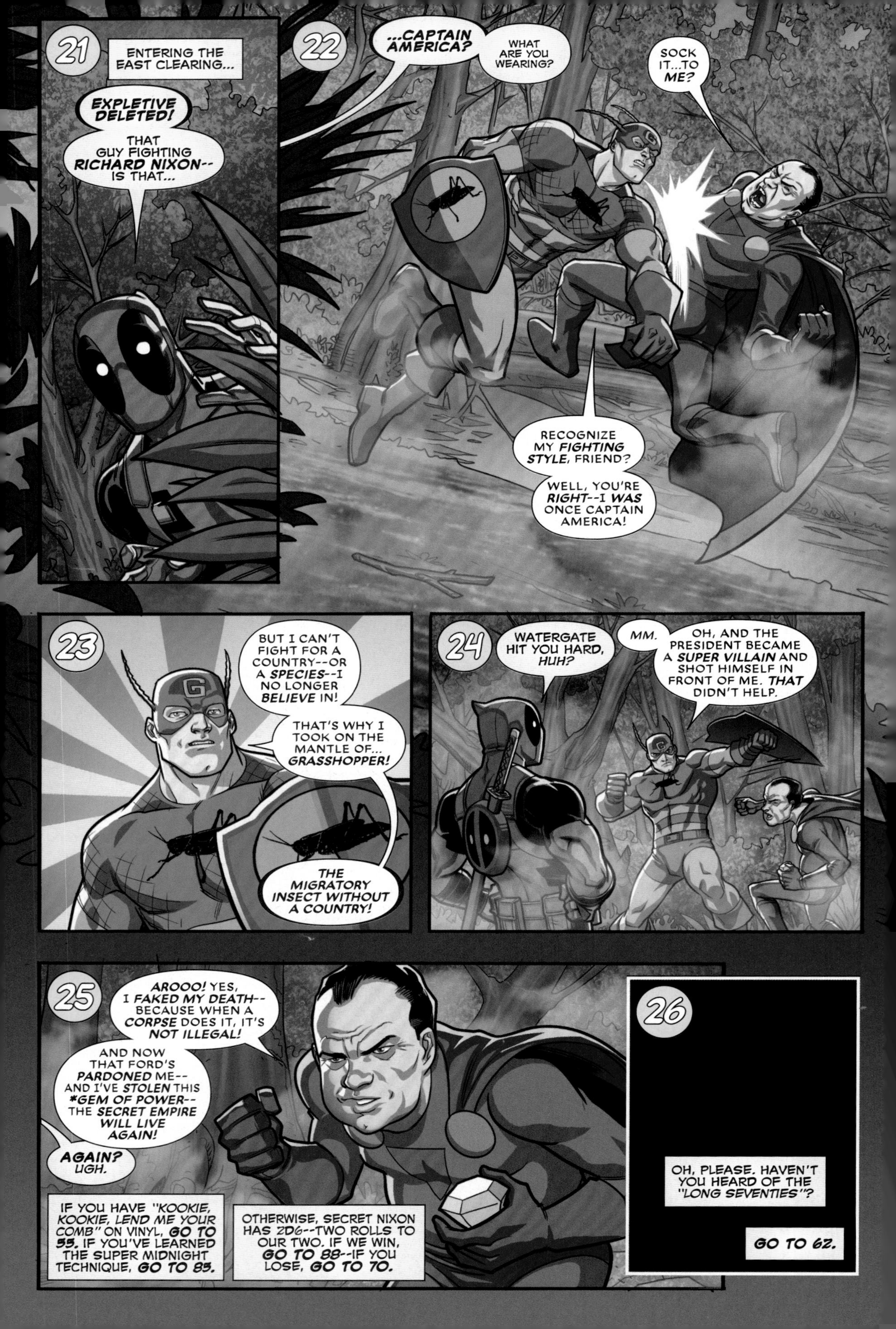
21
ENTERING THE EAST CLEARING...
EXPLETIVE DELETED!
THAT GUY FIGHTING RICHARD NIXON-- IS THAT...
22
...CAPTAIN AMERICA?
WHAT ARE YOU WEARING?
SOCK IT...TO ME?
RECOGNIZE MY FIGHTING STYLE, FRIEND?
WELL, YOU'RE RIGHT--I WAS ONCE CAPTAIN AMERICA!
23
BUT I CAN'T FIGHT FOR A COUNTRY--OR A SPECIES--I NO LONGER BELIEVE IN!
THAT'S WHY I TOOK ON THE MANTLE OF... GRASSHOPPER!
THE MIGRATORY INSECT WITHOUT A COUNTRY!
24
WATERGATE HIT YOU HARD, HUH?
MM.
OH, AND THE PRESIDENT BECAME A SUPER VILLAIN AND SHOT HIMSELF IN FRONT OF ME. THAT DIDN'T HELP.
25
AROOO! YES, I FAKED MY DEATH-- BECAUSE WHEN A CORPSE DOES IT, IT'S NOT ILLEGAL!
AND NOW THAT FORD'S PARDONED ME-- AND I'VE STOLEN THIS *GEM OF POWER-- THE SECRET EMPIRE WILL LIVE AGAIN!
AGAIN? UGH.
IF YOU HAVE "KOOKIE, KOOKIE, LEND ME YOUR COMB" ON VINYL, GO TO 55. IF YOU'VE LEARNED THE SUPER MIDNIGHT TECHNIQUE, GO TO 85.
OTHERWISE, SECRET NIXON HAS 2D6--TWO ROLLS TO OUR TWO. IF WE WIN, GO TO 88--IF YOU LOSE, GO TO 70.
26
OH, PLEASE. HAVEN'T YOU HEARD OF THE "LONG SEVENTIES"?
GO TO 62.

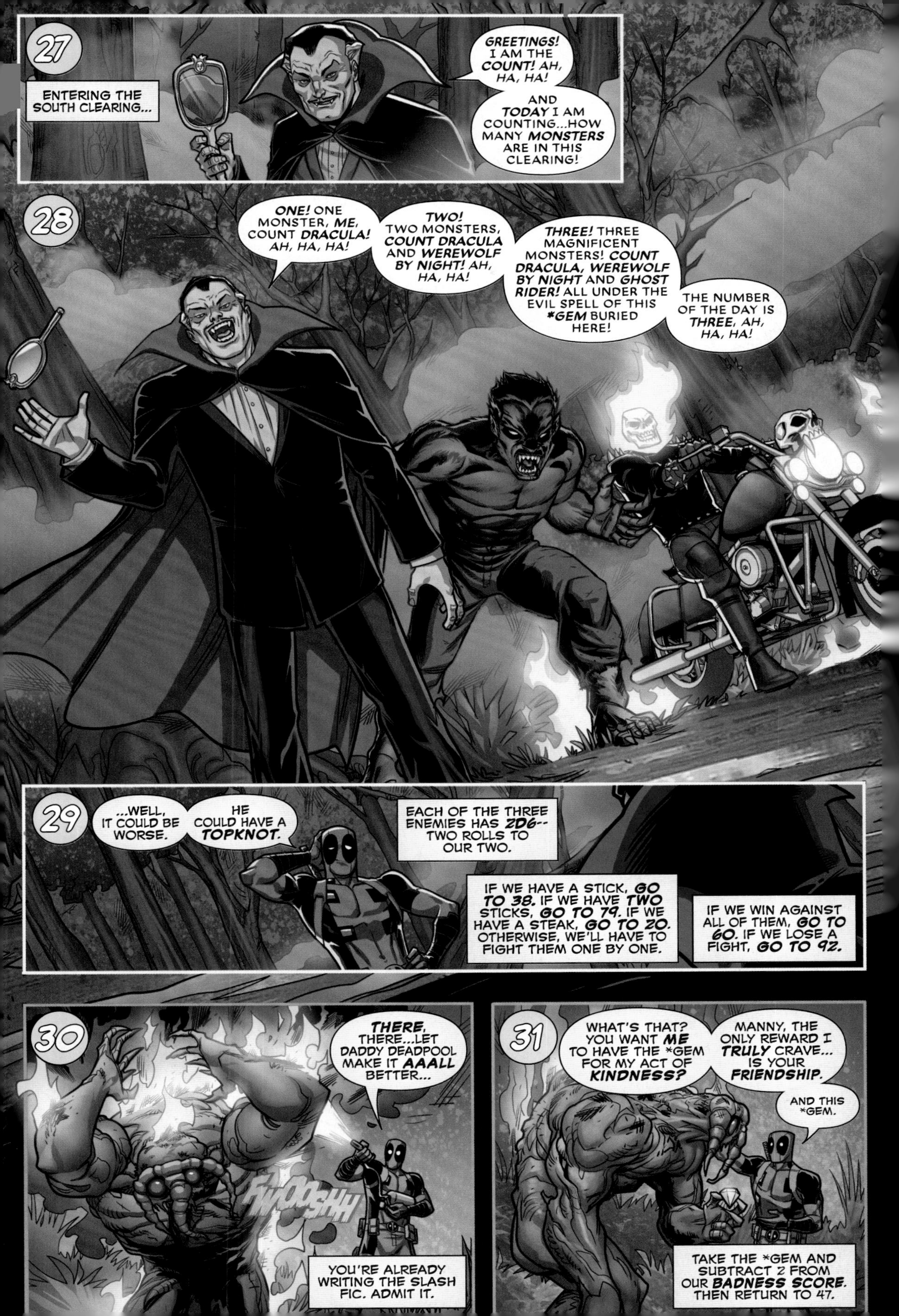
27
ENTERING THE SOUTH CLEARING...
GREETINGS! I AM THE COUNT! AH, HA, HA!
AND TODAY I AM COUNTING...HOW MANY MONSTERS ARE IN THIS CLEARING!
28
ONE! ONE MONSTER, ME, COUNT DRACULA! AH, HA, HA!
TWO! TWO MONSTERS, COUNT DRACULA AND WEREWOLF BY NIGHT! AH, HA, HA!
THREE! THREE MAGNIFICENT MONSTERS! COUNT DRACULA, WEREWOLF BY NIGHT AND GHOST RIDER! ALL UNDER THE EVIL SPELL OF THIS *GEM BURIED HERE!
THE NUMBER OF THE DAY IS THREE, AH, HA, HA!
29
...WELL, IT COULD BE WORSE.
HE COULD HAVE A TOPKNOT.
EACH OF THE THREE ENEMIES HAS 2D6-- TWO ROLLS TO OUR TWO.
IF WE HAVE A STICK, GO TO 38. IF WE HAVE TWO STICKS, GO TO 79. IF WE HAVE A STEAK, GO TO 20. OTHERWISE, WE'LL HAVE TO FIGHT THEM ONE BY ONE.
IF WE WIN AGAINST ALL OF THEM, GO TO 60. IF WE LOSE A FIGHT, GO TO 92.
30
THERE, THERE...LET DADDY DEADPOOL MAKE IT AAALL BETTER...
FWOOSHH
YOU'RE ALREADY WRITING THE SLASH FIC. ADMIT IT.
31
WHAT'S THAT? YOU WANT ME TO HAVE THE *GEM FOR MY ACT OF KINDNESS?
MANNY, THE ONLY REWARD I TRULY CRAVE... IS YOUR FRIENDSHIP.
AND THIS *GEM.
TAKE THE *GEM AND SUBTRACT 2 FROM OUR BADNESS SCORE. THEN RETURN TO 47.

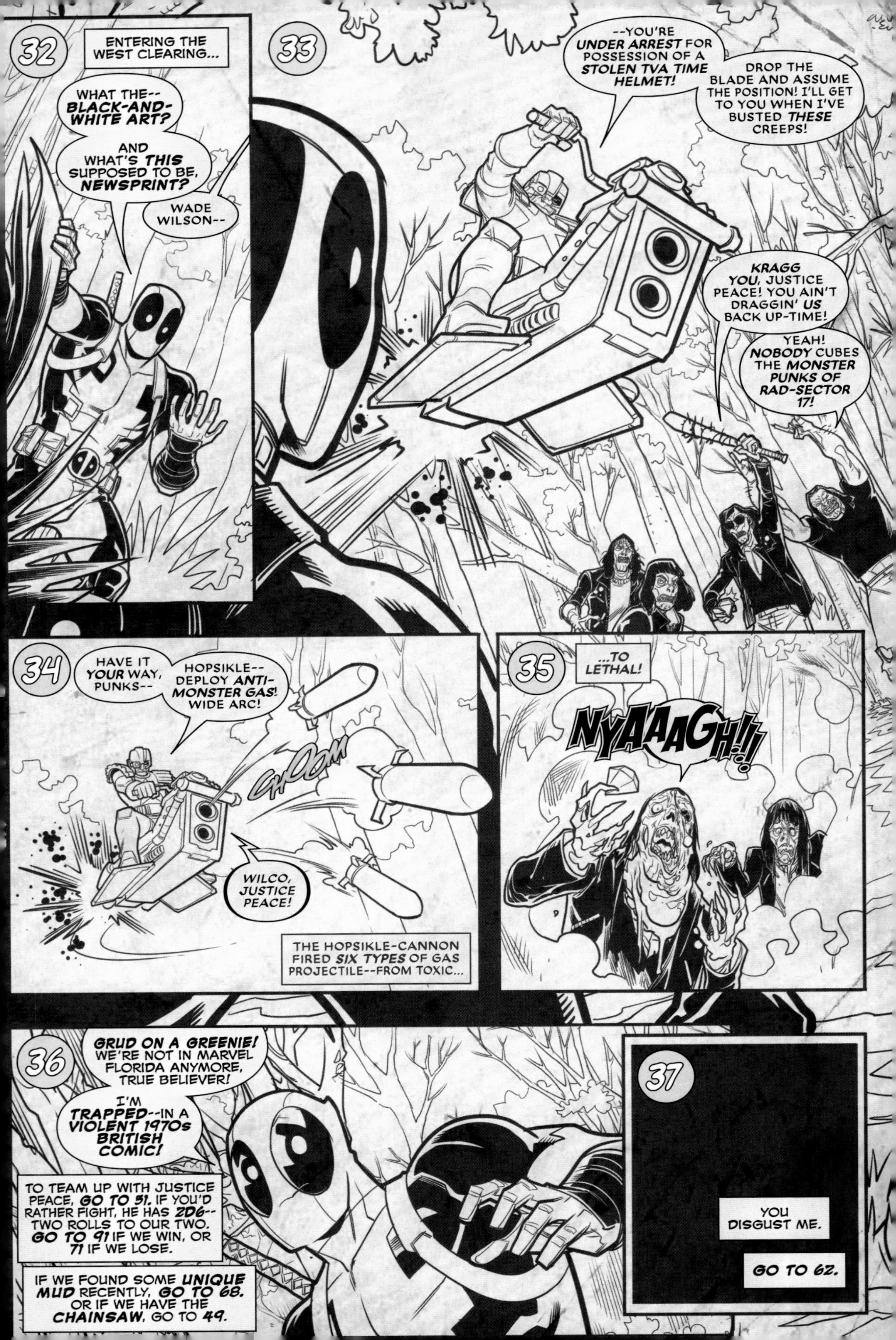
32
ENTERING THE WEST CLEARING...
WHAT THE-- BLACK-AND-WHITE ART?
AND WHAT'S THIS SUPPOSED TO BE, NEWSPRINT?
WADE WILSON--
33
--YOU'RE UNDER ARREST FOR POSSESSION OF A STOLEN TVA TIME HELMET!
DROP THE BLADE AND ASSUME THE POSITION! I'LL GET TO YOU WHEN I'VE BUSTED THESE CREEPS!
KRAGG YOU, JUSTICE PEACE! YOU AIN'T DRAGGIN' US BACK UP-TIME!
YEAH! NOBODY CUBES THE MONSTER PUNKS OF RAD-SECTOR 17!
34
HAVE IT YOUR WAY, PUNKS--
HOPSIKLE-- DEPLOY ANTI-MONSTER GAS! WIDE ARC!
SHOOM
WILCO, JUSTICE PEACE!
THE HOPSIKLE-CANNON FIRED SIX TYPES OF GAS PROJECTILE--FROM TOXIC...
35
...TO LETHAL!
NYAAAGH!!
36
GRUD ON A GREENIE! WE'RE NOT IN MARVEL FLORIDA ANYMORE, TRUE BELIEVER!
I'M TRAPPED--IN A VIOLENT 1970s BRITISH COMIC!
TO TEAM UP WITH JUSTICE PEACE, GO TO 51. IF YOU'D RATHER FIGHT, HE HAS 2D6--TWO ROLLS TO OUR TWO. GO TO 91 IF WE WIN, OR 71 IF WE LOSE.
IF WE FOUND SOME UNIQUE MUD RECENTLY, GO TO 68. OR IF WE HAVE THE CHAINSAW, GO TO 49.
37
YOU DISGUST ME.
GO TO 62.

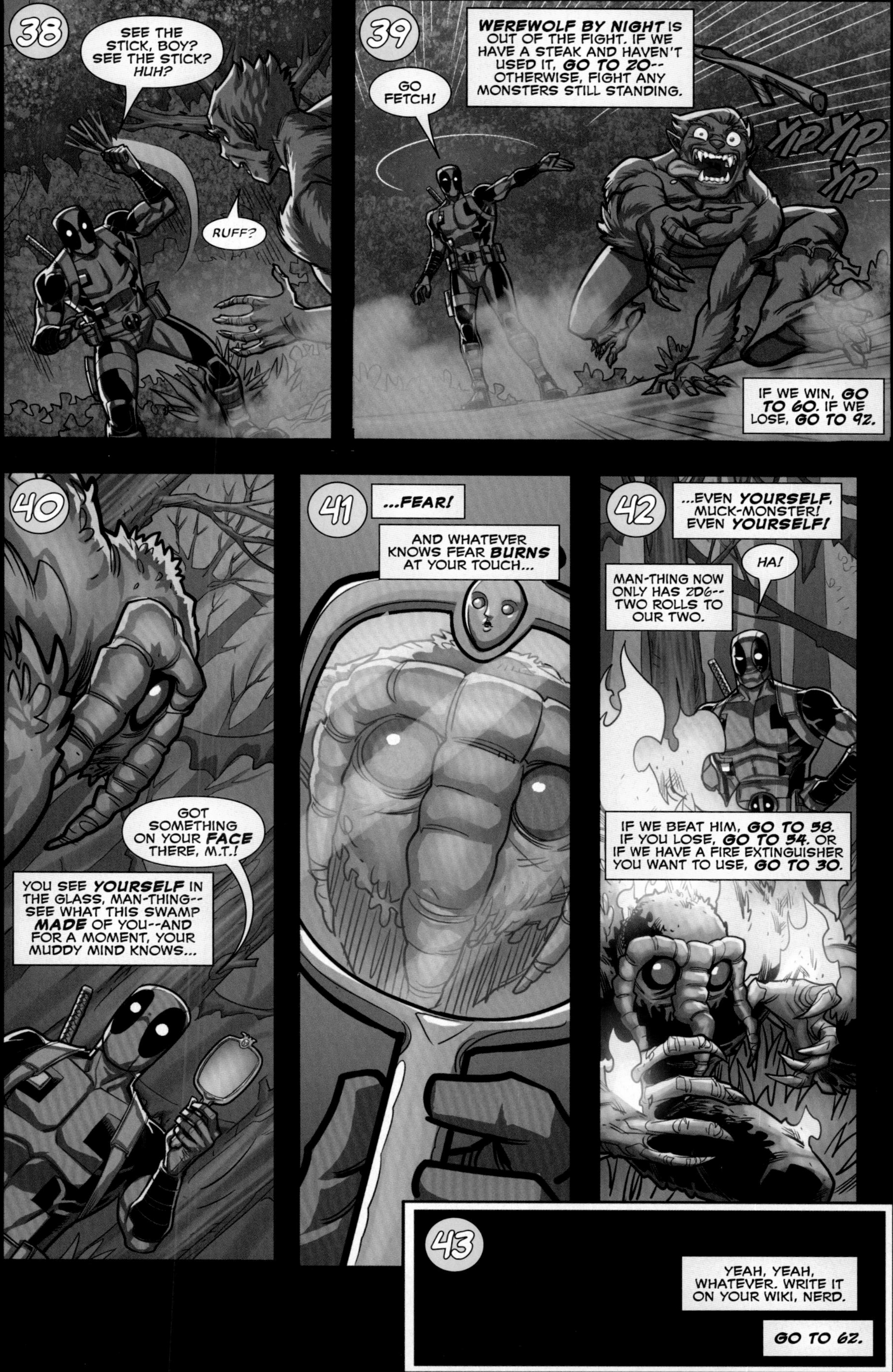

38
SEE THE STICK, BOY? SEE THE STICK? HUH?
RUFF?
39
WEREWOLF BY NIGHT IS OUT OF THE FIGHT. IF WE HAVE A STEAK AND HAVEN'T USED IT, GO TO 20-- OTHERWISE, FIGHT ANY MONSTERS STILL STANDING.
GO FETCH!
YIP YIP YIP
IF WE WIN, GO TO 60. IF WE LOSE, GO TO 92.
40
GOT SOMETHING ON YOUR FACE THERE, M.T.!
YOU SEE YOURSELF IN THE GLASS, MAN-THING-- SEE WHAT THIS SWAMP MADE OF YOU--AND FOR A MOMENT, YOUR MUDDY MIND KNOWS...
41
...FEAR!
AND WHATEVER KNOWS FEAR BURNS AT YOUR TOUCH...
42
...EVEN YOURSELF, MUCK-MONSTER! EVEN YOURSELF!
HA!
MAN-THING NOW ONLY HAS 2D6-- TWO ROLLS TO OUR TWO.
IF WE BEAT HIM, GO TO 58. IF YOU LOSE, GO TO 54. OR IF WE HAVE A FIRE EXTINGUISHER YOU WANT TO USE, GO TO 30.
43
YEAH, YEAH, WHATEVER. WRITE IT ON YOUR WIKI, NERD.
GO TO 62.

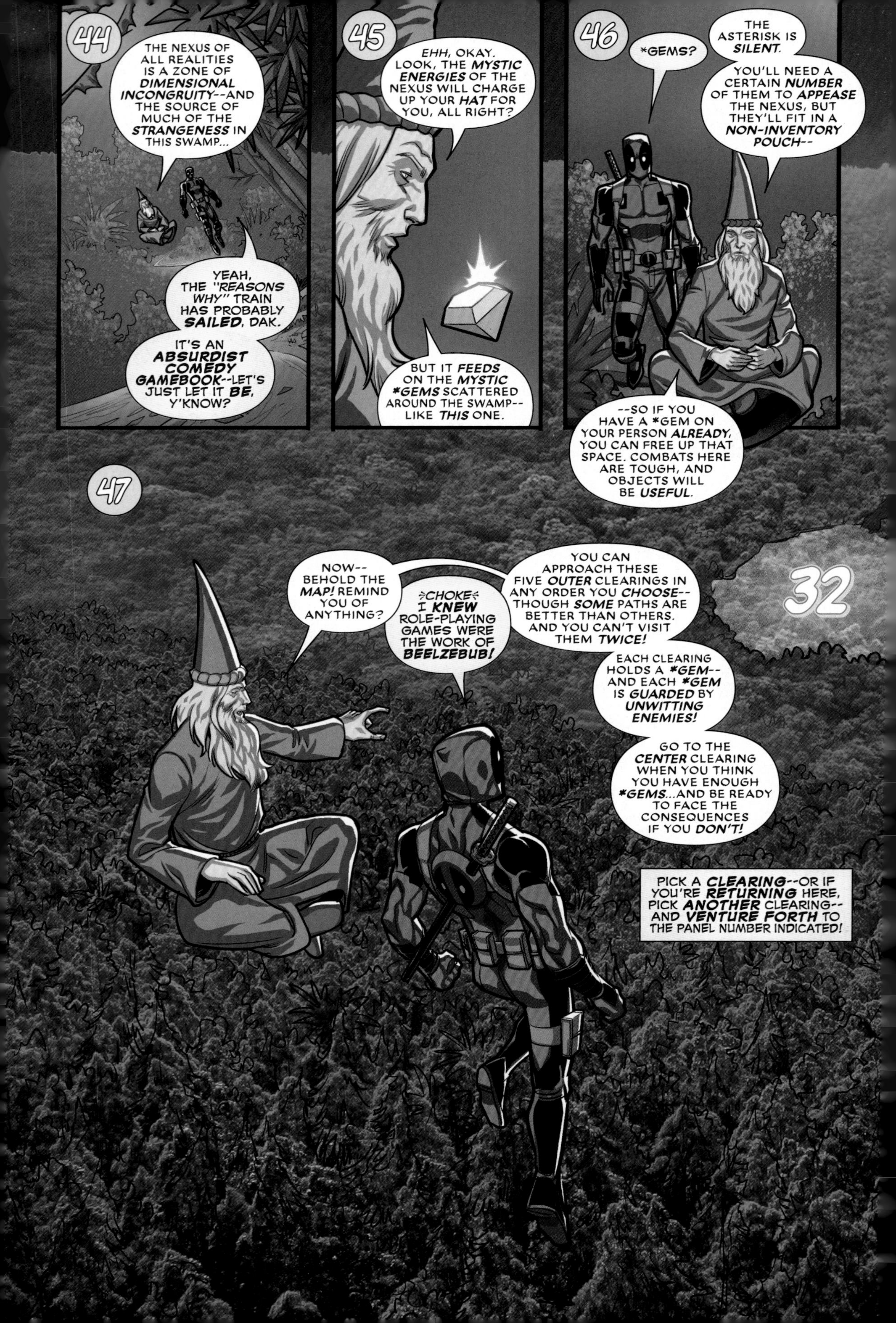

44
THE NEXUS OF ALL REALITIES IS A ZONE OF DIMENSIONAL INCONGRUITY--AND THE SOURCE OF MUCH OF THE STRANGENESS IN THIS SWAMP...
YEAH, THE "REASONS WHY" TRAIN HAS PROBABLY SAILED, DAK.
IT'S AN ABSURDIST COMEDY GAMEBOOK--LET'S JUST LET IT BE, Y'KNOW?
45
EHH, OKAY. LOOK, THE MYSTIC ENERGIES OF THE NEXUS WILL CHARGE UP YOUR HAT FOR YOU, ALL RIGHT?
BUT IT FEEDS ON THE MYSTIC *GEMS SCATTERED AROUND THE SWAMP--LIKE THIS ONE.
46
*GEMS?
THE ASTERISK IS SILENT.
YOU'LL NEED A CERTAIN NUMBER OF THEM TO APPEASE THE NEXUS, BUT THEY'LL FIT IN A NON-INVENTORY POUCH--
--SO IF YOU HAVE A *GEM ON YOUR PERSON ALREADY, YOU CAN FREE UP THAT SPACE. COMBATS HERE ARE TOUGH, AND OBJECTS WILL BE USEFUL.
47
NOW--BEHOLD THE MAP! REMIND YOU OF ANYTHING?
YOU CAN APPROACH THESE FIVE OUTER CLEARINGS IN ANY ORDER YOU CHOOSE--THOUGH SOME PATHS ARE BETTER THAN OTHERS. AND YOU CAN'T VISIT THEM TWICE!
CHOKE I KNEW ROLE-PLAYING GAMES WERE THE WORK OF BEELZEBUB!
EACH CLEARING HOLDS A *GEM--AND EACH *GEM IS GUARDED BY UNWITTING ENEMIES!
GO TO THE CENTER CLEARING WHEN YOU THINK YOU HAVE ENOUGH *GEMS...AND BE READY TO FACE THE CONSEQUENCES IF YOU DON'T!
32
PICK A CLEARING--OR IF YOU'RE RETURNING HERE, PICK ANOTHER CLEARING--AND VENTURE FORTH TO THE PANEL NUMBER INDICATED!

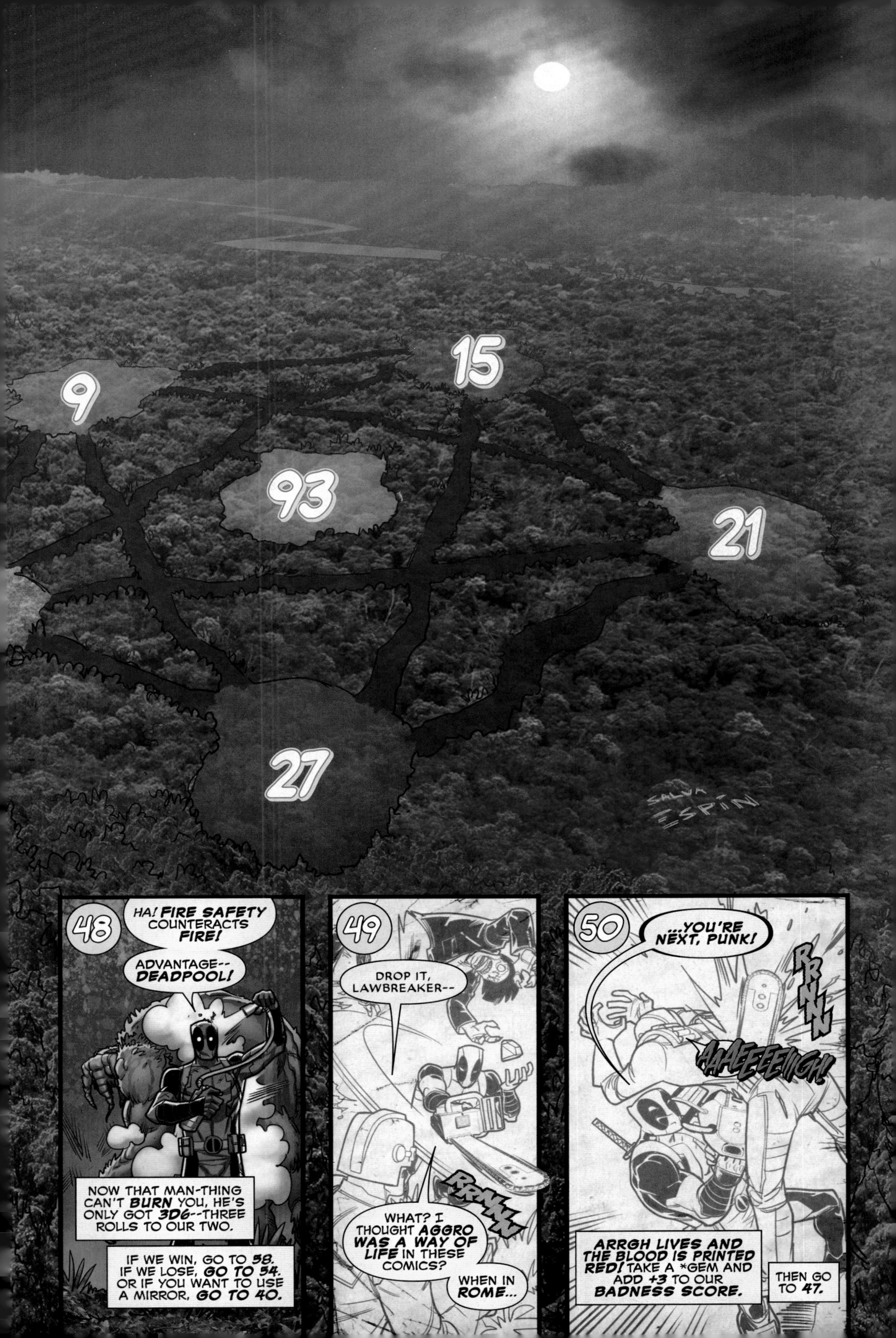

9
15
93
21
27
SALVA ESPIN
48
HA! FIRE SAFETY COUNTERACTS FIRE!
ADVANTAGE-- DEADPOOL!
NOW THAT MAN-THING CAN'T BURN YOU, HE'S ONLY GOT 3D6--THREE ROLLS TO OUR TWO.
IF WE WIN, GO TO 58. IF WE LOSE, GO TO 54. OR IF YOU WANT TO USE A MIRROR, GO TO 40.
49
DROP IT, LAWBREAKER--
RRNNN
WHAT? I THOUGHT AGGRO WAS A WAY OF LIFE IN THESE COMICS?
WHEN IN ROME...
50
...YOU'RE NEXT, PUNK!
RRNNN
AAAEEEEIIGH!
ARRGH LIVES AND THE BLOOD IS PRINTED RED! TAKE A *GEM AND ADD +3 TO OUR BADNESS SCORE.
THEN GO TO 47.

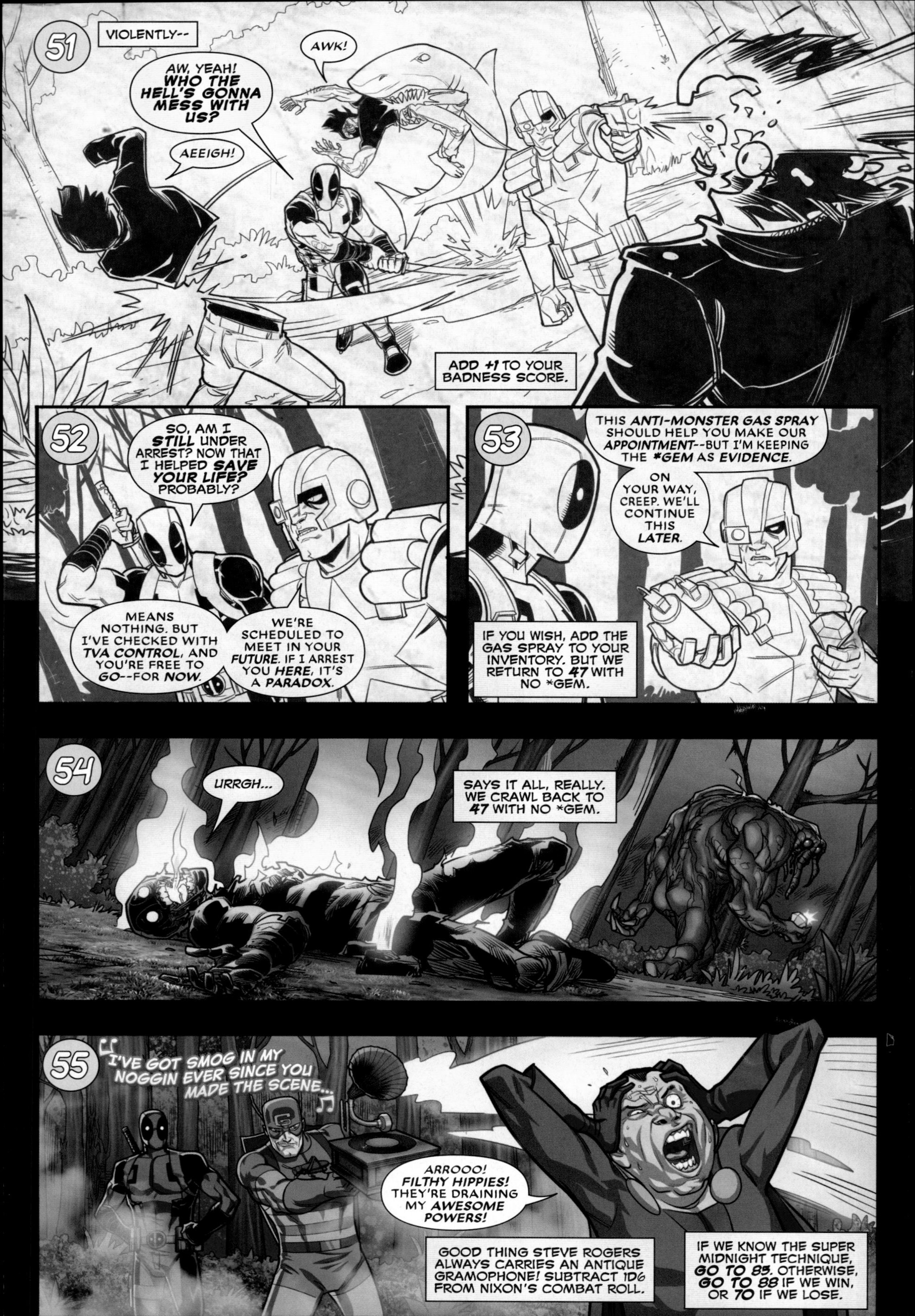
51
VIOLENTLY--
AW, YEAH! WHO THE HELL'S GONNA MESS WITH US?
AWK!
AEEIGH!
ADD +1 TO YOUR BADNESS SCORE.
52
SO, AM I STILL UNDER ARREST? NOW THAT I HELPED SAVE YOUR LIFE? PROBABLY?
MEANS NOTHING. BUT I'VE CHECKED WITH TVA CONTROL, AND YOU'RE FREE TO GO--FOR NOW.
WE'RE SCHEDULED TO MEET IN YOUR FUTURE. IF I ARREST YOU HERE, IT'S A PARADOX.
53
THIS ANTI-MONSTER GAS SPRAY SHOULD HELP YOU MAKE OUR APPOINTMENT--BUT I'M KEEPING THE *GEM AS EVIDENCE.
ON YOUR WAY, CREEP. WE'LL CONTINUE THIS LATER.
IF YOU WISH, ADD THE GAS SPRAY TO YOUR INVENTORY. BUT WE RETURN TO 47 WITH NO *GEM.
54
URRGH...
SAYS IT ALL, REALLY. WE CRAWL BACK TO 47 WITH NO *GEM.
55
I'VE GOT SMOG IN MY NOGGIN EVER SINCE YOU MADE THE SCENE...
ARROOO! FILTHY HIPPIES! THEY'RE DRAINING MY AWESOME POWERS!
GOOD THING STEVE ROGERS ALWAYS CARRIES AN ANTIQUE GRAMOPHONE! SUBTRACT 1D6 FROM NIXON'S COMBAT ROLL.
IF WE KNOW THE SUPER MIDNIGHT TECHNIQUE, GO TO 85. OTHERWISE, GO TO 88 IF WE WIN, OR 70 IF WE LOSE.

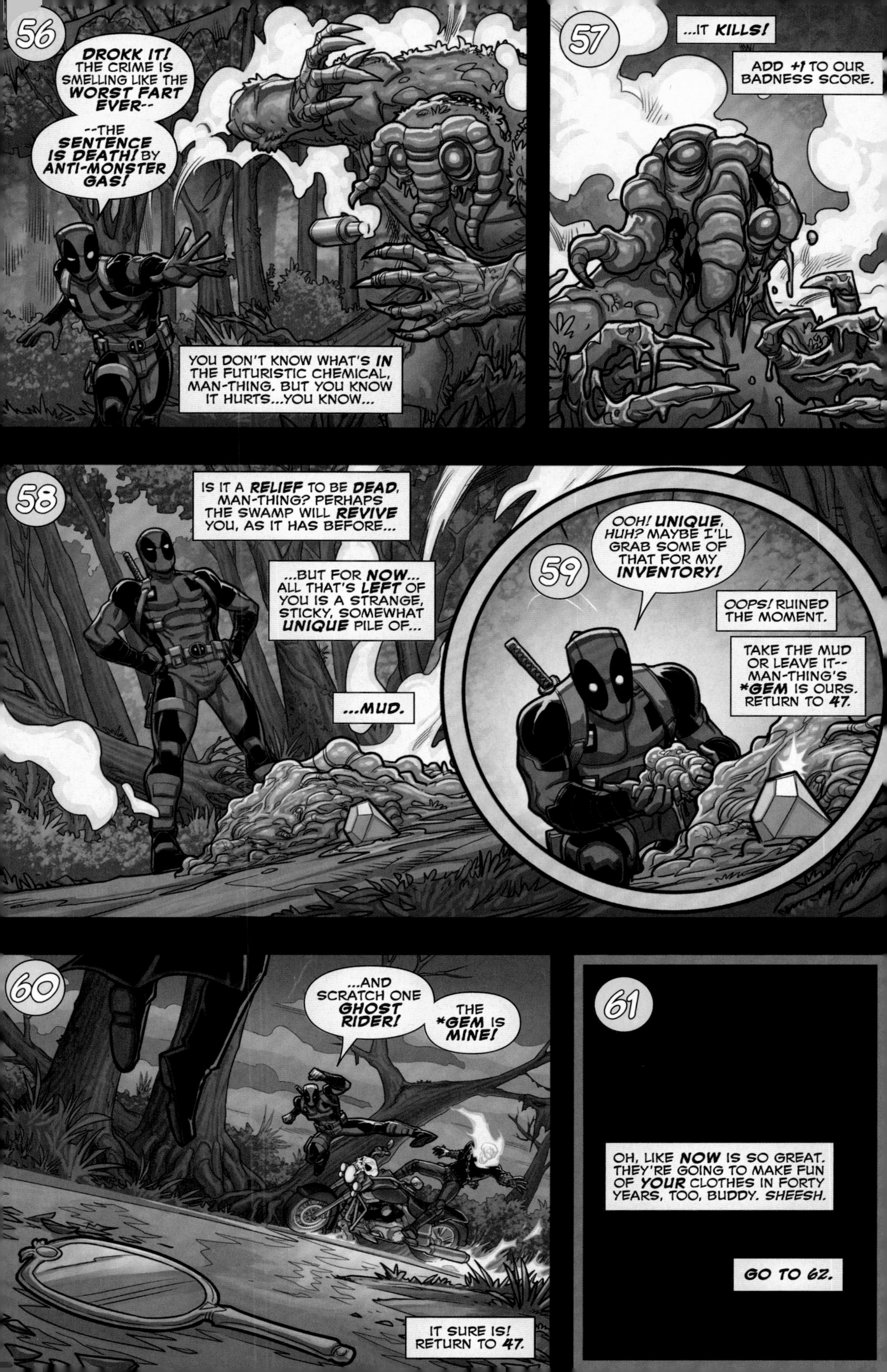
56
DROKK IT! THE CRIME IS SMELLING LIKE THE WORST FART EVER--
--THE SENTENCE IS DEATH! BY ANTI-MONSTER GAS!
YOU DON'T KNOW WHAT'S IN THE FUTURISTIC CHEMICAL, MAN-THING. BUT YOU KNOW IT HURTS...YOU KNOW...
57
...IT KILLS!
ADD +1 TO OUR BADNESS SCORE.
58
IS IT A RELIEF TO BE DEAD, MAN-THING? PERHAPS THE SWAMP WILL REVIVE YOU, AS IT HAS BEFORE...
...BUT FOR NOW... ALL THAT'S LEFT OF YOU IS A STRANGE, STICKY, SOMEWHAT UNIQUE PILE OF...
...MUD.
59
OOH! UNIQUE, HUH? MAYBE I'LL GRAB SOME OF THAT FOR MY INVENTORY!
OOPS! RUINED THE MOMENT.
TAKE THE MUD OR LEAVE IT-- MAN-THING'S *GEM IS OURS. RETURN TO 47.
60
...AND SCRATCH ONE GHOST RIDER!
THE *GEM IS MINE!
IT SURE IS! RETURN TO 47.
61
OH, LIKE NOW IS SO GREAT. THEY'RE GOING TO MAKE FUN OF YOUR CLOTHES IN FORTY YEARS, TOO, BUDDY. SHEESH.
GO TO 62.

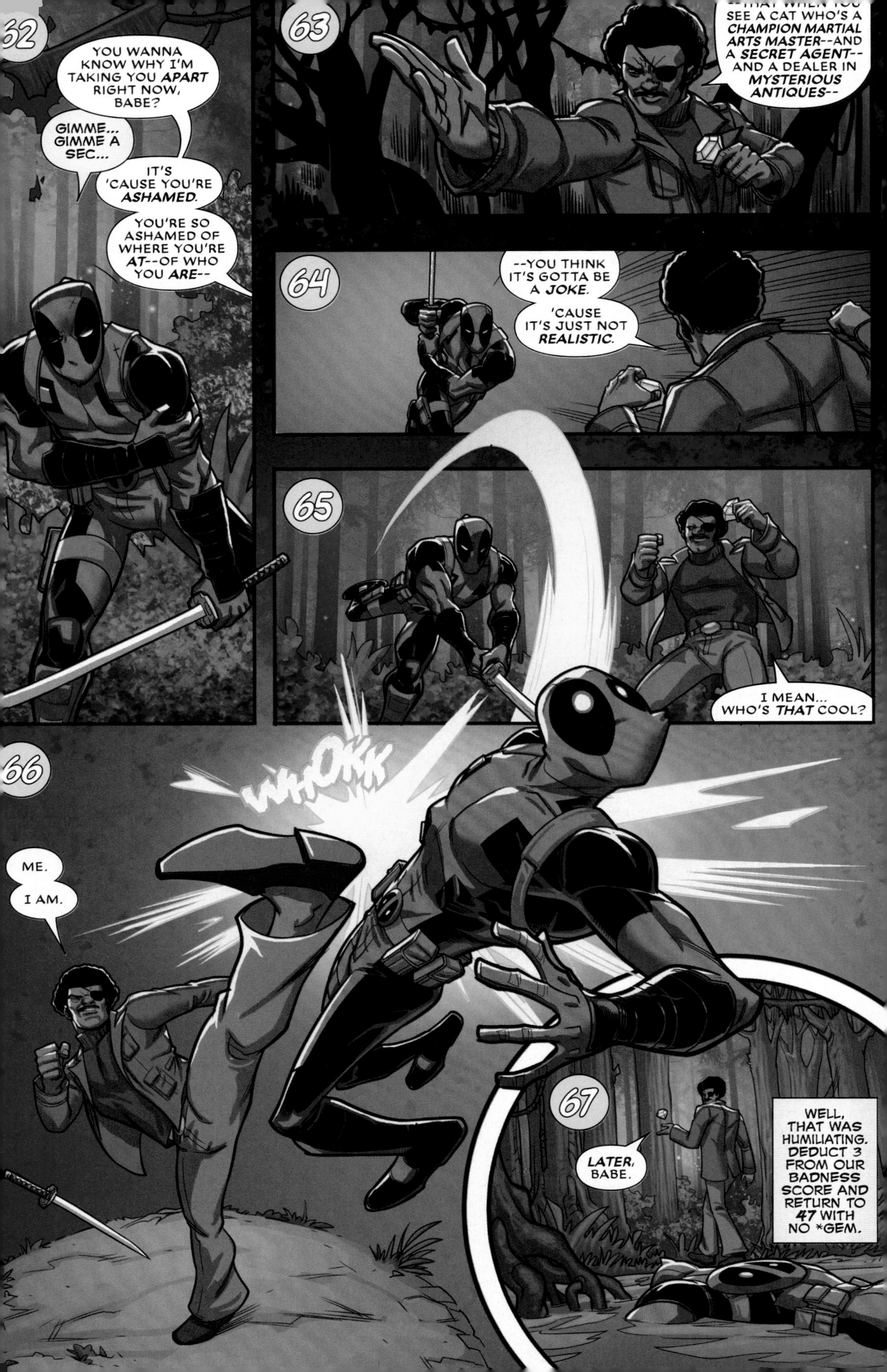
62
YOU WANNA KNOW WHY I'M TAKING YOU APART RIGHT NOW, BABE?
GIMME... GIMME A SEC...
IT'S 'CAUSE YOU'RE ASHAMED.
YOU'RE SO ASHAMED OF WHERE YOU'RE AT--OF WHO YOU ARE--
63
SEE A CAT WHO'S A CHAMPION MARTIAL ARTS MASTER--AND A SECRET AGENT--AND A DEALER IN MYSTERIOUS ANTIQUES--
64
--YOU THINK IT'S GOTTA BE A JOKE.
'CAUSE IT'S JUST NOT REALISTIC.
65
I MEAN... WHO'S THAT COOL?
66
WHOKK
ME.
I AM.
67
LATER, BABE.
WELL, THAT WAS HUMILIATING. DEDUCT 3 FROM OUR BADNESS SCORE AND RETURN TO 47 WITH NO *GEM.

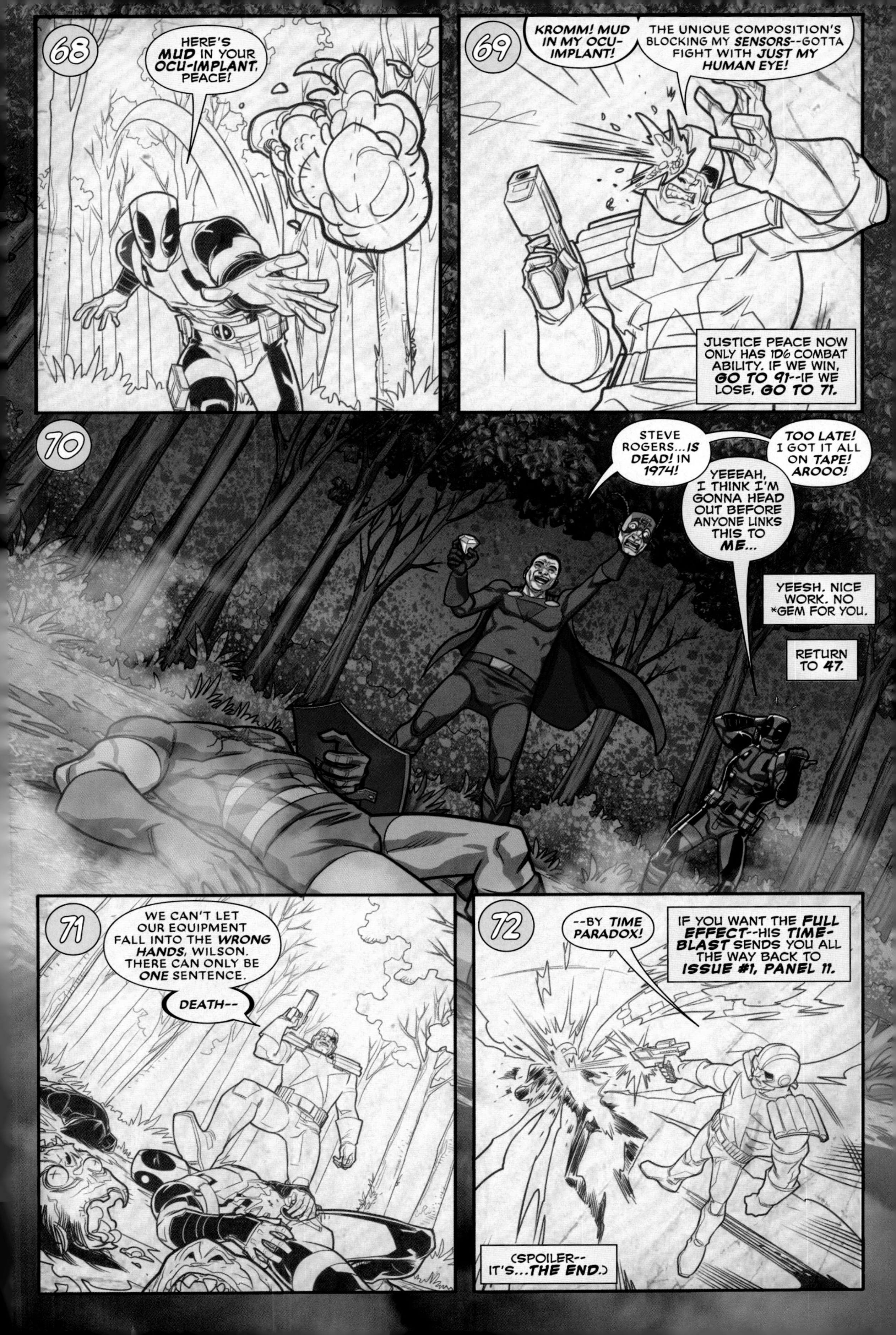
68
HERE'S MUD IN YOUR OCU-IMPLANT, PEACE!
69
KROMM! MUD IN MY OCU-IMPLANT!
THE UNIQUE COMPOSITION'S BLOCKING MY SENSORS--GOTTA FIGHT WITH JUST MY HUMAN EYE!
JUSTICE PEACE NOW ONLY HAS 1D6 COMBAT ABILITY. IF WE WIN, GO TO 91--IF WE LOSE, GO TO 71.
70
STEVE ROGERS...IS DEAD! IN 1974!
TOO LATE! I GOT IT ALL ON TAPE! AROOO!
YEEEAH, I THINK I'M GONNA HEAD OUT BEFORE ANYONE LINKS THIS TO ME...
YEESH. NICE WORK. NO *GEM FOR YOU.
RETURN TO 47.
71
WE CAN'T LET OUR EQUIPMENT FALL INTO THE WRONG HANDS, WILSON. THERE CAN ONLY BE ONE SENTENCE.
DEATH--
72
--BY TIME PARADOX!
IF YOU WANT THE FULL EFFECT--HIS TIME-BLAST SENDS YOU ALL THE WAY BACK TO ISSUE #1, PANEL 11.
(SPOILER-- IT'S...THE END.)

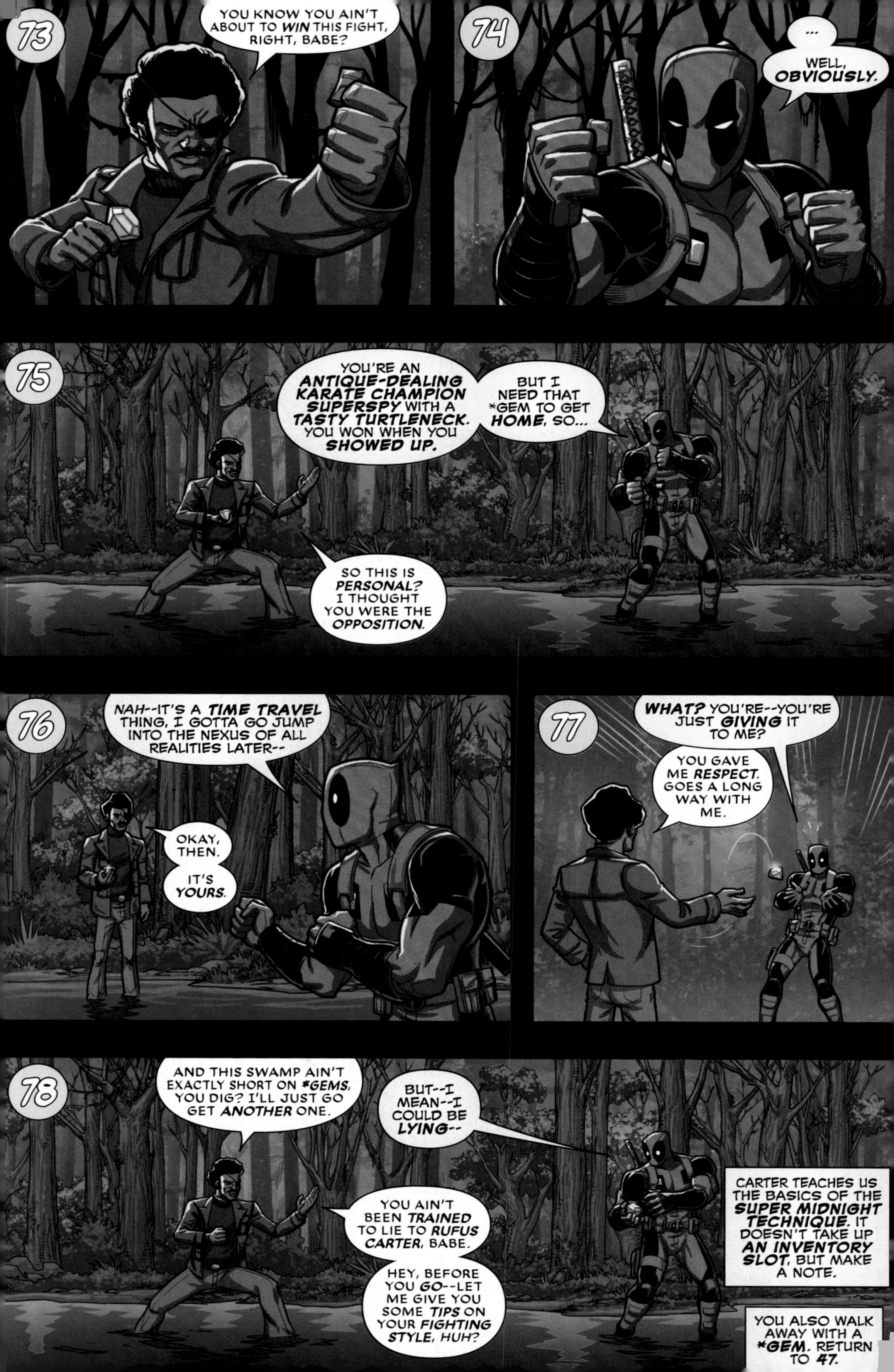
73
YOU KNOW YOU AIN'T ABOUT TO WIN THIS FIGHT, RIGHT, BABE?
74
...
WELL, OBVIOUSLY.
75
YOU'RE AN ANTIQUE-DEALING KARATE CHAMPION SUPERSPY WITH A TASTY TURTLENECK. YOU WON WHEN YOU SHOWED UP.
BUT I NEED THAT *GEM TO GET HOME, SO...
SO THIS IS PERSONAL? I THOUGHT YOU WERE THE OPPOSITION.
76
NAH--IT'S A TIME TRAVEL THING, I GOTTA GO JUMP INTO THE NEXUS OF ALL REALITIES LATER--
OKAY, THEN.
IT'S YOURS.
77
WHAT? YOU'RE--YOU'RE JUST GIVING IT TO ME?
YOU GAVE ME RESPECT. GOES A LONG WAY WITH ME.
78
AND THIS SWAMP AIN'T EXACTLY SHORT ON *GEMS, YOU DIG? I'LL JUST GO GET ANOTHER ONE.
BUT--I MEAN--I COULD BE LYING--
YOU AIN'T BEEN TRAINED TO LIE TO RUFUS CARTER, BABE.
HEY, BEFORE YOU GO--LET ME GIVE YOU SOME TIPS ON YOUR FIGHTING STYLE, HUH?
CARTER TEACHES US THE BASICS OF THE SUPER MIDNIGHT TECHNIQUE. IT DOESN'T TAKE UP AN INVENTORY SLOT, BUT MAKE A NOTE.
YOU ALSO WALK AWAY WITH A *GEM. RETURN TO 47.

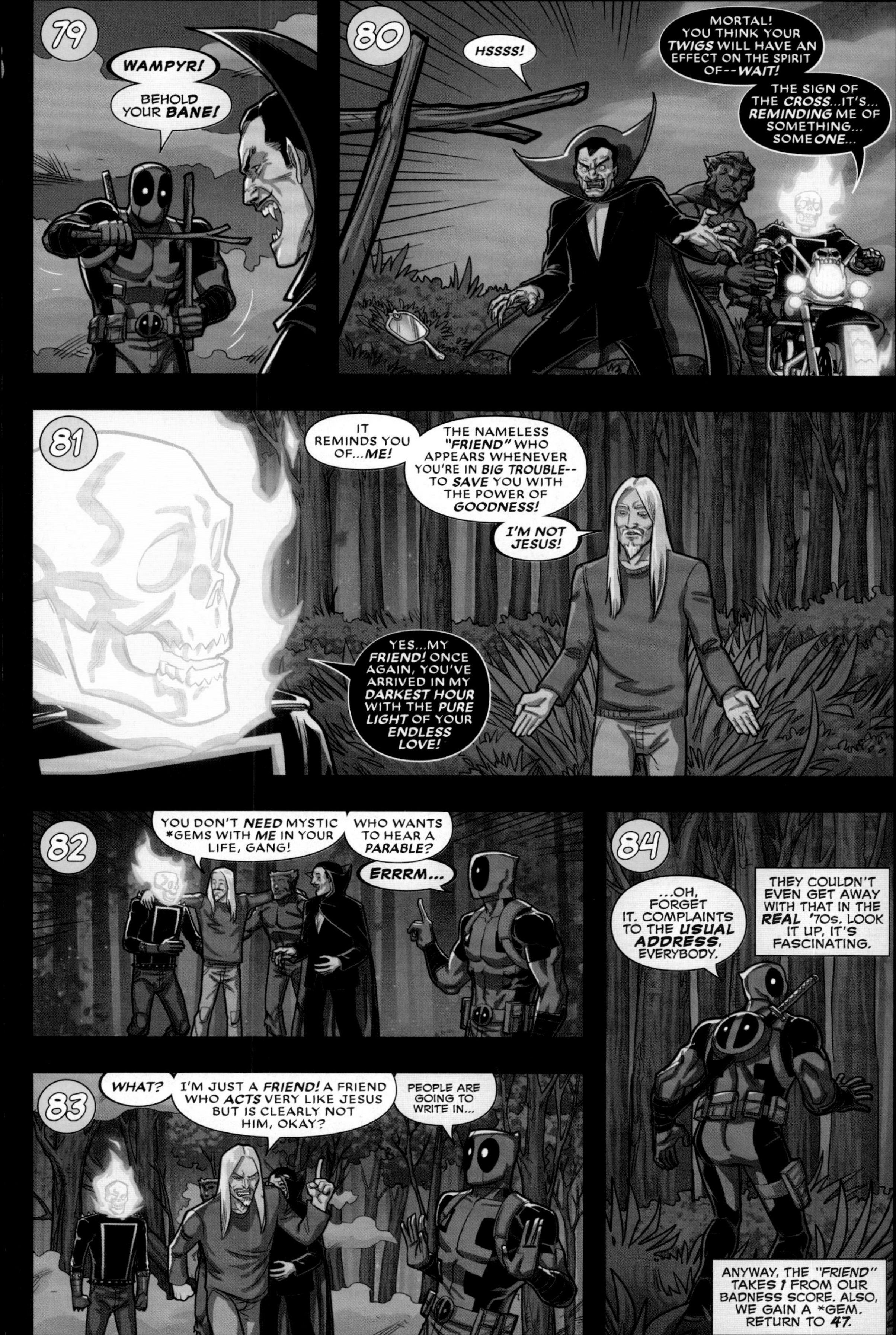
79
WAMPYR!
BEHOLD YOUR BANE!
80
HSSSS!
MORTAL! YOU THINK YOUR TWIGS WILL HAVE AN EFFECT ON THE SPIRIT OF--WAIT!
THE SIGN OF THE CROSS...IT'S... REMINDING ME OF SOMETHING... SOMEONE...
81
IT REMINDS YOU OF...ME!
THE NAMELESS "FRIEND" WHO APPEARS WHENEVER YOU'RE IN BIG TROUBLE--TO SAVE YOU WITH THE POWER OF GOODNESS!
I'M NOT JESUS!
YES...MY FRIEND! ONCE AGAIN, YOU'VE ARRIVED IN MY DARKEST HOUR WITH THE PURE LIGHT OF YOUR ENDLESS LOVE!
82
YOU DON'T NEED MYSTIC *GEMS WITH ME IN YOUR LIFE, GANG!
WHO WANTS TO HEAR A PARABLE?
ERRRM...
83
WHAT?
I'M JUST A FRIEND! A FRIEND WHO ACTS VERY LIKE JESUS BUT IS CLEARLY NOT HIM, OKAY?
PEOPLE ARE GOING TO WRITE IN...
84
...OH, FORGET IT. COMPLAINTS TO THE USUAL ADDRESS, EVERYBODY.
THEY COULDN'T EVEN GET AWAY WITH THAT IN THE REAL '70s. LOOK IT UP, IT'S FASCINATING.
ANYWAY, THE "FRIEND" TAKES 1 FROM OUR BADNESS SCORE. ALSO, WE GAIN A *GEM. RETURN TO 47.

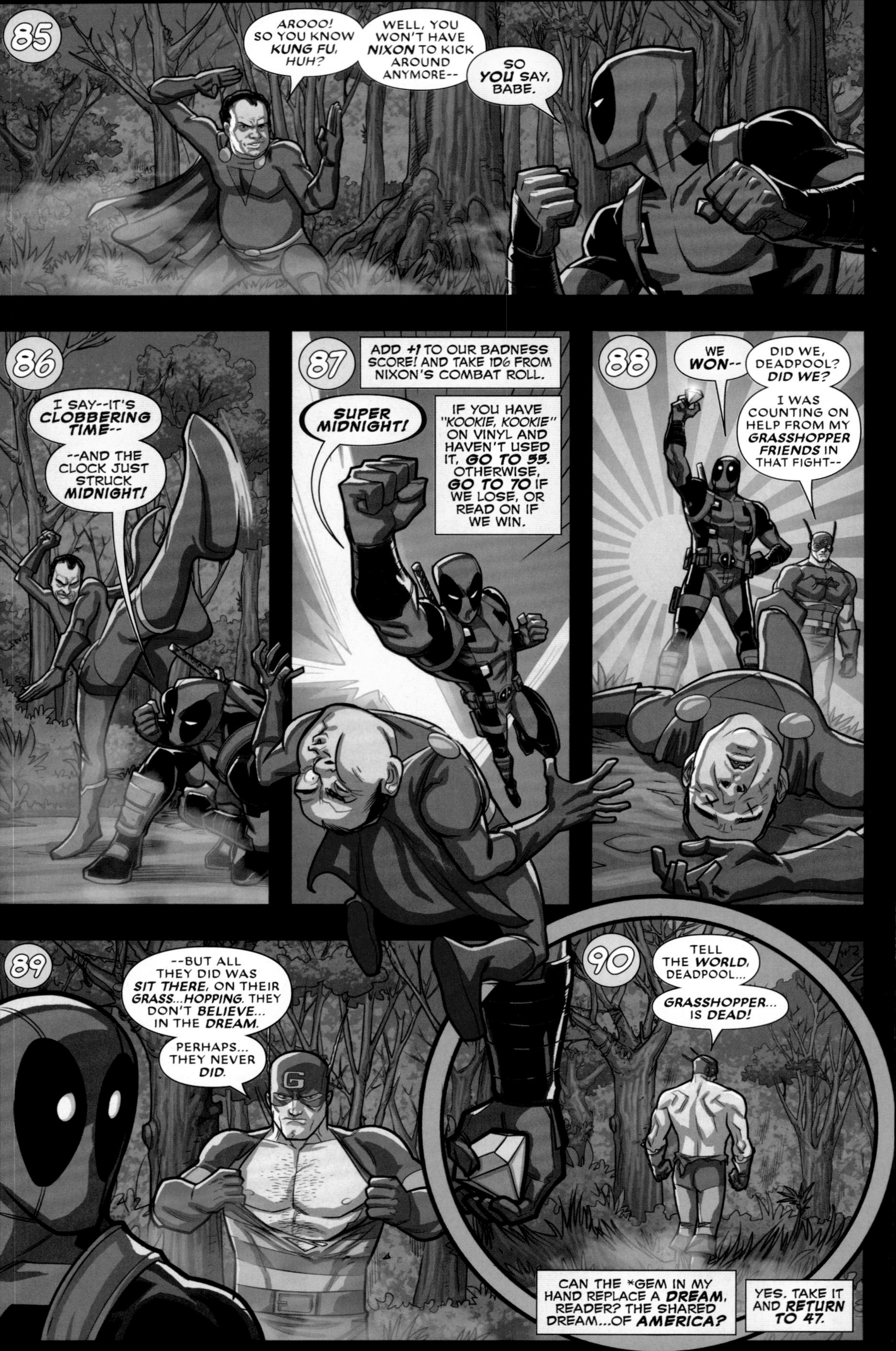
85
AROOO! SO YOU KNOW KUNG FU, HUH?
WELL, YOU WON'T HAVE NIXON TO KICK AROUND ANYMORE--
SO YOU SAY, BABE.
86
I SAY--IT'S CLOBBERING TIME--
--AND THE CLOCK JUST STRUCK MIDNIGHT!
87
ADD +1 TO OUR BADNESS SCORE! AND TAKE 1D6 FROM NIXON'S COMBAT ROLL.
SUPER MIDNIGHT!
IF YOU HAVE "KOOKIE, KOOKIE" ON VINYL AND HAVEN'T USED IT, GO TO 55. OTHERWISE, GO TO 70 IF WE LOSE, OR READ ON IF WE WIN.
88
WE WON--
DID WE, DEADPOOL? DID WE?
I WAS COUNTING ON HELP FROM MY GRASSHOPPER FRIENDS IN THAT FIGHT--
89
--BUT ALL THEY DID WAS SIT THERE, ON THEIR GRASS...HOPPING. THEY DON'T BELIEVE... IN THE DREAM.
PERHAPS... THEY NEVER DID.
90
TELL THE WORLD, DEADPOOL...
GRASSHOPPER... IS DEAD!
CAN THE *GEM IN MY HAND REPLACE A DREAM, READER? THE SHARED DREAM...OF AMERICA?
YES. TAKE IT AND RETURN TO 47.

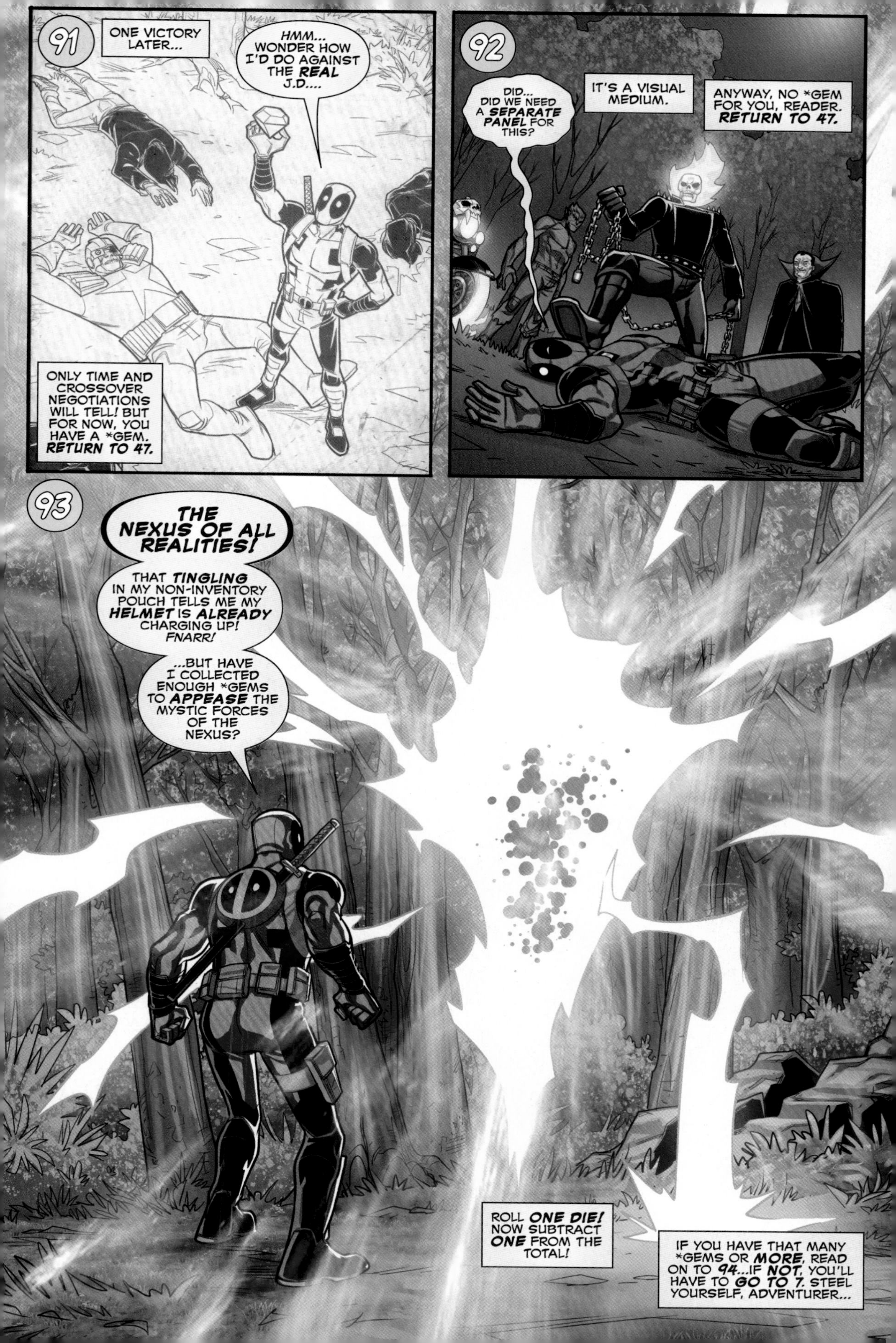
91
ONE VICTORY LATER...
HMM... WONDER HOW I'D DO AGAINST THE REAL J.D....
ONLY TIME AND CROSSOVER NEGOTIATIONS WILL TELL! BUT FOR NOW, YOU HAVE A *GEM. RETURN TO 47.
92
DID... DID WE NEED A SEPARATE PANEL FOR THIS?
IT'S A VISUAL MEDIUM.
ANYWAY, NO *GEM FOR YOU, READER. RETURN TO 47.
93
THE NEXUS OF ALL REALITIES!
THAT TINGLING IN MY NON-INVENTORY POUCH TELLS ME MY HELMET IS ALREADY CHARGING UP! FNARR!
...BUT HAVE I COLLECTED ENOUGH *GEMS TO APPEASE THE MYSTIC FORCES OF THE NEXUS?
ROLL ONE DIE! NOW SUBTRACT ONE FROM THE TOTAL!
IF YOU HAVE THAT MANY *GEMS OR MORE, READ ON TO 94...IF NOT, YOU'LL HAVE TO GO TO 7. STEEL YOURSELF, ADVENTURER...

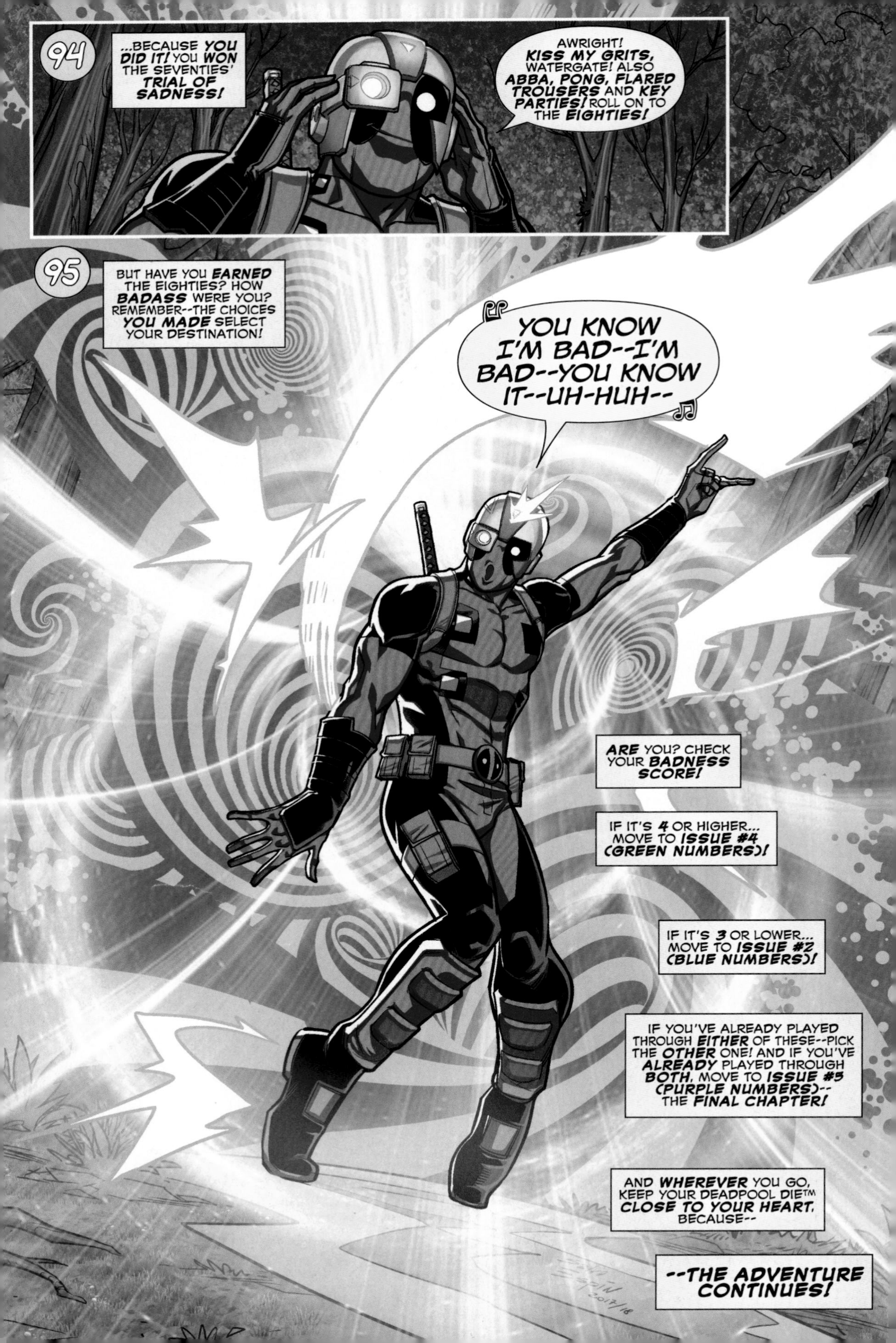
94
...BECAUSE YOU DID IT! YOU WON THE SEVENTIES' TRIAL OF SADNESS!
AWRIGHT! KISS MY GRITS, WATERGATE! ALSO ABBA, PONG, FLARED TROUSERS AND KEY PARTIES! ROLL ON TO THE EIGHTIES!
95
BUT HAVE YOU EARNED THE EIGHTIES? HOW BADASS WERE YOU? REMEMBER--THE CHOICES YOU MADE SELECT YOUR DESTINATION!
YOU KNOW I'M BAD--I'M BAD--YOU KNOW IT--UH-HUH--
ARE YOU? CHECK YOUR BADNESS SCORE!
IF IT'S 4 OR HIGHER... MOVE TO ISSUE #4 (GREEN NUMBERS)!
IF IT'S 3 OR LOWER... MOVE TO ISSUE #2 (BLUE NUMBERS)!
IF YOU'VE ALREADY PLAYED THROUGH EITHER OF THESE--PICK THE OTHER ONE! AND IF YOU'VE ALREADY PLAYED THROUGH BOTH, MOVE TO ISSUE #5 (PURPLE NUMBERS)-- THE FINAL CHAPTER!
AND WHEREVER YOU GO, KEEP YOUR DEADPOOL DIE™ CLOSE TO YOUR HEART, BECAUSE--
--THE ADVENTURE CONTINUES!

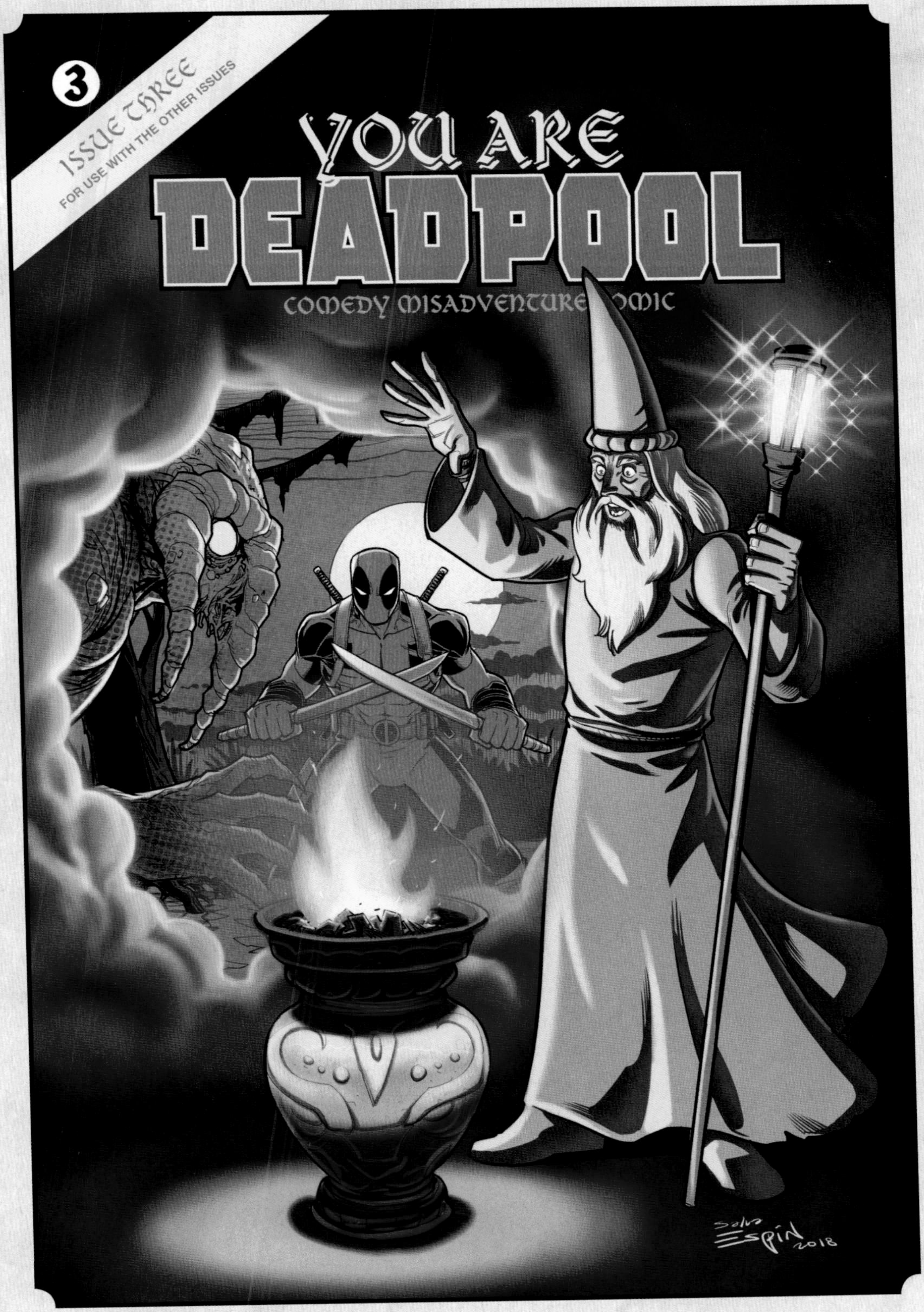

3 VARIANT BY **SALVA ESPIN**

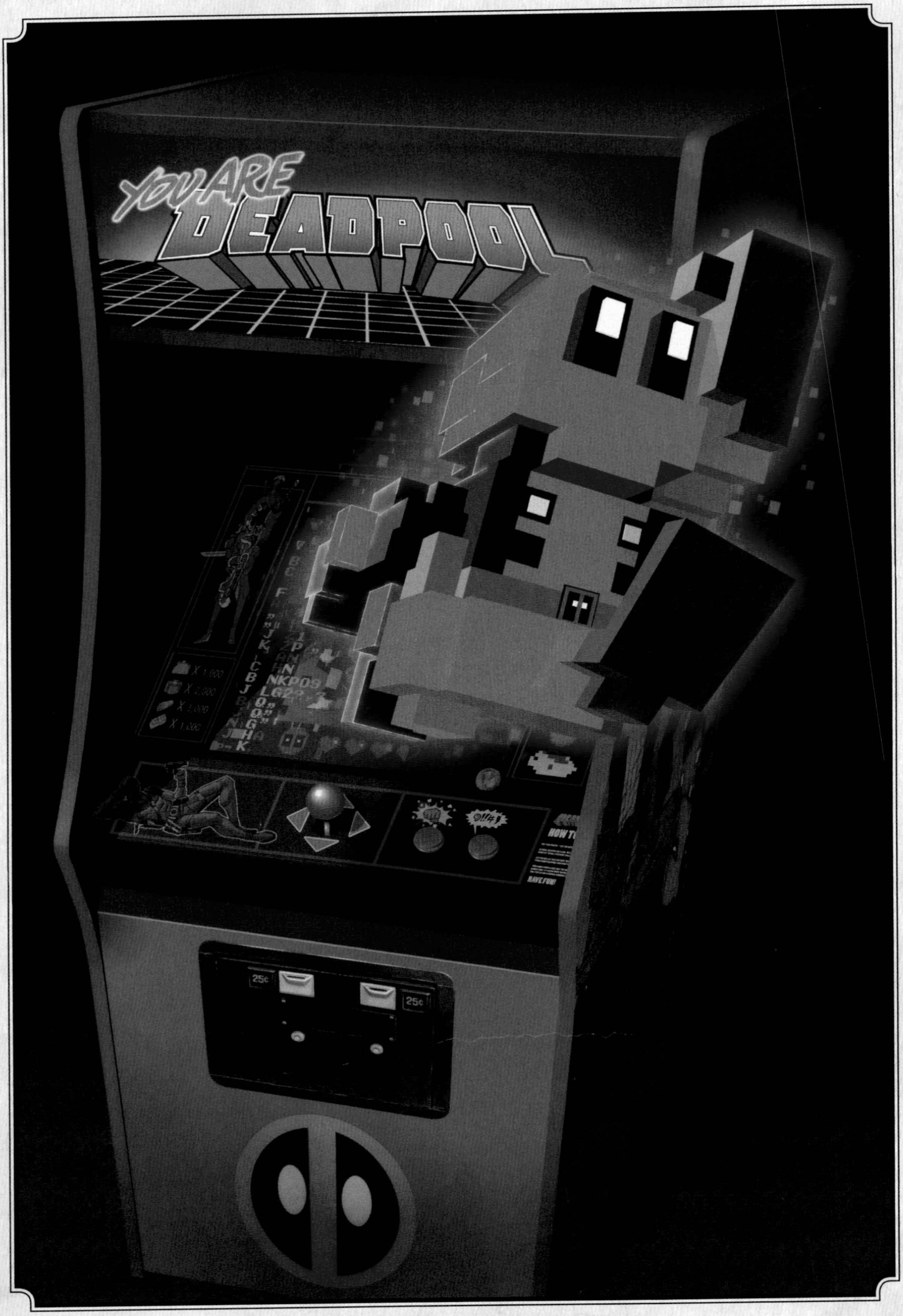
YOU ARE
DEADPOOL
25¢
25¢

four

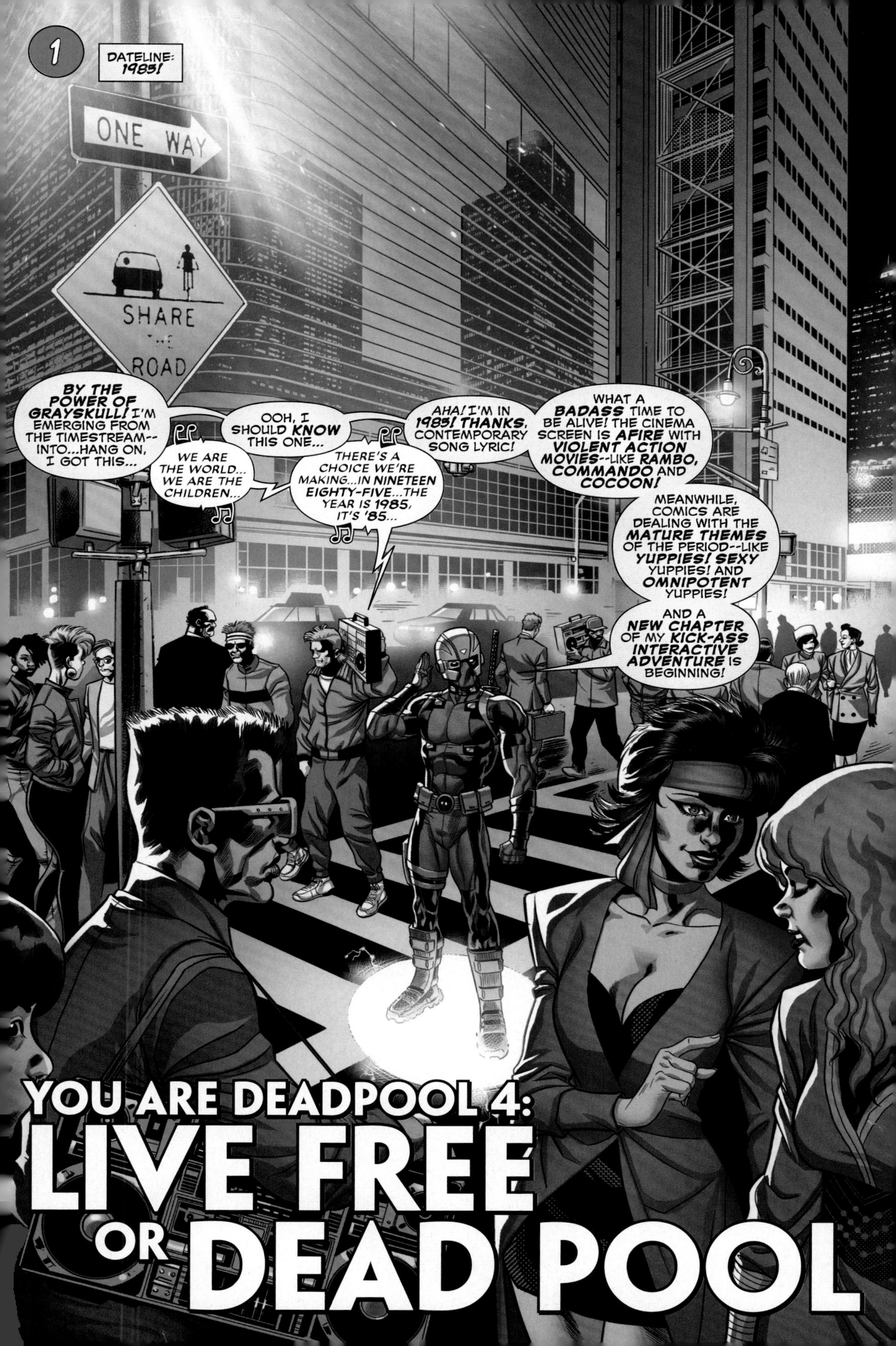
1
DATELINE: 1985!
ONE WAY
SHARE THE ROAD
BY THE POWER OF GRAYSKULL! I'M EMERGING FROM THE TIMESTREAM--INTO...HANG ON, I GOT THIS...
WE ARE THE WORLD... WE ARE THE CHILDREN...
OOH, I SHOULD KNOW THIS ONE...
THERE'S A CHOICE WE'RE MAKING...IN NINETEEN EIGHTY-FIVE...THE YEAR IS 1985, IT'S '85...
AHA! I'M IN 1985! THANKS, CONTEMPORARY SONG LYRIC!
WHAT A BADASS TIME TO BE ALIVE! THE CINEMA SCREEN IS AFIRE WITH VIOLENT ACTION MOVIES--LIKE RAMBO, COMMANDO AND COCOON!
MEANWHILE, COMICS ARE DEALING WITH THE MATURE THEMES OF THE PERIOD--LIKE YUPPIES! SEXY YUPPIES! AND OMNIPOTENT YUPPIES!
AND A NEW CHAPTER OF MY KICK-ASS INTERACTIVE ADVENTURE IS BEGINNING!
YOU ARE DEADPOOL 4:
LIVE FREE OR DEAD POOL

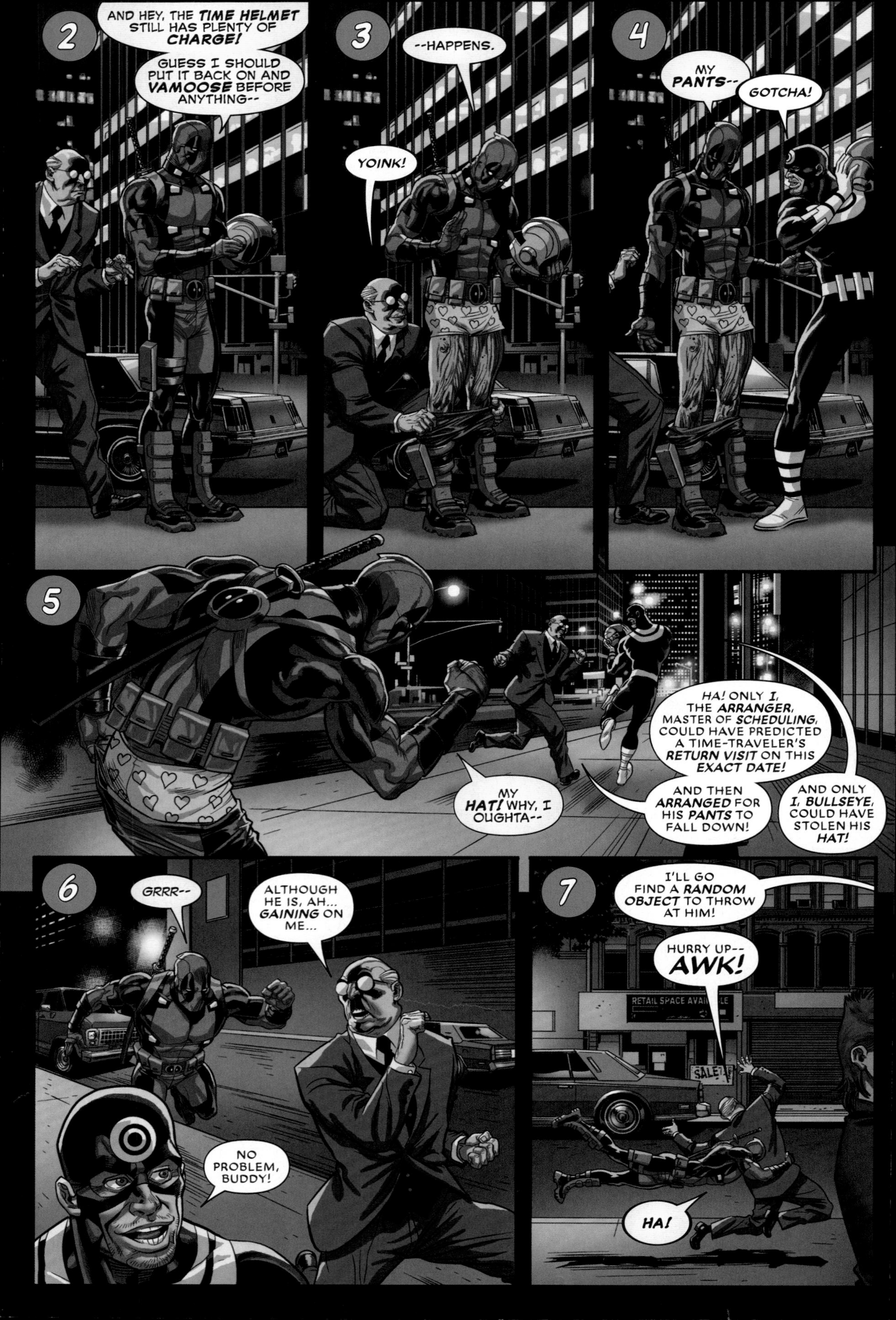
2
AND HEY, THE TIME HELMET STILL HAS PLENTY OF CHARGE!
GUESS I SHOULD PUT IT BACK ON AND VAMOOSE BEFORE ANYTHING--
3
--HAPPENS.
YOINK!
4
MY PANTS--
GOTCHA!
5
MY HAT! WHY, I OUGHTA--
HA! ONLY I, THE ARRANGER, MASTER OF SCHEDULING, COULD HAVE PREDICTED A TIME-TRAVELER'S RETURN VISIT ON THIS EXACT DATE!
AND THEN ARRANGED FOR HIS PANTS TO FALL DOWN!
AND ONLY I, BULLSEYE, COULD HAVE STOLEN HIS HAT!
6
GRRR--
ALTHOUGH HE IS, AH... GAINING ON ME...
NO PROBLEM, BUDDY!
7
I'LL GO FIND A RANDOM OBJECT TO THROW AT HIM!
HURRY UP-- AWK!
SALE
HA!

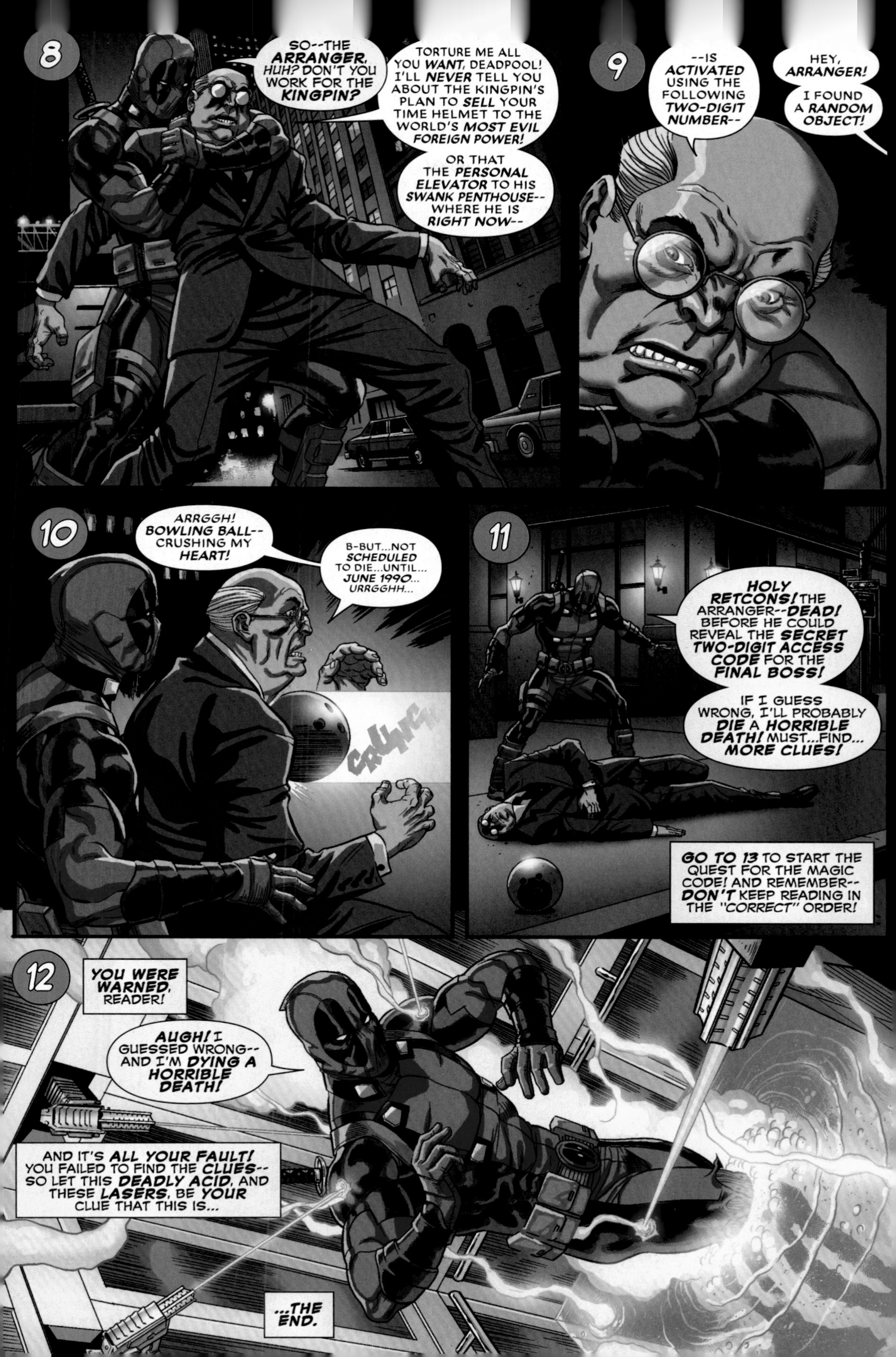
8
SO--THE ARRANGER, HUH? DON'T YOU WORK FOR THE KINGPIN?
TORTURE ME ALL YOU WANT, DEADPOOL! I'LL NEVER TELL YOU ABOUT THE KINGPIN'S PLAN TO SELL YOUR TIME HELMET TO THE WORLD'S MOST EVIL FOREIGN POWER!
OR THAT THE PERSONAL ELEVATOR TO HIS SWANK PENTHOUSE-- WHERE HE IS RIGHT NOW--
9
--IS ACTIVATED USING THE FOLLOWING TWO-DIGIT NUMBER--
HEY, ARRANGER!
I FOUND A RANDOM OBJECT!
10
ARRGGH! BOWLING BALL-- CRUSHING MY HEART!
B-BUT...NOT SCHEDULED TO DIE...UNTIL... JUNE 1990... URRGGHH...
11
HOLY RETCONS! THE ARRANGER--DEAD! BEFORE HE COULD REVEAL THE SECRET TWO-DIGIT ACCESS CODE FOR THE FINAL BOSS!
IF I GUESS WRONG, I'LL PROBABLY DIE A HORRIBLE DEATH! MUST...FIND... MORE CLUES!
GO TO 13 TO START THE QUEST FOR THE MAGIC CODE! AND REMEMBER-- DON'T KEEP READING IN THE "CORRECT" ORDER!
12
YOU WERE WARNED, READER!
AUGH! I GUESSED WRONG-- AND I'M DYING A HORRIBLE DEATH!
AND IT'S ALL YOUR FAULT! YOU FAILED TO FIND THE CLUES-- SO LET THIS DEADLY ACID, AND THESE LASERS, BE YOUR CLUE THAT THIS IS...
...THE END.

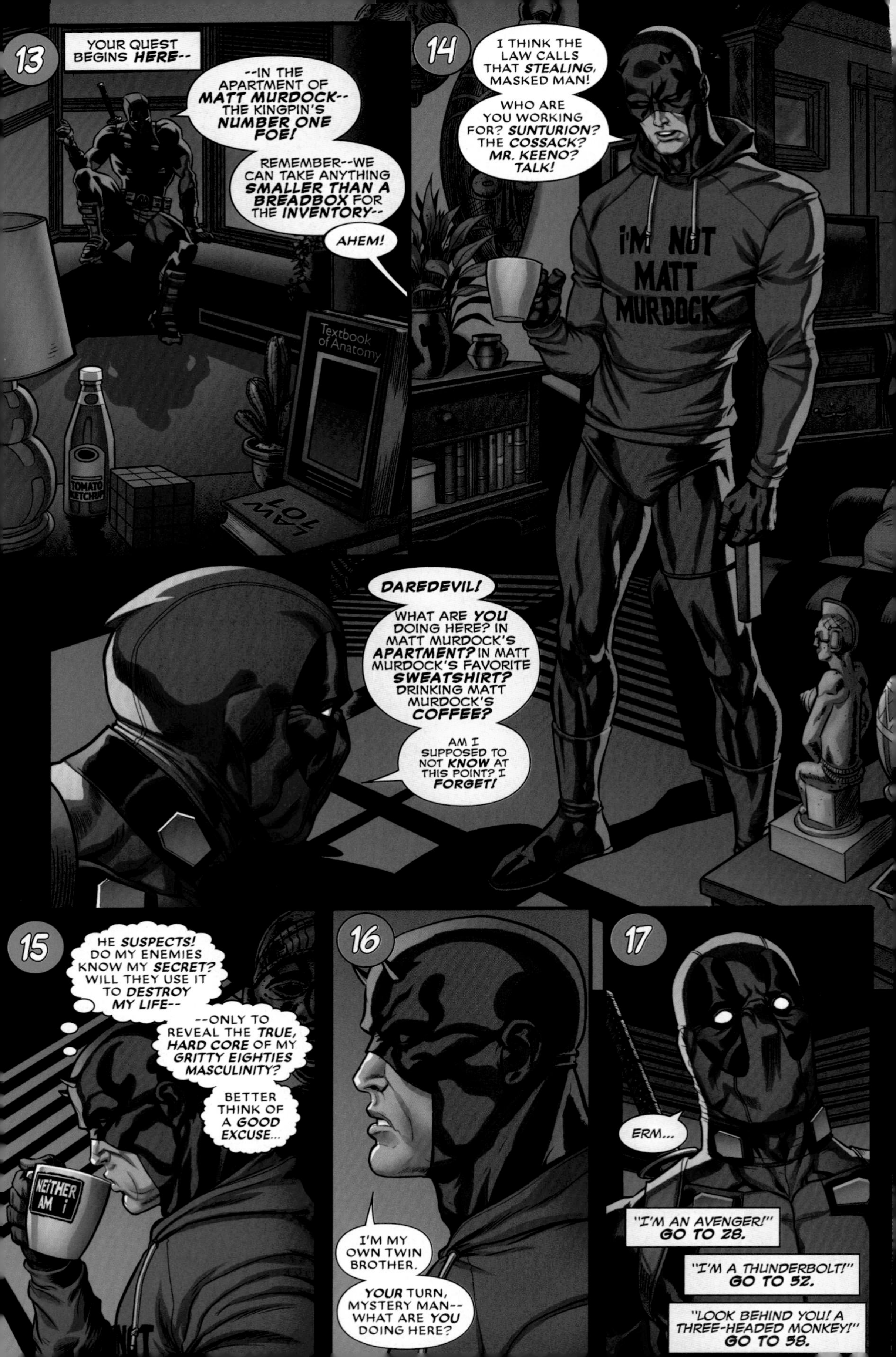
13
YOUR QUEST BEGINS HERE--
--IN THE APARTMENT OF MATT MURDOCK-- THE KINGPIN'S NUMBER ONE FOE!
REMEMBER--WE CAN TAKE ANYTHING SMALLER THAN A BREADBOX FOR THE INVENTORY--
AHEM!
Textbook of Anatomy
LAW 101
TOMATO KETCHUP
14
I THINK THE LAW CALLS THAT STEALING, MASKED MAN!
WHO ARE YOU WORKING FOR? SUNTURION? THE COSSACK? MR. KEENO? TALK!
I'M NOT MATT MURDOCK
DAREDEVIL!
WHAT ARE YOU DOING HERE? IN MATT MURDOCK'S APARTMENT? IN MATT MURDOCK'S FAVORITE SWEATSHIRT? DRINKING MATT MURDOCK'S COFFEE?
AM I SUPPOSED TO NOT KNOW AT THIS POINT? I FORGET!
15
HE SUSPECTS! DO MY ENEMIES KNOW MY SECRET? WILL THEY USE IT TO DESTROY MY LIFE--
--ONLY TO REVEAL THE TRUE, HARD CORE OF MY GRITTY EIGHTIES MASCULINITY?
BETTER THINK OF A GOOD EXCUSE...
NEITHER AM I
16
I'M MY OWN TWIN BROTHER.
YOUR TURN, MYSTERY MAN-- WHAT ARE YOU DOING HERE?
17
ERM...
"I'M AN AVENGER!" GO TO 28.
"I'M A THUNDERBOLT!" GO TO 52.
"LOOK BEHIND YOU! A THREE-HEADED MONKEY!" GO TO 58.

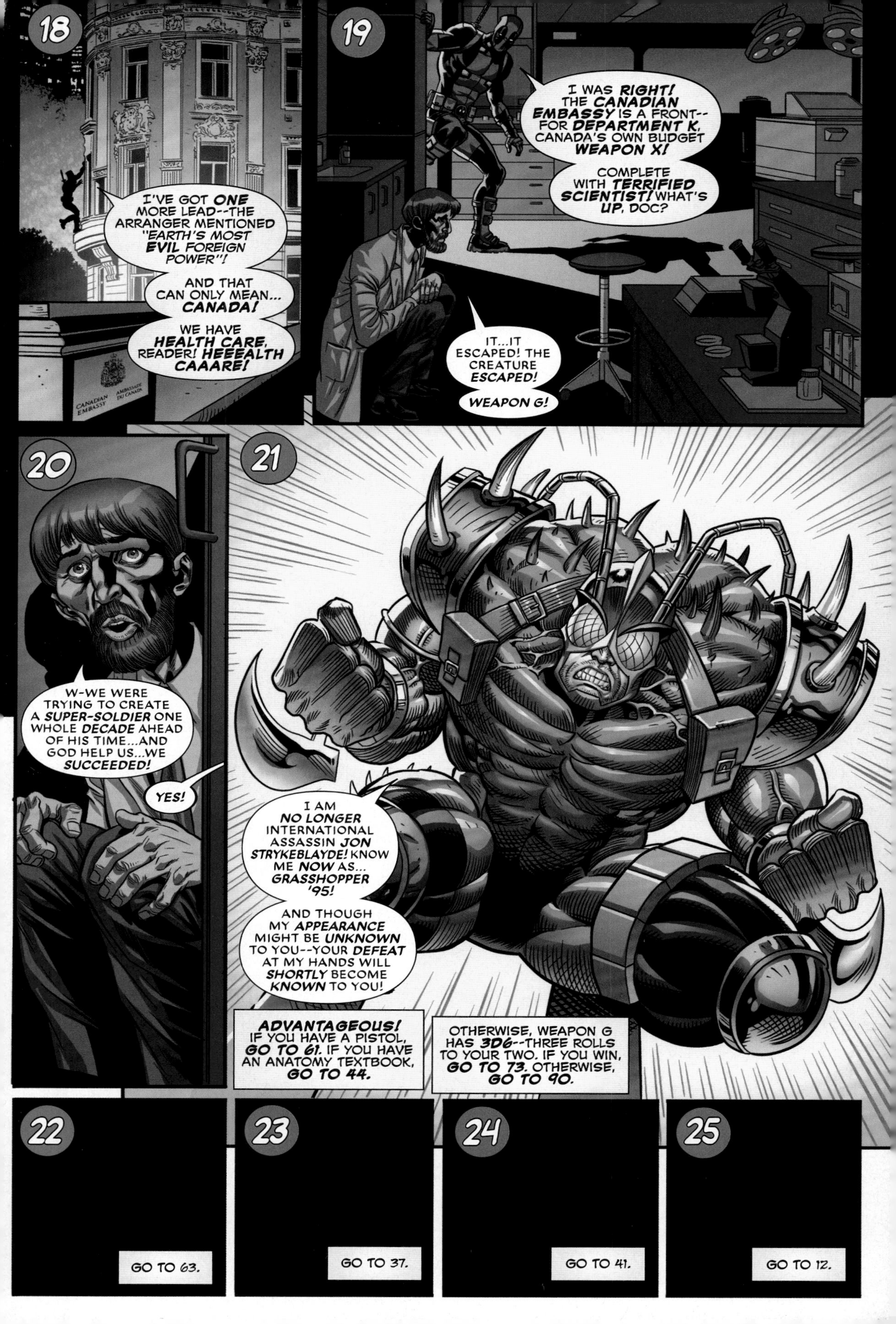
18
I'VE GOT ONE MORE LEAD--THE ARRANGER MENTIONED "EARTH'S MOST EVIL FOREIGN POWER"!
AND THAT CAN ONLY MEAN... CANADA!
WE HAVE HEALTH CARE, READER! HEEEALTH CAAARE!
CANADIAN EMBASSY
AMBASSADE DU CANADA
19
I WAS RIGHT! THE CANADIAN EMBASSY IS A FRONT-- FOR DEPARTMENT K, CANADA'S OWN BUDGET WEAPON X!
COMPLETE WITH TERRIFIED SCIENTIST! WHAT'S UP, DOC?
IT...IT ESCAPED! THE CREATURE ESCAPED!
WEAPON G!
20
W-WE WERE TRYING TO CREATE A SUPER-SOLDIER ONE WHOLE DECADE AHEAD OF HIS TIME...AND GOD HELP US...WE SUCCEEDED!
YES!
21
I AM NO LONGER INTERNATIONAL ASSASSIN JON STRYKEBLAYDE! KNOW ME NOW AS... GRASSHOPPER '95!
AND THOUGH MY APPEARANCE MIGHT BE UNKNOWN TO YOU--YOUR DEFEAT AT MY HANDS WILL SHORTLY BECOME KNOWN TO YOU!
ADVANTAGEOUS! IF YOU HAVE A PISTOL, GO TO 61. IF YOU HAVE AN ANATOMY TEXTBOOK, GO TO 44.
OTHERWISE, WEAPON G HAS 3D6--THREE ROLLS TO YOUR TWO. IF YOU WIN, GO TO 73. OTHERWISE, GO TO 90.
22
GO TO 63.
23
GO TO 37.
24
GO TO 41.
25
GO TO 12.

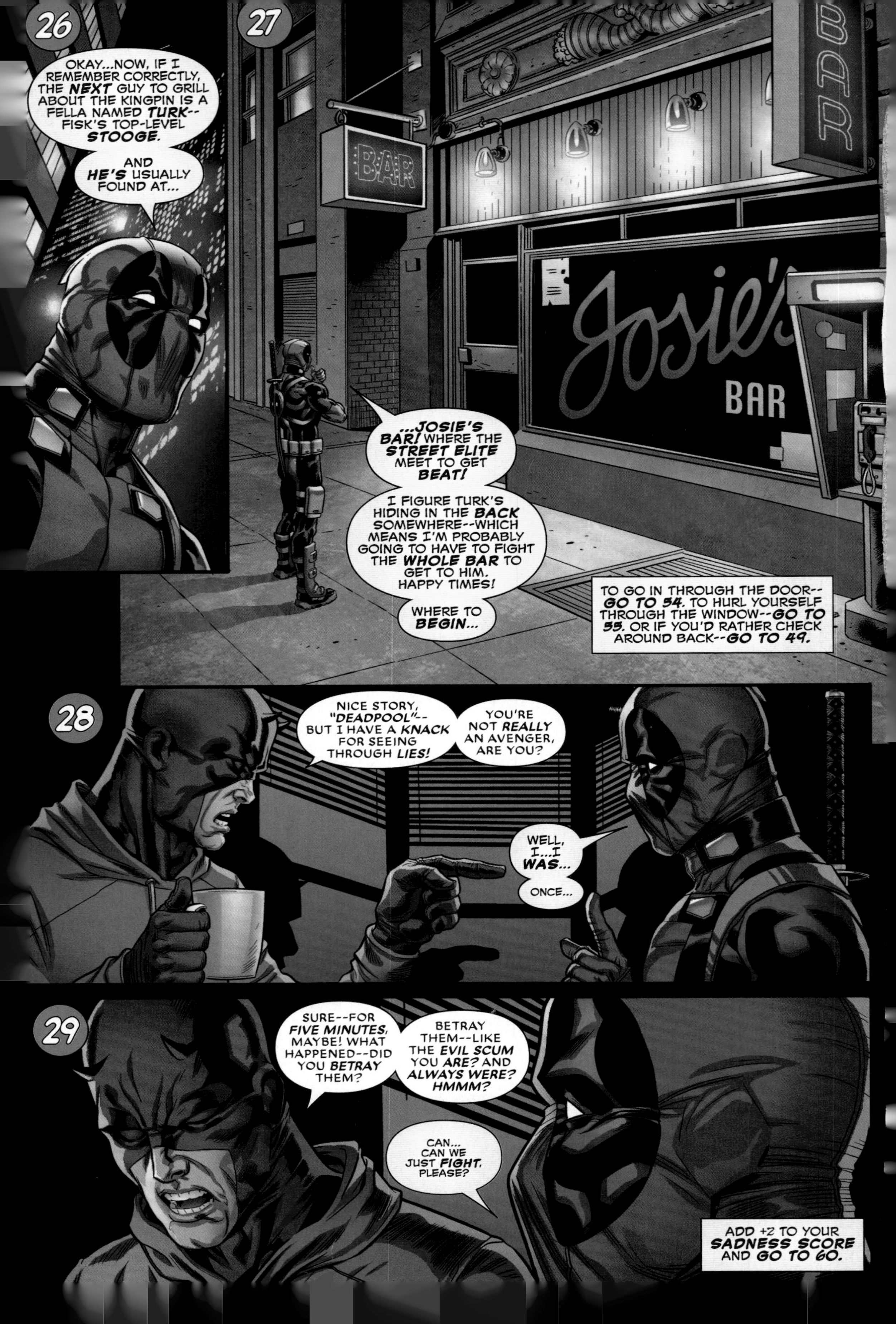
26
OKAY...NOW, IF I REMEMBER CORRECTLY, THE NEXT GUY TO GRILL ABOUT THE KINGPIN IS A FELLA NAMED TURK-- FISK'S TOP-LEVEL STOOGE.
AND HE'S USUALLY FOUND AT...
27
BAR
BAR
Josie's
BAR
...JOSIE'S BAR! WHERE THE STREET ELITE MEET TO GET BEAT!
I FIGURE TURK'S HIDING IN THE BACK SOMEWHERE--WHICH MEANS I'M PROBABLY GOING TO HAVE TO FIGHT THE WHOLE BAR TO GET TO HIM. HAPPY TIMES!
WHERE TO BEGIN...
TO GO IN THROUGH THE DOOR-- GO TO 54. TO HURL YOURSELF THROUGH THE WINDOW--GO TO 55. OR IF YOU'D RATHER CHECK AROUND BACK--GO TO 49.
28
NICE STORY, "DEADPOOL"-- BUT I HAVE A KNACK FOR SEEING THROUGH LIES!
YOU'RE NOT REALLY AN AVENGER, ARE YOU?
WELL, I...I WAS...
ONCE...
29
SURE--FOR FIVE MINUTES, MAYBE! WHAT HAPPENED--DID YOU BETRAY THEM?
BETRAY THEM--LIKE THE EVIL SCUM YOU ARE? AND ALWAYS WERE? HMMM?
CAN... CAN WE JUST FIGHT, PLEASE?
ADD +2 TO YOUR SADNESS SCORE AND GO TO 60.

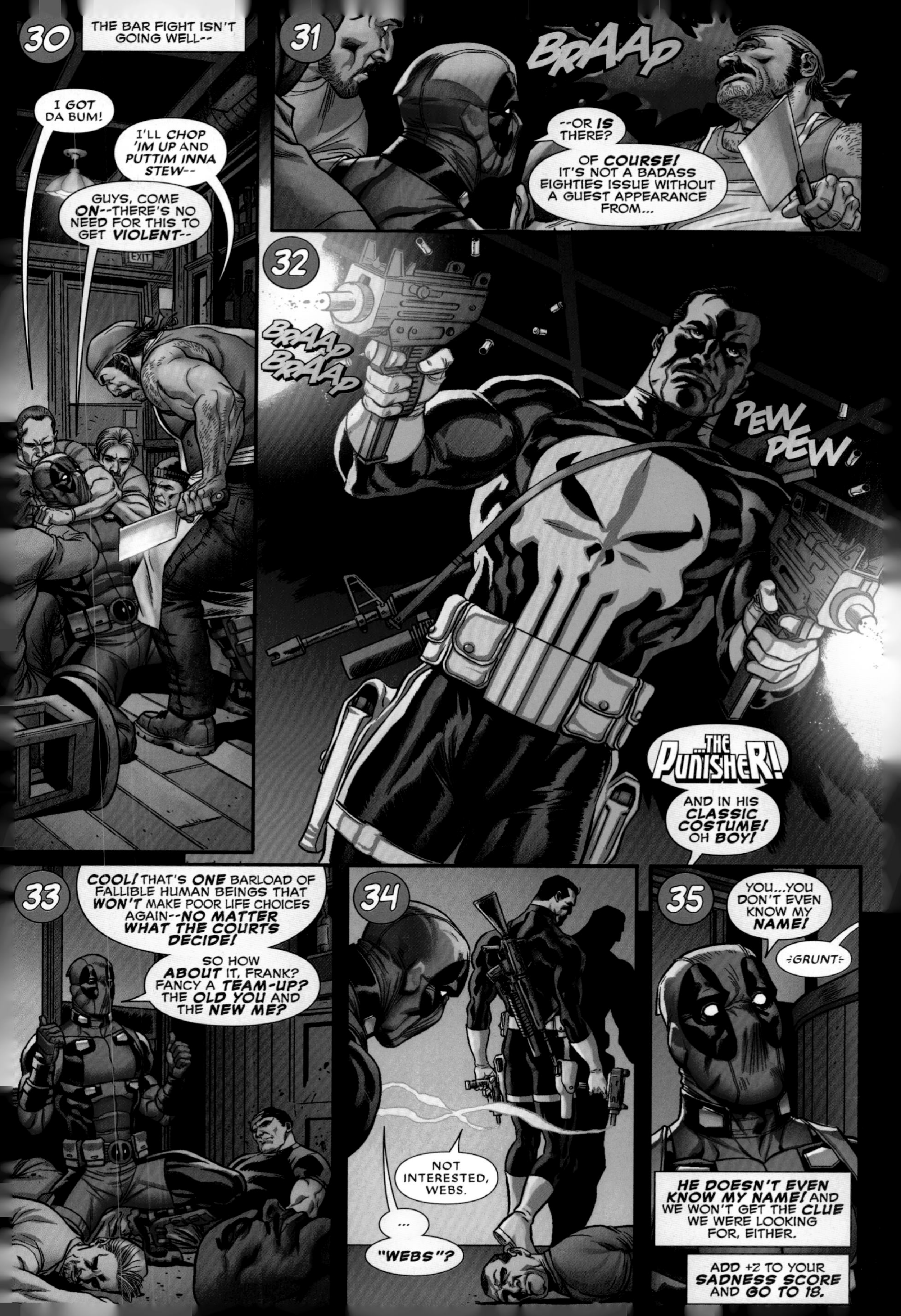
30
THE BAR FIGHT ISN'T GOING WELL--
I GOT DA BUM!
I'LL CHOP 'IM UP AND PUTTIM INNA STEW--
GUYS, COME ON--THERE'S NO NEED FOR THIS TO GET VIOLENT--
EXIT
31
BRAAAP
--OR IS THERE?
OF COURSE! IT'S NOT A BADASS EIGHTIES ISSUE WITHOUT A GUEST APPEARANCE FROM...
32
BRAAAP BRAAAP
PEW PEW
...THE PUNISHER!
AND IN HIS CLASSIC COSTUME! OH BOY!
33
COOL! THAT'S ONE BARLOAD OF FALLIBLE HUMAN BEINGS THAT WON'T MAKE POOR LIFE CHOICES AGAIN--NO MATTER WHAT THE COURTS DECIDE!
SO HOW ABOUT IT, FRANK? FANCY A TEAM-UP? THE OLD YOU AND THE NEW ME?
34
NOT INTERESTED, WEBS.
...
"WEBS"?
35
YOU...YOU DON'T EVEN KNOW MY NAME!
=GRUNT=
HE DOESN'T EVEN KNOW MY NAME! AND WE WON'T GET THE CLUE WE WERE LOOKING FOR, EITHER.
ADD +2 TO YOUR SADNESS SCORE AND GO TO 18.

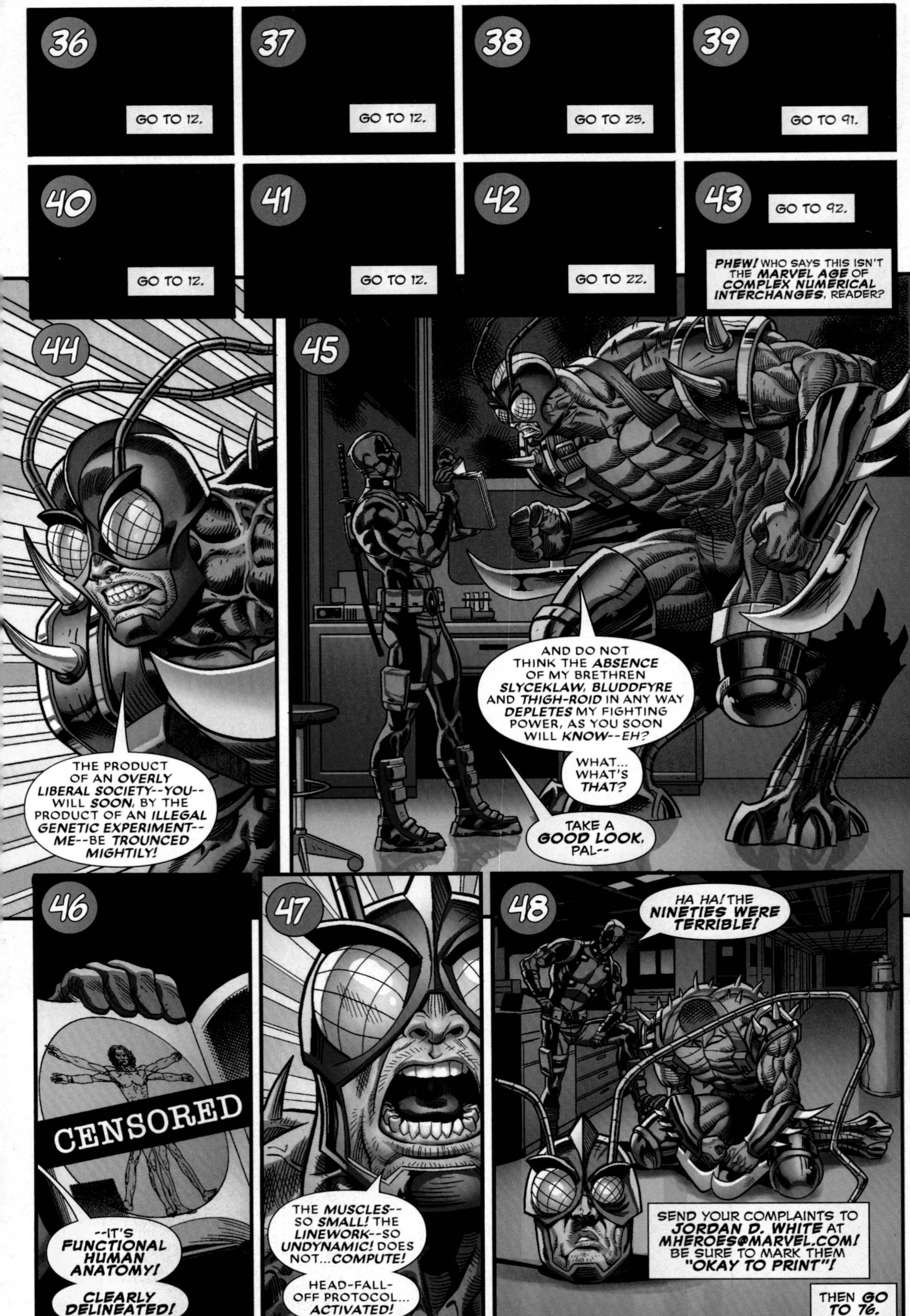

36
GO TO 12.
37
GO TO 12.
38
GO TO 25.
39
GO TO 91.
40
GO TO 12.
41
GO TO 12.
42
GO TO 22.
43
GO TO 92.
PHEW! WHO SAYS THIS ISN'T THE MARVEL AGE OF COMPLEX NUMERICAL INTERCHANGES, READER?
44
THE PRODUCT OF AN OVERLY LIBERAL SOCIETY--YOU--WILL SOON, BY THE PRODUCT OF AN ILLEGAL GENETIC EXPERIMENT--ME--BE TROUNCED MIGHTILY!
45
AND DO NOT THINK THE ABSENCE OF MY BRETHREN SLYCEKLAW, BLUDDFYRE AND THIGH-ROID IN ANY WAY DEPLETES MY FIGHTING POWER, AS YOU SOON WILL KNOW--EH?
WHAT... WHAT'S THAT?
TAKE A GOOD LOOK, PAL--
46
CENSORED
--IT'S FUNCTIONAL HUMAN ANATOMY!
CLEARLY DELINEATED!
47
THE MUSCLES--SO SMALL! THE LINEWORK--SO UNDYNAMIC! DOES NOT...COMPUTE!
HEAD-FALL-OFF PROTOCOL... ACTIVATED!
48
HA HA! THE NINETIES WERE TERRIBLE!
SEND YOUR COMPLAINTS TO JORDAN D. WHITE AT MHEROES@MARVEL.COM! BE SURE TO MARK THEM "OKAY TO PRINT"!
THEN GO TO 76.

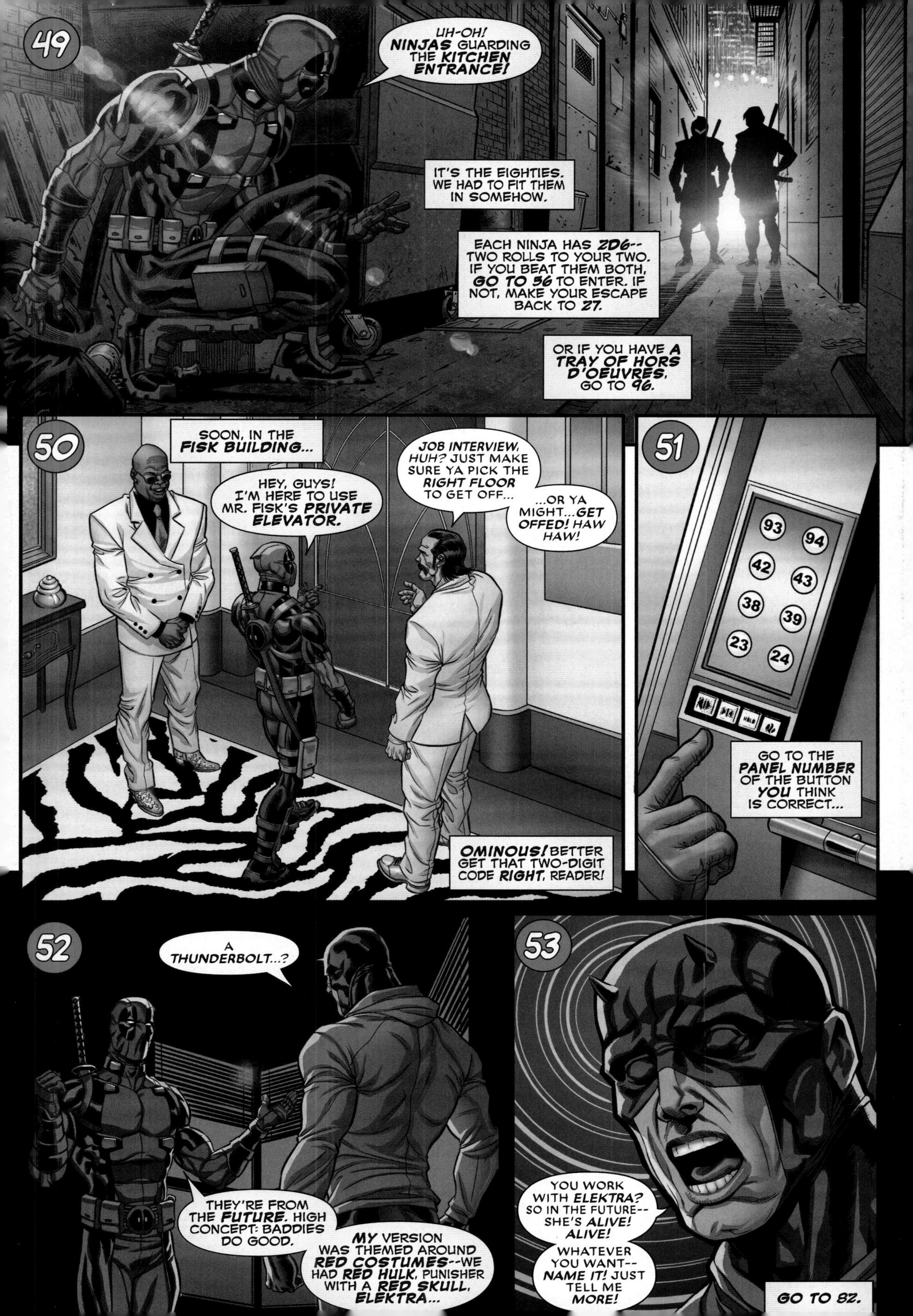
49
UH-OH! NINJAS GUARDING THE KITCHEN ENTRANCE!
IT'S THE EIGHTIES. WE HAD TO FIT THEM IN SOMEHOW.
EACH NINJA HAS 2D6-- TWO ROLLS TO YOUR TWO. IF YOU BEAT THEM BOTH, GO TO 56 TO ENTER. IF NOT, MAKE YOUR ESCAPE BACK TO 27.
OR IF YOU HAVE A TRAY OF HORS D'OEUVRES, GO TO 96.
50
SOON, IN THE FISK BUILDING...
HEY, GUYS! I'M HERE TO USE MR. FISK'S PRIVATE ELEVATOR.
JOB INTERVIEW, HUH? JUST MAKE SURE YA PICK THE RIGHT FLOOR TO GET OFF...
...OR YA MIGHT...GET OFFED! HAW HAW!
OMINOUS! BETTER GET THAT TWO-DIGIT CODE RIGHT, READER!
51
93
94
42
43
38
39
23
24
GO TO THE PANEL NUMBER OF THE BUTTON YOU THINK IS CORRECT...
52
A THUNDERBOLT...?
THEY'RE FROM THE FUTURE. HIGH CONCEPT: BADDIES DO GOOD.
MY VERSION WAS THEMED AROUND RED COSTUMES--WE HAD RED HULK, PUNISHER WITH A RED SKULL, ELEKTRA...
53
YOU WORK WITH ELEKTRA? SO IN THE FUTURE-- SHE'S ALIVE! ALIVE!
WHATEVER YOU WANT-- NAME IT! JUST TELL ME MORE!
GO TO 82.

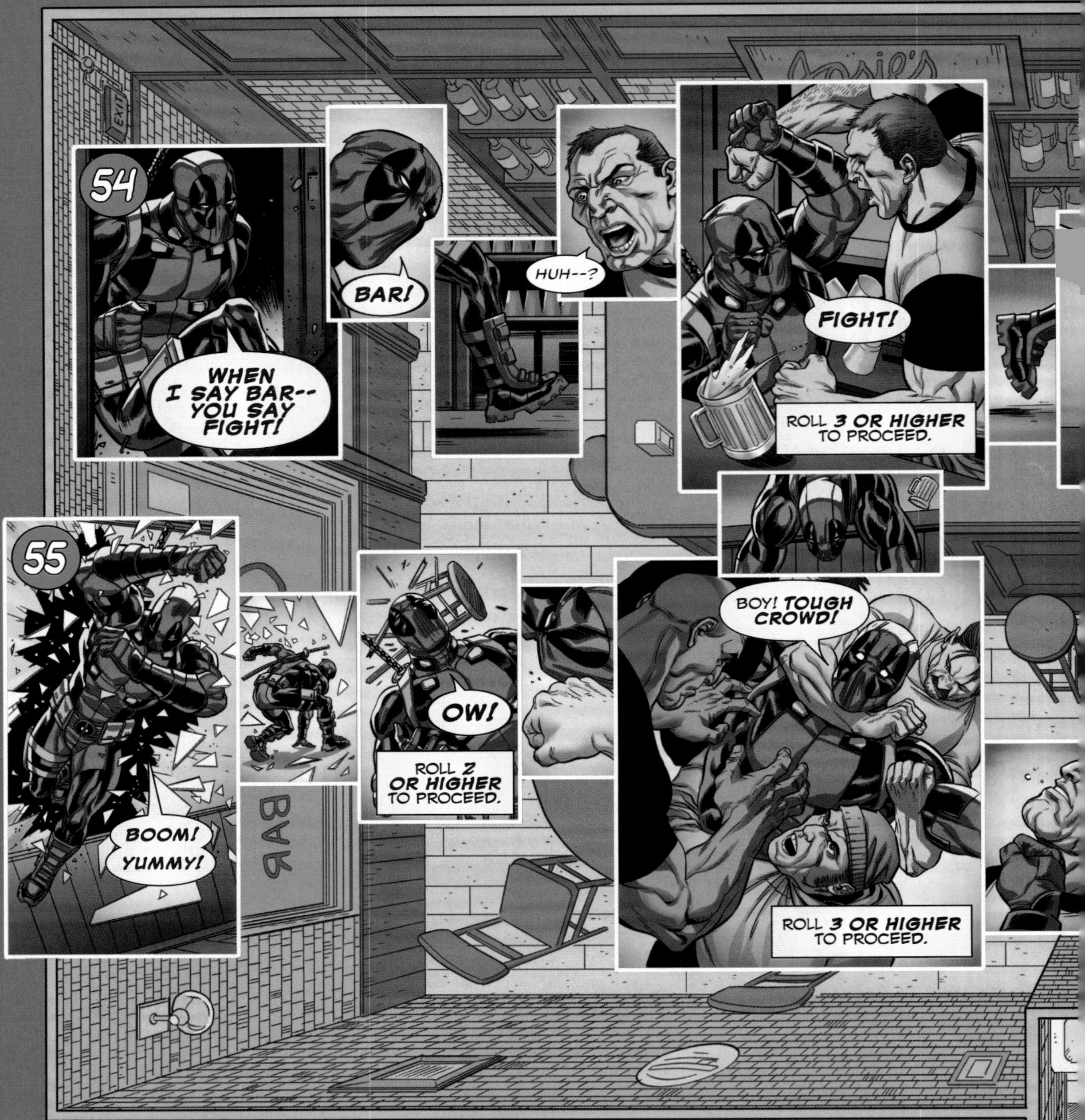
54
WHEN I SAY BAR-- YOU SAY FIGHT!
BAR!
HUH--?
FIGHT!
ROLL 3 OR HIGHER TO PROCEED.
55
BOOM! YUMMY!
OW!
ROLL 2 OR HIGHER TO PROCEED.
BOY! TOUGH CROWD!
ROLL 3 OR HIGHER TO PROCEED.

WELCOME TO THE *JOSIE'S BAR FIGHT RAMPAGE MINIGAME*, TRUE BELIEVER!

THE RULES COULDN'T BE ***SIMPLER***--STARTING AT YOUR CHOSEN ***ENTRYPOINT***, FOLLOW THE PANELS IN ***ANY DIRECTION*** TO RAMPAGE THROUGH THE BAR IN SEARCH OF ***TURK***, WHO'S HIDING IN THE ***BACK OFFICE!***

ALONG THE WAY, YOU'LL HAVE TO MAKE ***DICE ROLLS*** TO PROCEED--FAIL ONE, AND YOU ***LOSE*** THE BAR BRAWL AND GO STRAIGHT TO ***PANEL 30!*** GOOD LUCK--AND ***GOOD FIGHT!***

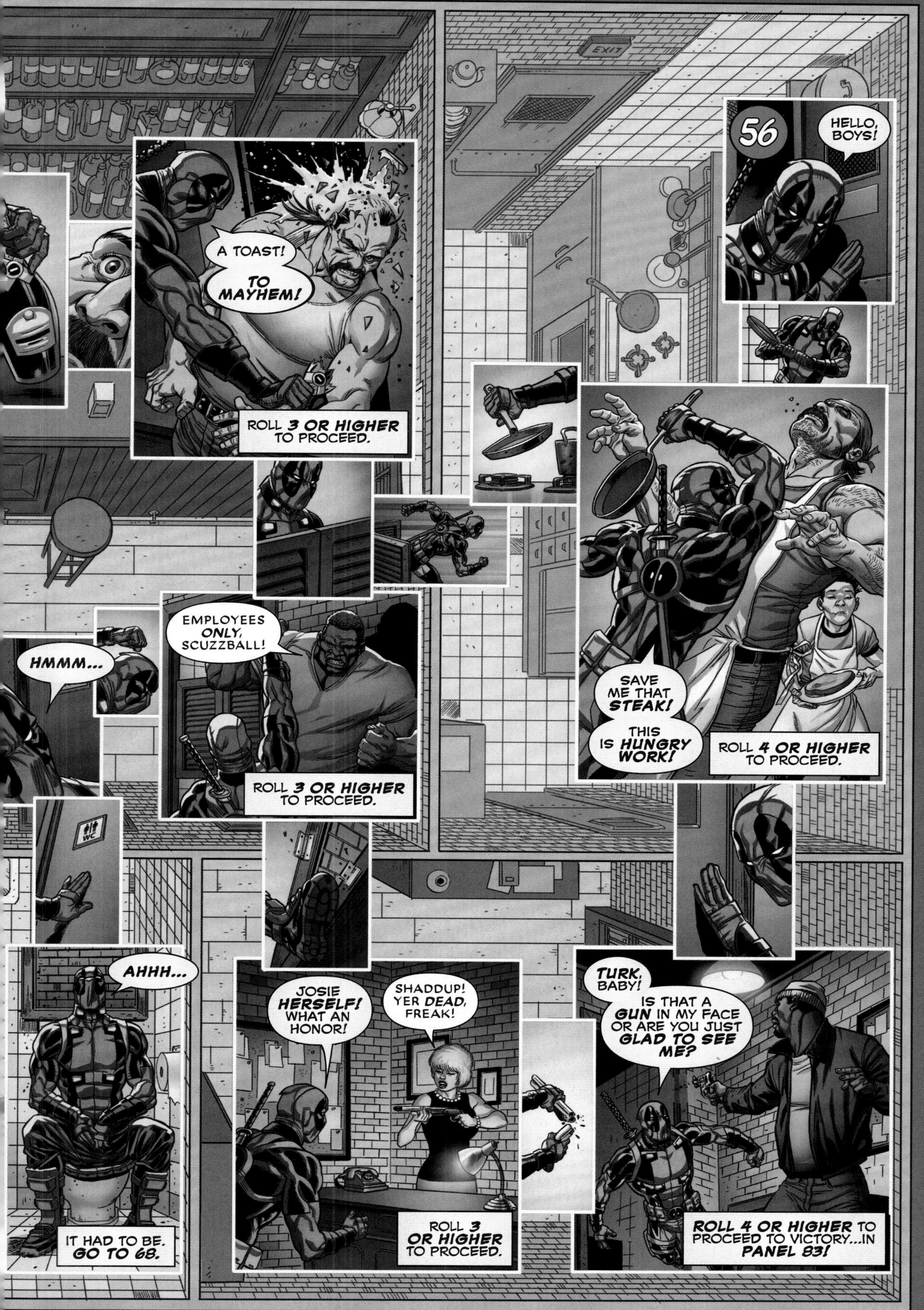
A TOAST!
TO MAYHEM!
ROLL 3 OR HIGHER TO PROCEED.
56
HELLO, BOYS!
SAVE ME THAT STEAK!
THIS IS HUNGRY WORK!
ROLL 4 OR HIGHER TO PROCEED.
HMMM...
EMPLOYEES ONLY, SCUZZBALL!
ROLL 3 OR HIGHER TO PROCEED.
AHHH...
IT HAD TO BE. GO TO 68.
JOSIE HERSELF! WHAT AN HONOR!
SHADDUP! YER DEAD, FREAK!
ROLL 3 OR HIGHER TO PROCEED.
TURK, BABY!
IS THAT A GUN IN MY FACE OR ARE YOU JUST GLAD TO SEE ME?
ROLL 4 OR HIGHER TO PROCEED TO VICTORY...IN PANEL 83!

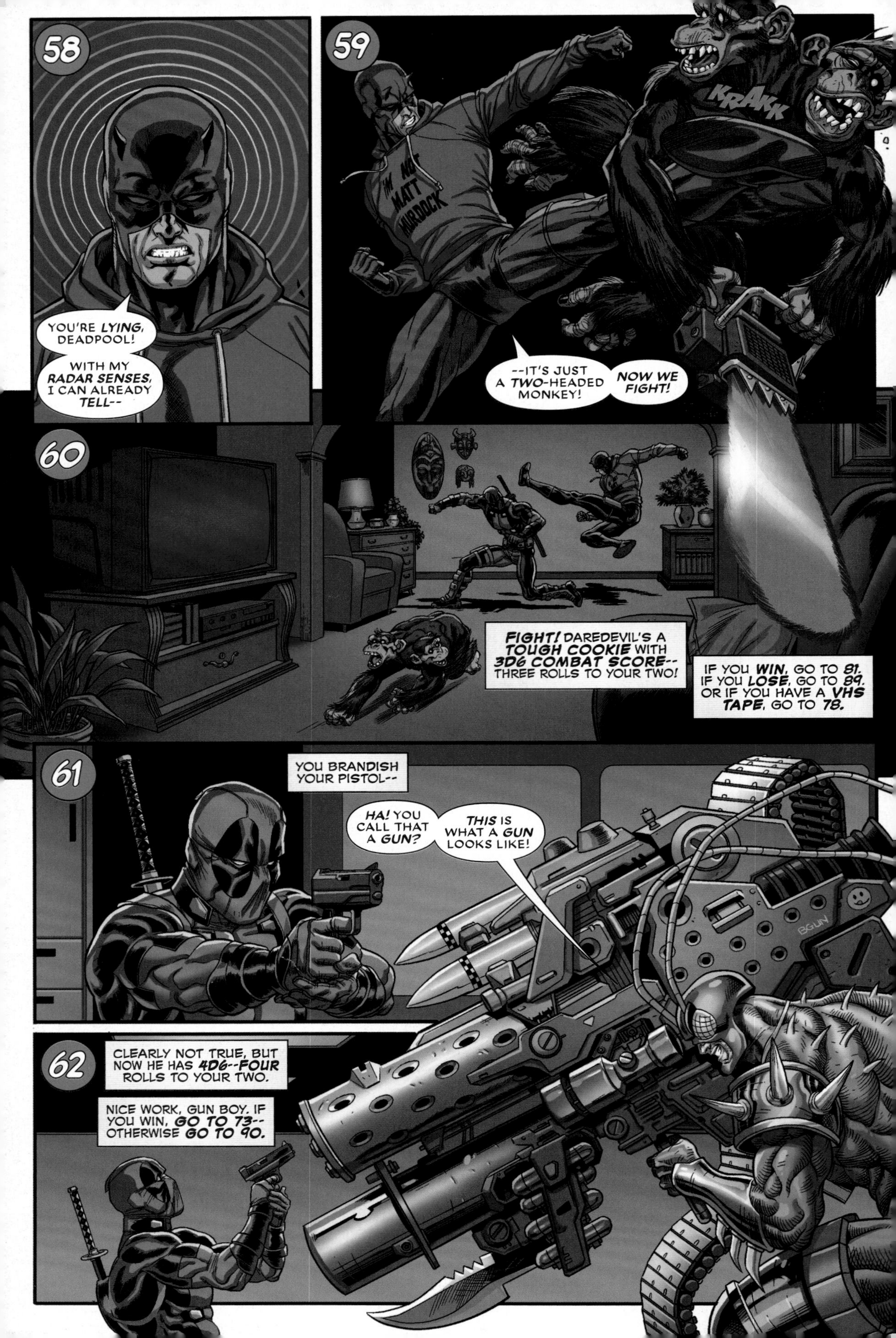
58
YOU'RE LYING, DEADPOOL!
WITH MY RADAR SENSES, I CAN ALREADY TELL--
59
I'M NOT MATT MURDOCK
KRAKK
--IT'S JUST A TWO-HEADED MONKEY!
NOW WE FIGHT!
60
FIGHT! DAREDEVIL'S A TOUGH COOKIE WITH 3D6 COMBAT SCORE-- THREE ROLLS TO YOUR TWO!
IF YOU WIN, GO TO 81. IF YOU LOSE, GO TO 89. OR IF YOU HAVE A VHS TAPE, GO TO 78.
61
YOU BRANDISH YOUR PISTOL--
HA! YOU CALL THAT A GUN?
THIS IS WHAT A GUN LOOKS LIKE!
62
CLEARLY NOT TRUE, BUT NOW HE HAS 4D6--FOUR ROLLS TO YOUR TWO.
NICE WORK, GUN BOY. IF YOU WIN, GO TO 73-- OTHERWISE GO TO 90.

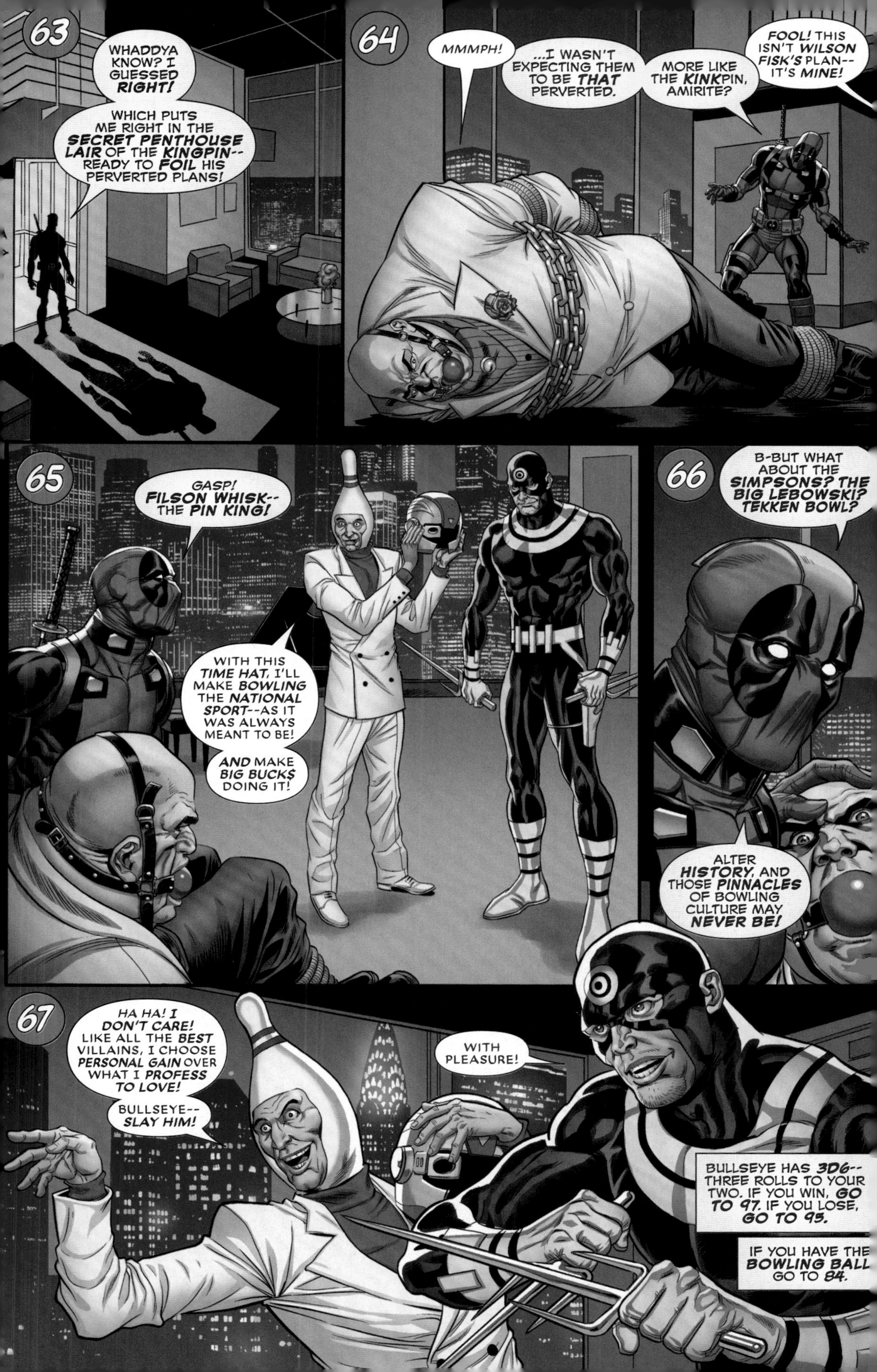
63
WHADDYA KNOW? I GUESSED RIGHT!
WHICH PUTS ME RIGHT IN THE SECRET PENTHOUSE LAIR OF THE KINGPIN--READY TO FOIL HIS PERVERTED PLANS!
64
MMMPH!
...I WASN'T EXPECTING THEM TO BE THAT PERVERTED.
MORE LIKE THE KINKPIN, AMIRITE?
FOOL! THIS ISN'T WILSON FISK'S PLAN--IT'S MINE!
65
GASP! FILSON WHISK--THE PIN KING!
WITH THIS TIME HAT, I'LL MAKE BOWLING THE NATIONAL SPORT--AS IT WAS ALWAYS MEANT TO BE!
AND MAKE BIG BUCK$ DOING IT!
66
B-BUT WHAT ABOUT THE SIMPSONS? THE BIG LEBOWSKI? TEKKEN BOWL?
ALTER HISTORY, AND THOSE PINNACLES OF BOWLING CULTURE MAY NEVER BE!
67
HA HA! I DON'T CARE! LIKE ALL THE BEST VILLAINS, I CHOOSE PERSONAL GAIN OVER WHAT I PROFESS TO LOVE!
BULLSEYE--SLAY HIM!
WITH PLEASURE!
BULLSEYE HAS 3D6--THREE ROLLS TO YOUR TWO. IF YOU WIN, GO TO 97. IF YOU LOSE, GO TO 95.
IF YOU HAVE THE BOWLING BALL GO TO 84.

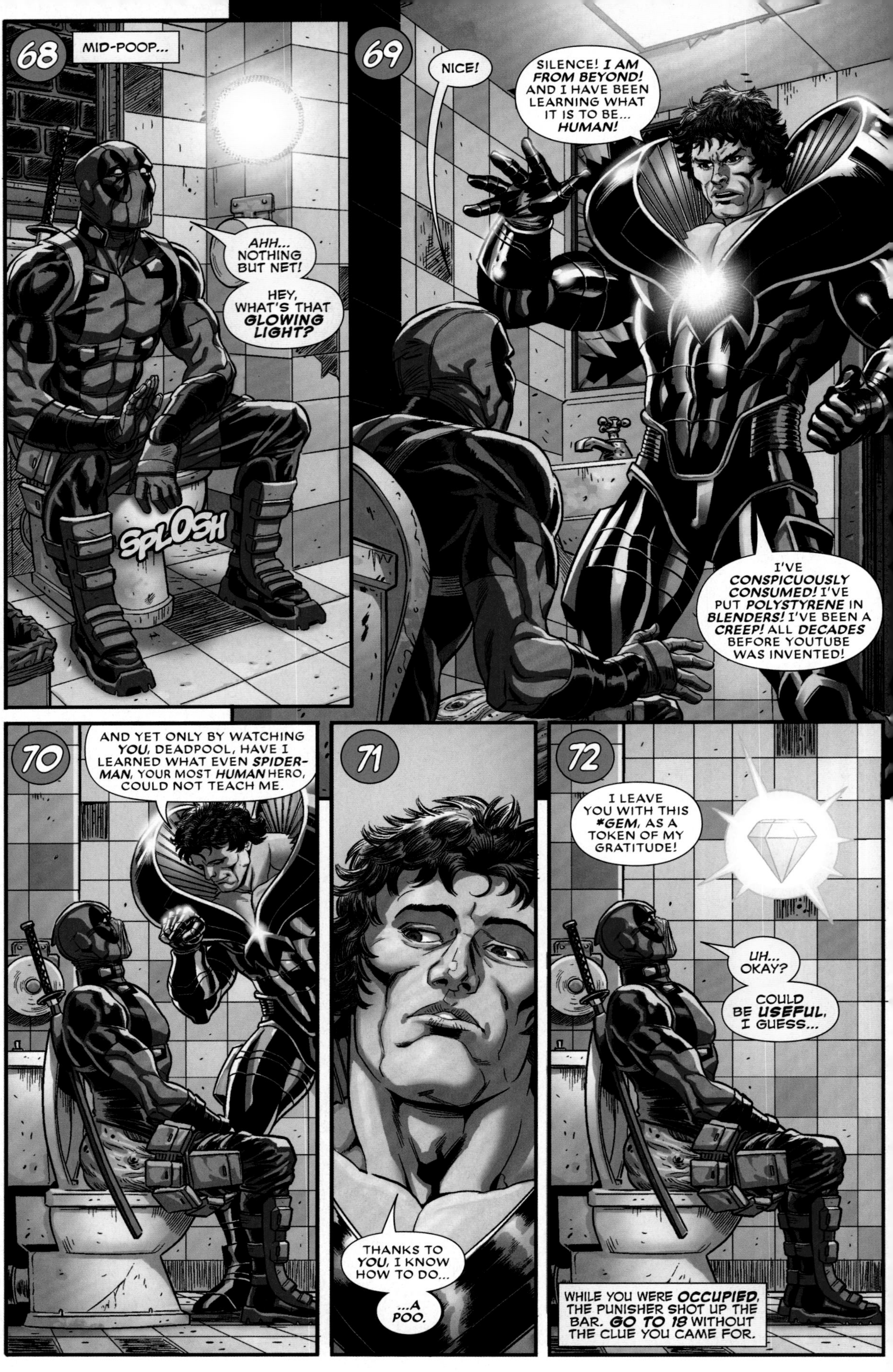
68
MID-POOP...
AHH... NOTHING BUT NET!
HEY, WHAT'S THAT GLOWING LIGHT?
SPLOSH
69
NICE!
SILENCE! I AM FROM BEYOND! AND I HAVE BEEN LEARNING WHAT IT IS TO BE... HUMAN!
I'VE CONSPICUOUSLY CONSUMED! I'VE PUT POLYSTYRENE IN BLENDERS! I'VE BEEN A CREEP! ALL DECADES BEFORE YOUTUBE WAS INVENTED!
70
AND YET ONLY BY WATCHING YOU, DEADPOOL, HAVE I LEARNED WHAT EVEN SPIDER-MAN, YOUR MOST HUMAN HERO, COULD NOT TEACH ME.
71
THANKS TO YOU, I KNOW HOW TO DO...
...A POO.
72
I LEAVE YOU WITH THIS *GEM, AS A TOKEN OF MY GRATITUDE!
UH... OKAY?
COULD BE USEFUL, I GUESS...
WHILE YOU WERE OCCUPIED, THE PUNISHER SHOT UP THE BAR. GO TO 18 WITHOUT THE CLUE YOU CAME FOR.

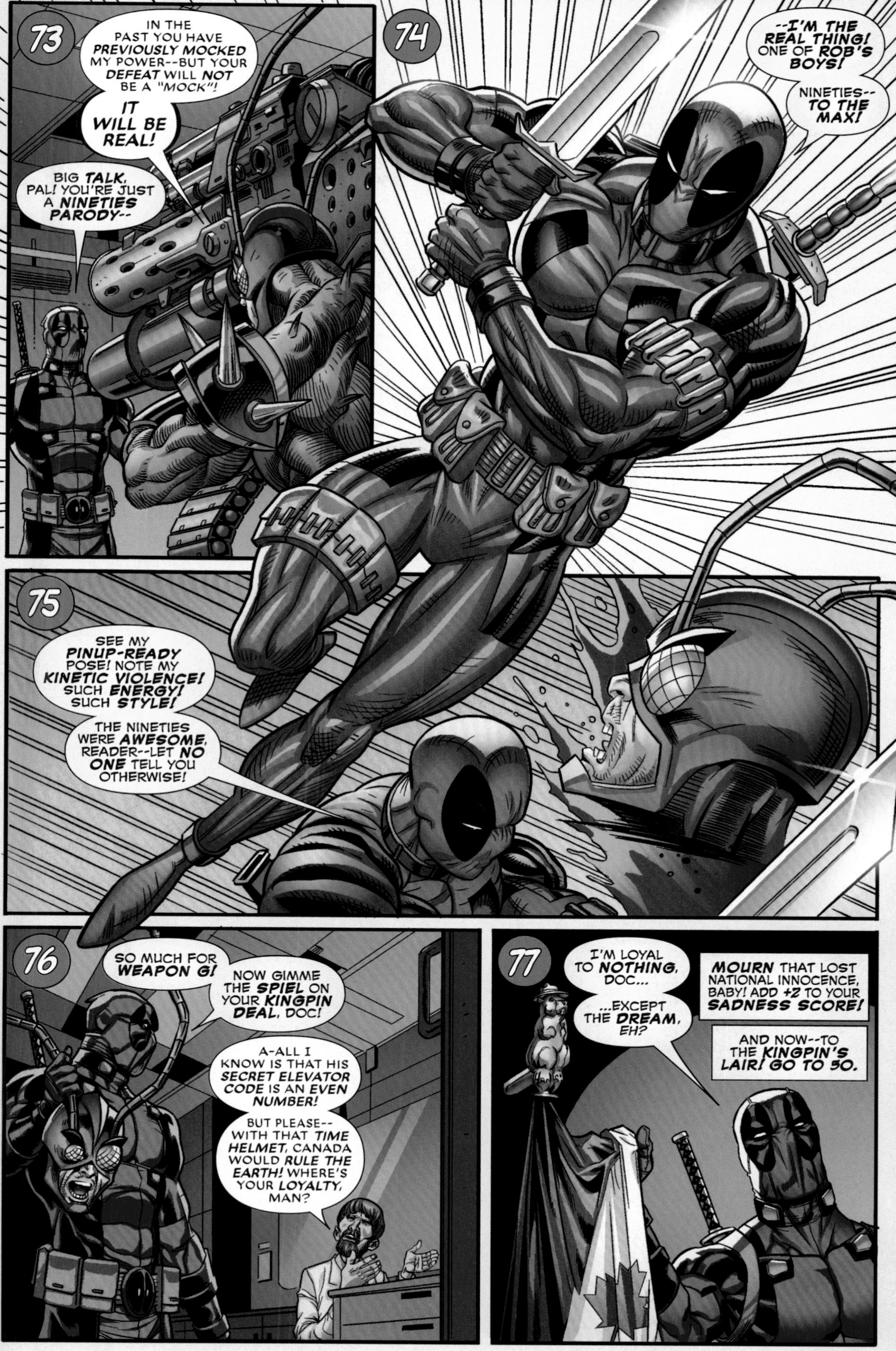
73
IN THE PAST YOU HAVE PREVIOUSLY MOCKED MY POWER--BUT YOUR DEFEAT WILL NOT BE A "MOCK"!
IT WILL BE REAL!
BIG TALK, PAL! YOU'RE JUST A NINETIES PARODY--
74
--I'M THE REAL THING! ONE OF ROB'S BOYS!
NINETIES-- TO THE MAX!
75
SEE MY PINUP-READY POSE! NOTE MY KINETIC VIOLENCE! SUCH ENERGY! SUCH STYLE!
THE NINETIES WERE AWESOME, READER--LET NO ONE TELL YOU OTHERWISE!
76
SO MUCH FOR WEAPON G!
NOW GIMME THE SPIEL ON YOUR KINGPIN DEAL, DOC!
A-ALL I KNOW IS THAT HIS SECRET ELEVATOR CODE IS AN EVEN NUMBER!
BUT PLEASE-- WITH THAT TIME HELMET, CANADA WOULD RULE THE EARTH! WHERE'S YOUR LOYALTY, MAN?
77
I'M LOYAL TO NOTHING, DOC...
...EXCEPT THE DREAM, EH?
MOURN THAT LOST NATIONAL INNOCENCE, BABY! ADD +2 TO YOUR SADNESS SCORE!
AND NOW--TO THE KINGPIN'S LAIR! GO TO 50.

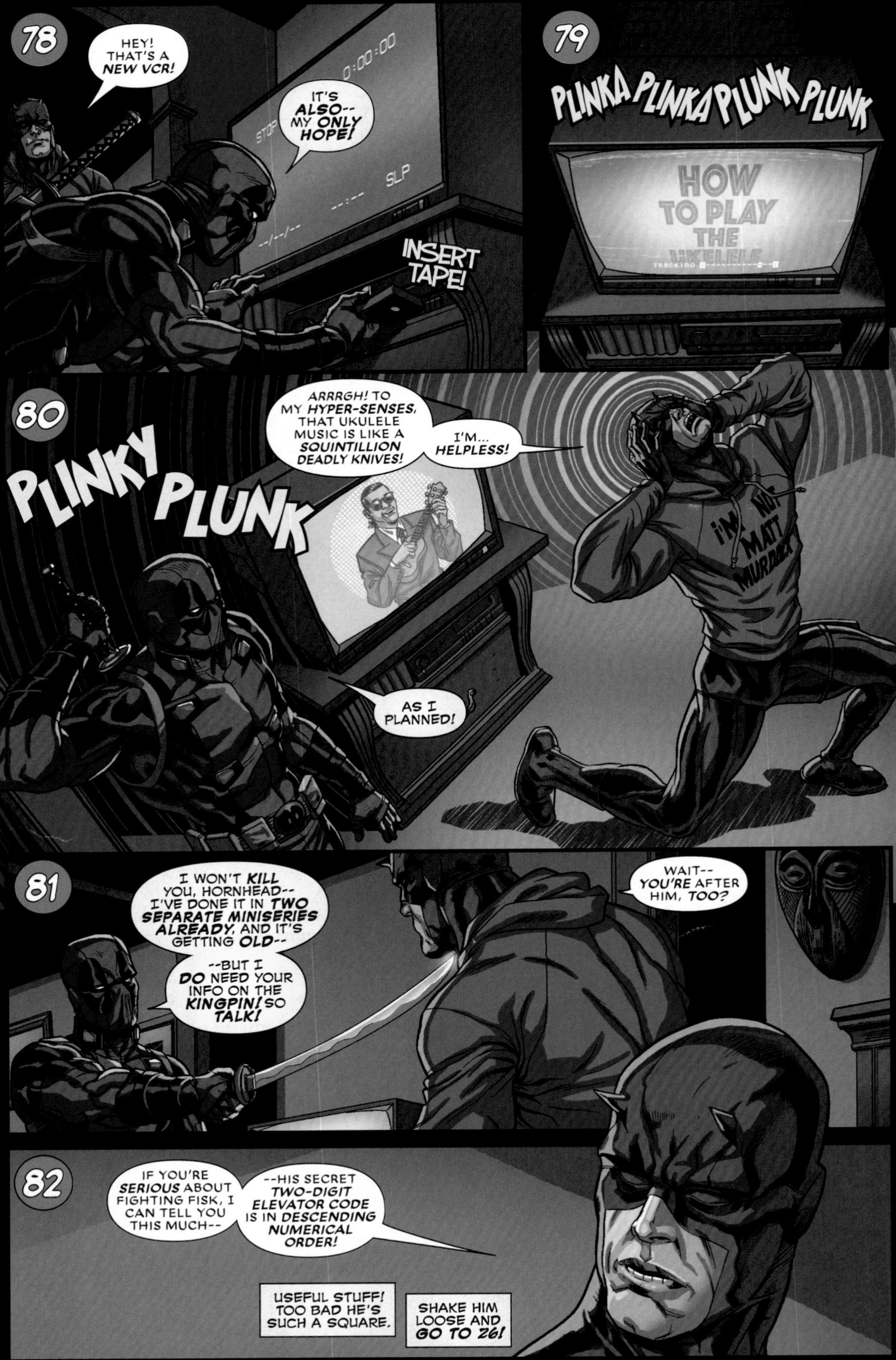
78
HEY! THAT'S A NEW VCR!
IT'S ALSO-- MY ONLY HOPE!
INSERT TAPE!
79
PLINKA PLINKA PLUNK PLUNK
HOW TO PLAY THE
80
PLINKY PLUNK
ARRRGH! TO MY HYPER-SENSES, THAT UKULELE MUSIC IS LIKE A SQUINTILLION DEADLY KNIVES!
I'M... HELPLESS!
AS I PLANNED!
I'M NOT MATT MURDOCK
81
I WON'T KILL YOU, HORNHEAD-- I'VE DONE IT IN TWO SEPARATE MINISERIES ALREADY, AND IT'S GETTING OLD--
--BUT I DO NEED YOUR INFO ON THE KINGPIN! SO TALK!
WAIT-- YOU'RE AFTER HIM, TOO?
82
IF YOU'RE SERIOUS ABOUT FIGHTING FISK, I CAN TELL YOU THIS MUCH--
--HIS SECRET TWO-DIGIT ELEVATOR CODE IS IN DESCENDING NUMERICAL ORDER!
USEFUL STUFF! TOO BAD HE'S SUCH A SQUARE.
SHAKE HIM LOOSE AND GO TO 26!

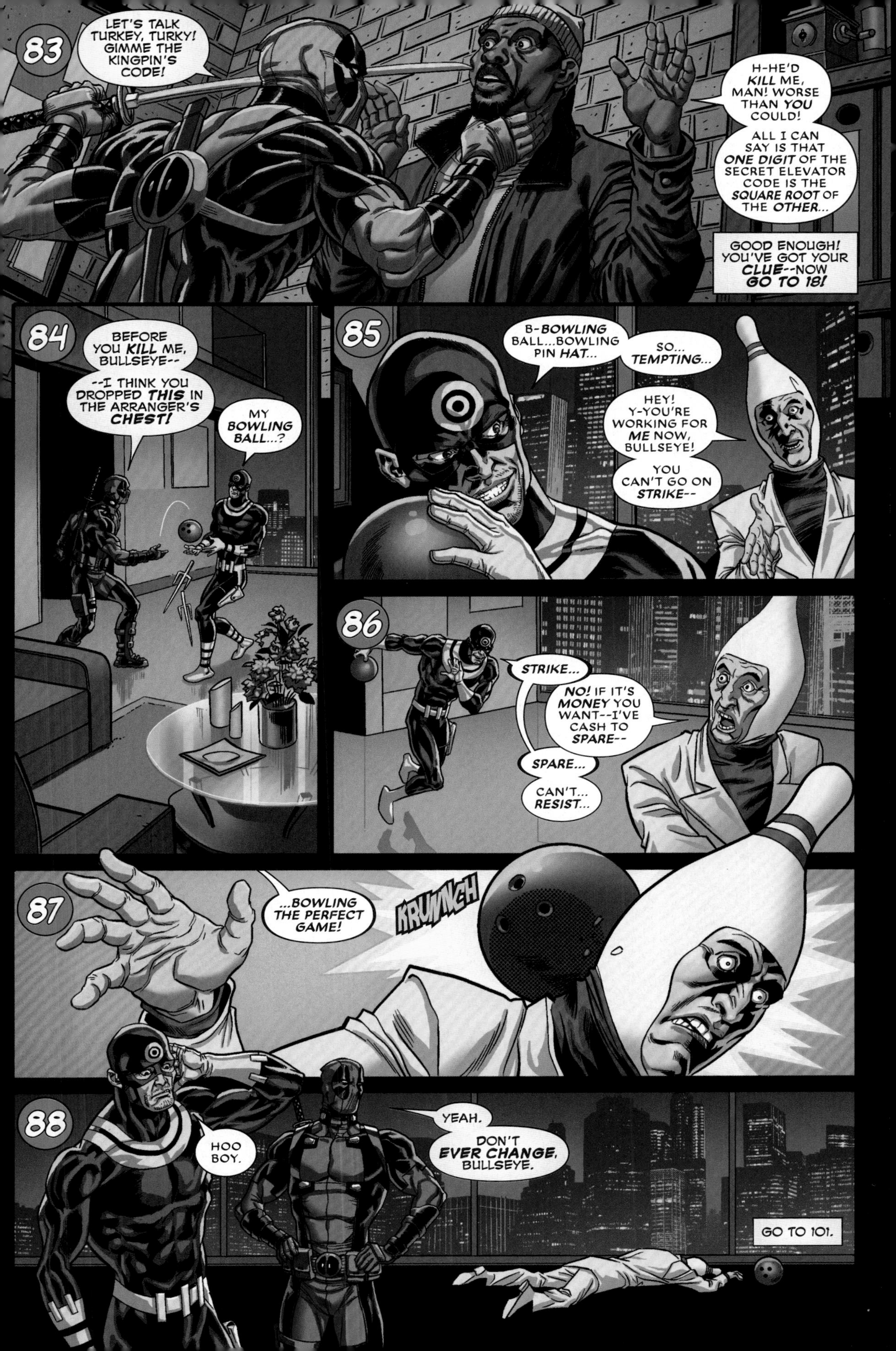
83
LET'S TALK TURKEY, TURKY! GIMME THE KINGPIN'S CODE!
H-HE'D KILL ME, MAN! WORSE THAN YOU COULD!
ALL I CAN SAY IS THAT ONE DIGIT OF THE SECRET ELEVATOR CODE IS THE SQUARE ROOT OF THE OTHER...
GOOD ENOUGH! YOU'VE GOT YOUR CLUE--NOW GO TO 18!
84
BEFORE YOU KILL ME, BULLSEYE--
--I THINK YOU DROPPED THIS IN THE ARRANGER'S CHEST!
MY BOWLING BALL...?
85
B-BOWLING BALL...BOWLING PIN HAT...
SO... TEMPTING...
HEY! Y-YOU'RE WORKING FOR ME NOW, BULLSEYE!
YOU CAN'T GO ON STRIKE--
86
STRIKE...
NO! IF IT'S MONEY YOU WANT--I'VE CASH TO SPARE--
SPARE...
CAN'T... RESIST...
87
...BOWLING THE PERFECT GAME!
KRUNNCH
88
HOO BOY.
YEAH.
DON'T EVER CHANGE, BULLSEYE.
GO TO 101.

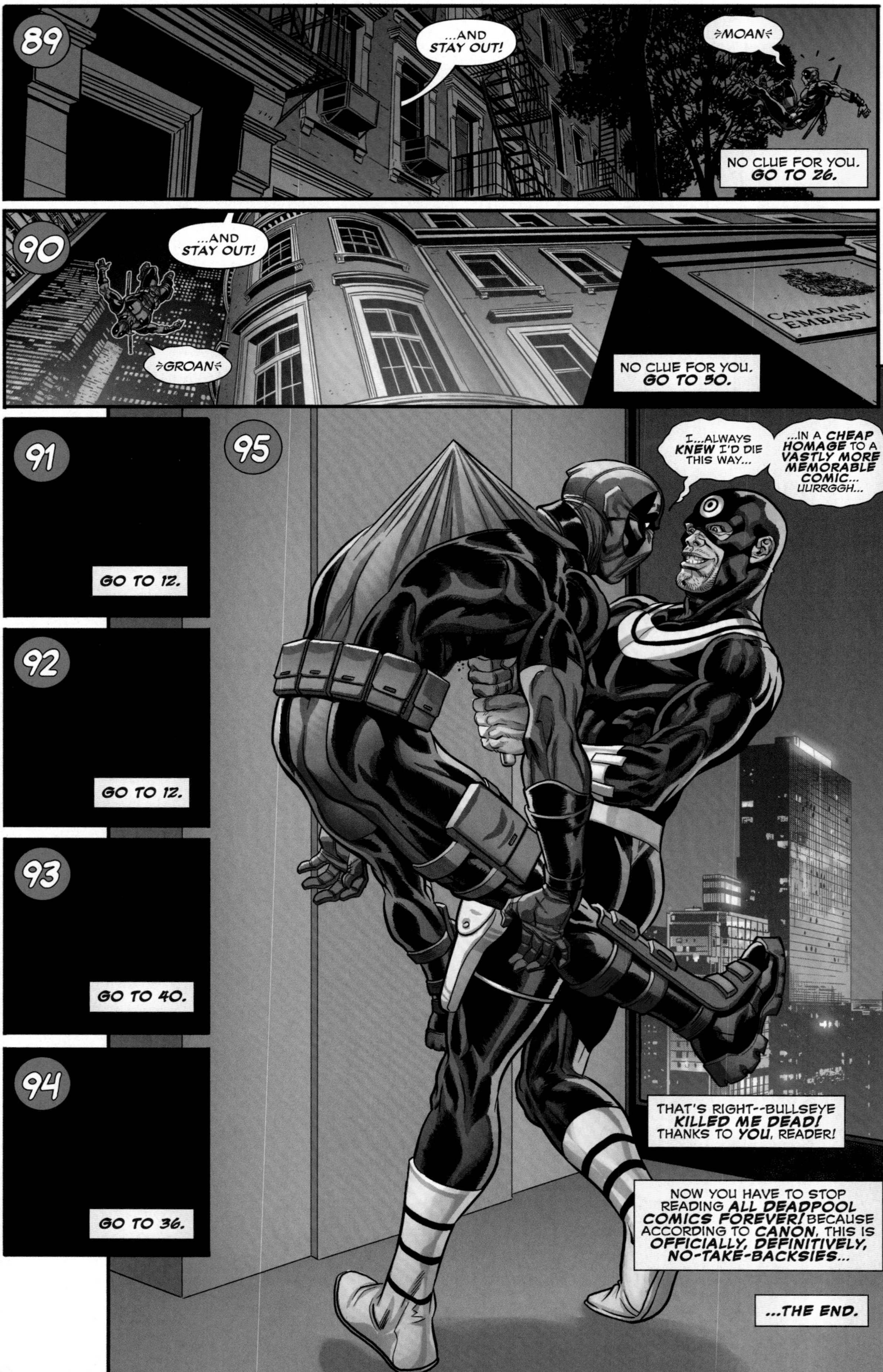

89
...AND STAY OUT!
⋟MOAN⋞
NO CLUE FOR YOU. GO TO 26.
90
...AND STAY OUT!
⋟GROAN⋞
CANADIAN EMBASSY
NO CLUE FOR YOU. GO TO 50.
91
GO TO 12.
92
GO TO 12.
93
GO TO 40.
94
GO TO 36.
95
I...ALWAYS KNEW I'D DIE THIS WAY...
...IN A CHEAP HOMAGE TO A VASTLY MORE MEMORABLE COMIC... UURRGGH...
THAT'S RIGHT--BULLSEYE KILLED ME DEAD! THANKS TO YOU, READER!
NOW YOU HAVE TO STOP READING ALL DEADPOOL COMICS FOREVER! BECAUSE ACCORDING TO CANON, THIS IS OFFICIALLY, DEFINITIVELY, NO-TAKE-BACKSIES...
...THE END.

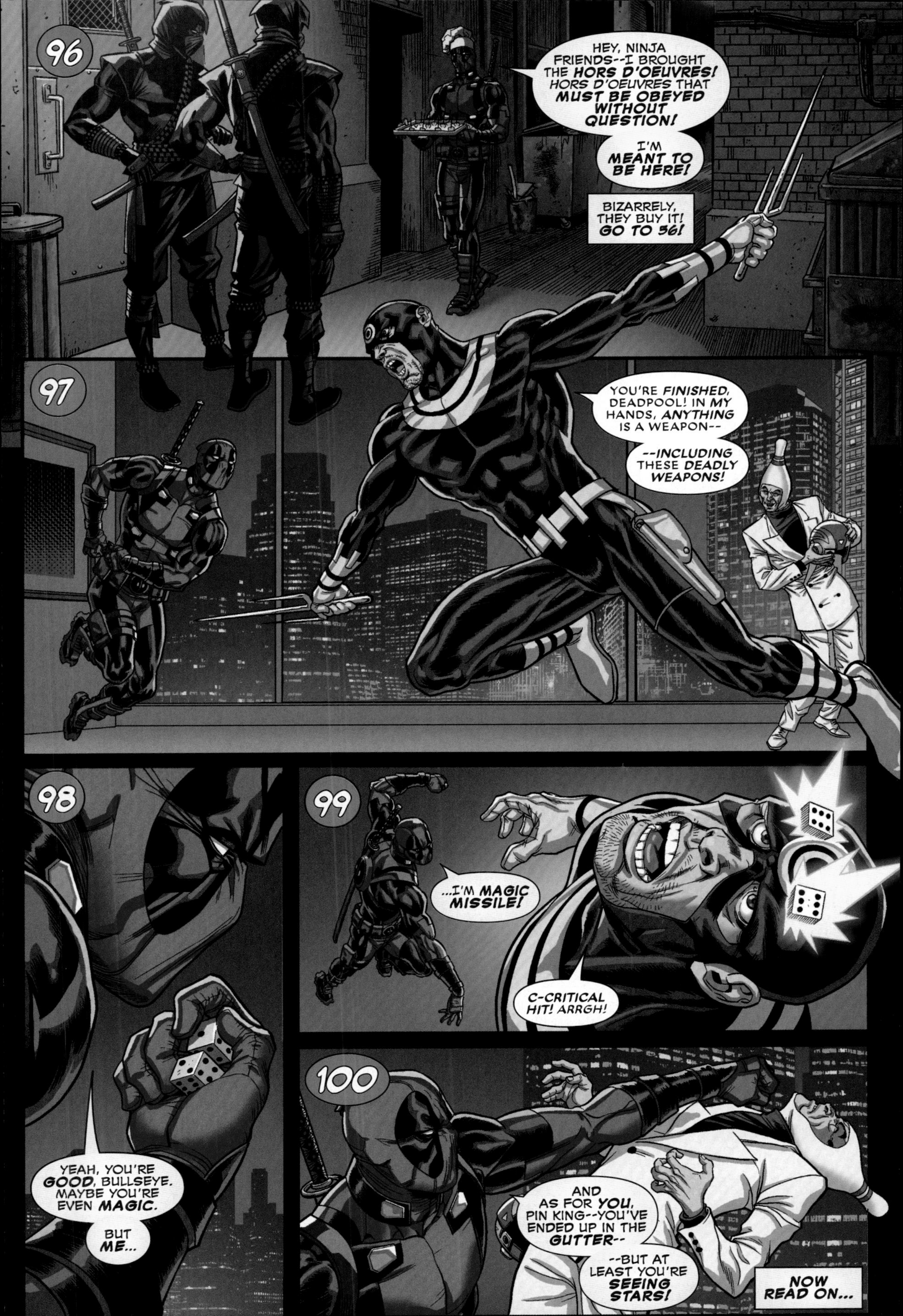
96
HEY, NINJA FRIENDS--I BROUGHT THE HORS D'OEUVRES! HORS D'OEUVRES THAT MUST BE OBEYED WITHOUT QUESTION!
I'M MEANT TO BE HERE!
BIZARRELY, THEY BUY IT! GO TO 56!
97
YOU'RE FINISHED, DEADPOOL! IN MY HANDS, ANYTHING IS A WEAPON--
--INCLUDING THESE DEADLY WEAPONS!
98
YEAH, YOU'RE GOOD, BULLSEYE. MAYBE YOU'RE EVEN MAGIC.
BUT ME...
99
...I'M MAGIC MISSILE!
C-CRITICAL HIT! ARRGH!
100
AND AS FOR YOU, PIN KING--YOU'VE ENDED UP IN THE GUTTER--
--BUT AT LEAST YOU'RE SEEING STARS!
NOW READ ON...

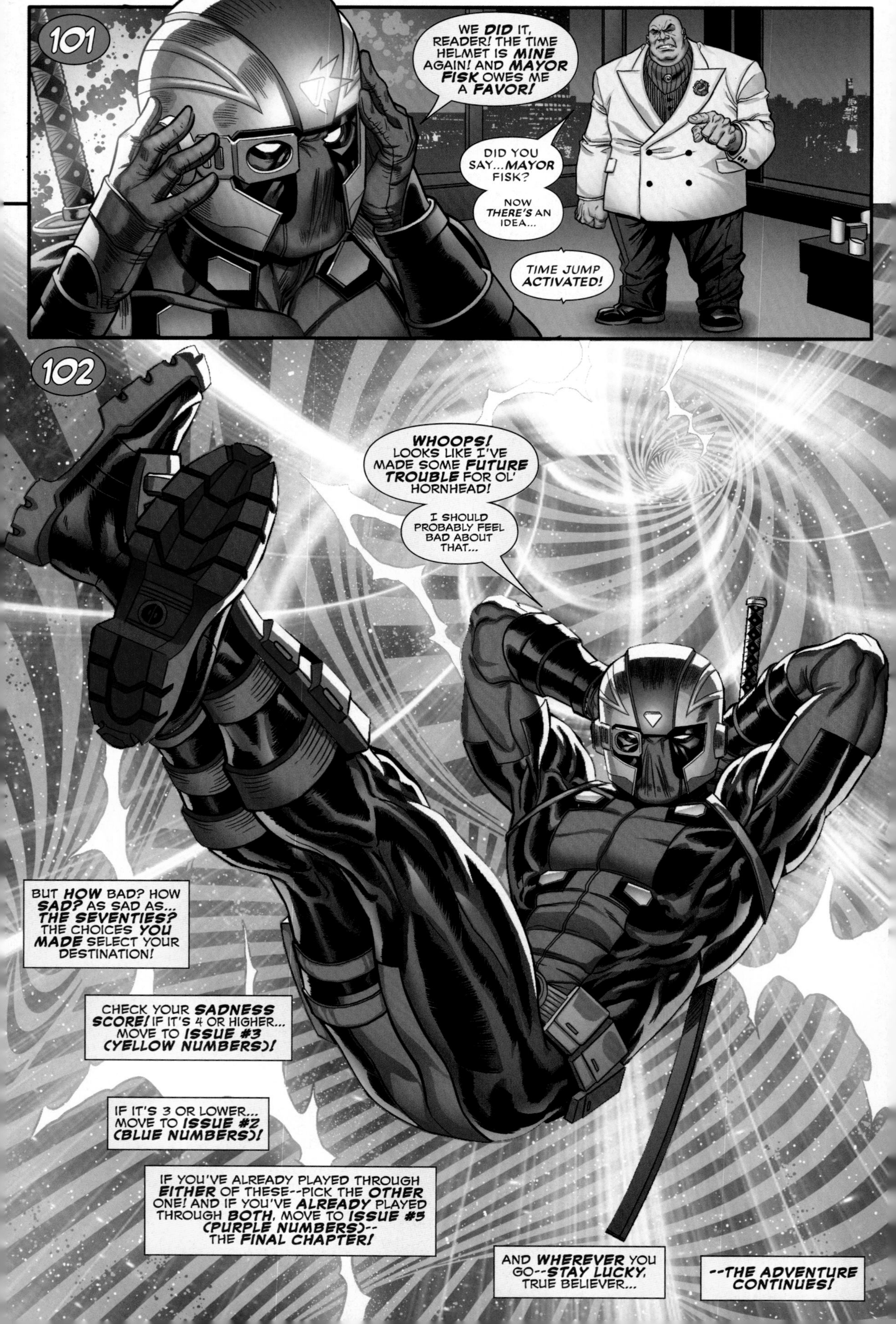
101
WE DID IT, READER! THE TIME HELMET IS MINE AGAIN! AND MAYOR FISK OWES ME A FAVOR!
DID YOU SAY...MAYOR FISK?
NOW THERE'S AN IDEA...
TIME JUMP ACTIVATED!
102
WHOOPS! LOOKS LIKE I'VE MADE SOME FUTURE TROUBLE FOR OL' HORNHEAD!
I SHOULD PROBABLY FEEL BAD ABOUT THAT...
BUT HOW BAD? HOW SAD? AS SAD AS... THE SEVENTIES? THE CHOICES YOU MADE SELECT YOUR DESTINATION!
CHECK YOUR SADNESS SCORE! IF IT'S 4 OR HIGHER... MOVE TO ISSUE #3 (YELLOW NUMBERS)!
IF IT'S 3 OR LOWER... MOVE TO ISSUE #2 (BLUE NUMBERS)!
IF YOU'VE ALREADY PLAYED THROUGH EITHER OF THESE--PICK THE OTHER ONE! AND IF YOU'VE ALREADY PLAYED THROUGH BOTH, MOVE TO ISSUE #5 (PURPLE NUMBERS)-- THE FINAL CHAPTER!
AND WHEREVER YOU GO--STAY LUCKY, TRUE BELIEVER...
--THE ADVENTURE CONTINUES!

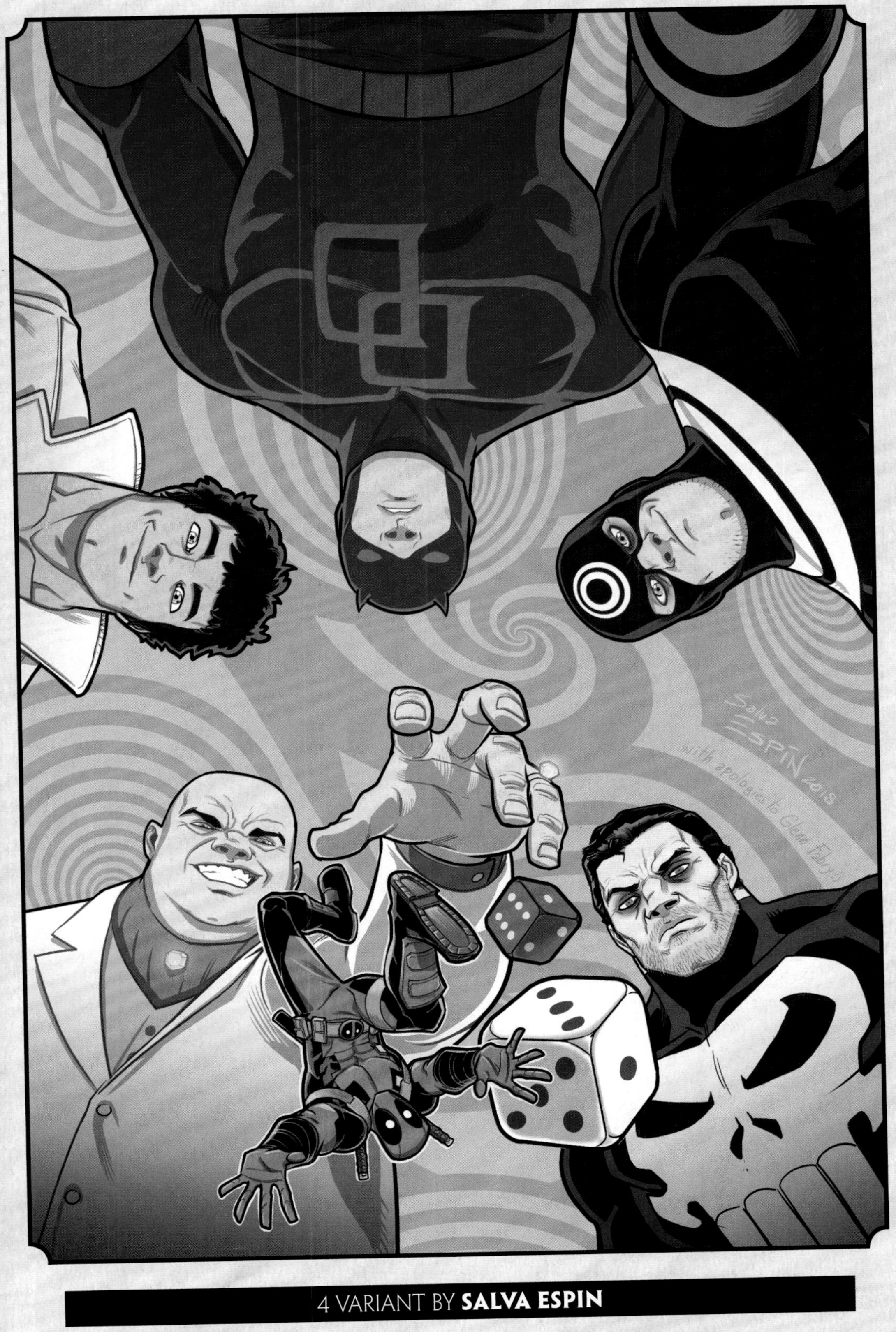
Salva ESPIN 2018
with apologies to Glenn Fabry :)

4 VARIANT BY **SALVA ESPIN**

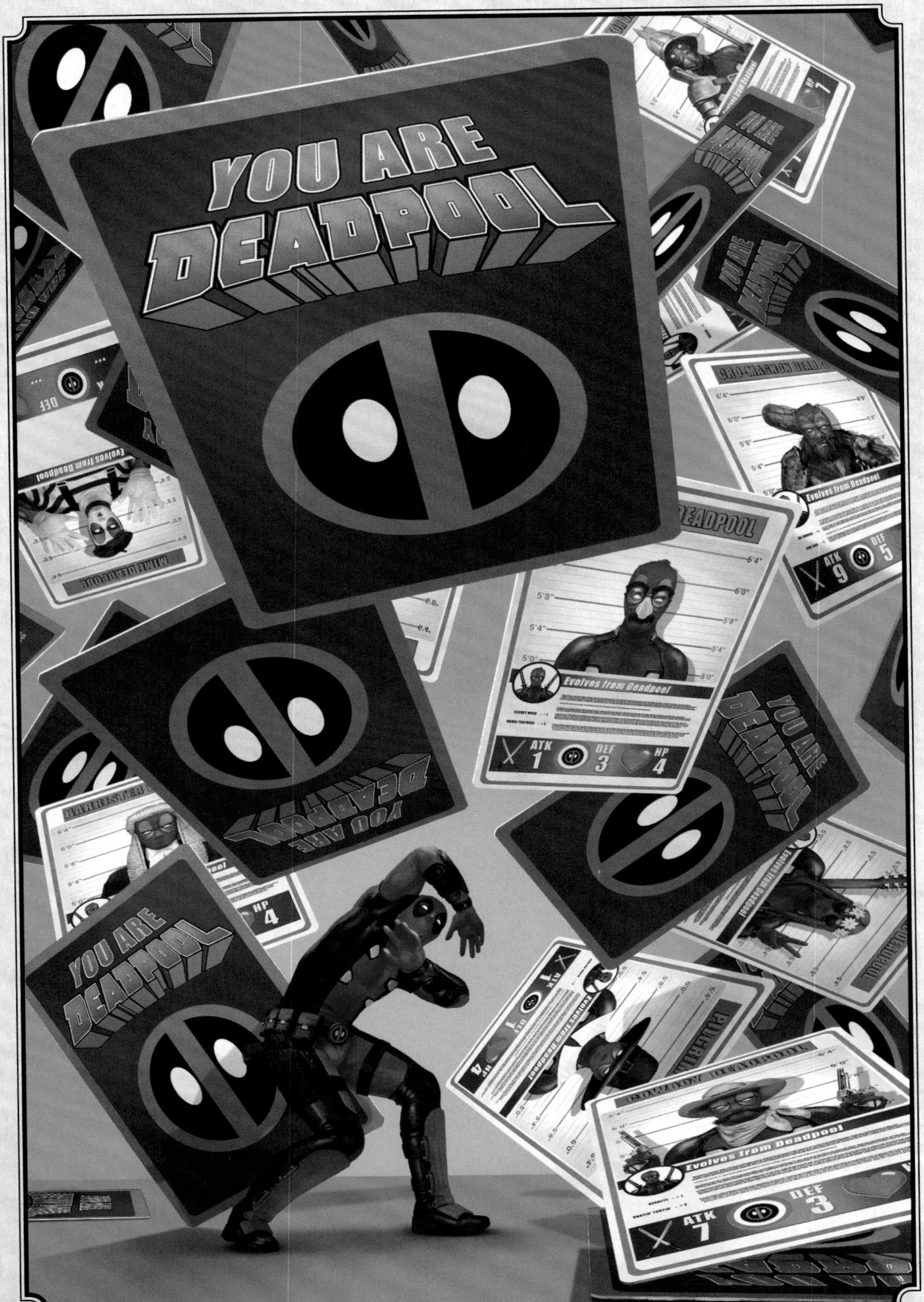
YOU ARE DEADPOOL
DEADPOOL
Evolves from Deadpool
ATK 1
DEF 3
HP 4
YOU ARE DEADPOOL
YOU ARE DEADPOOL
YOU ARE DEADPOOL
CRO-MAGNON DEADPOOL
Evolves from Deadpool
ATK 9
DEF 5
HP 4
Evolves from Deadpool
ATK 7
DEF 3

five

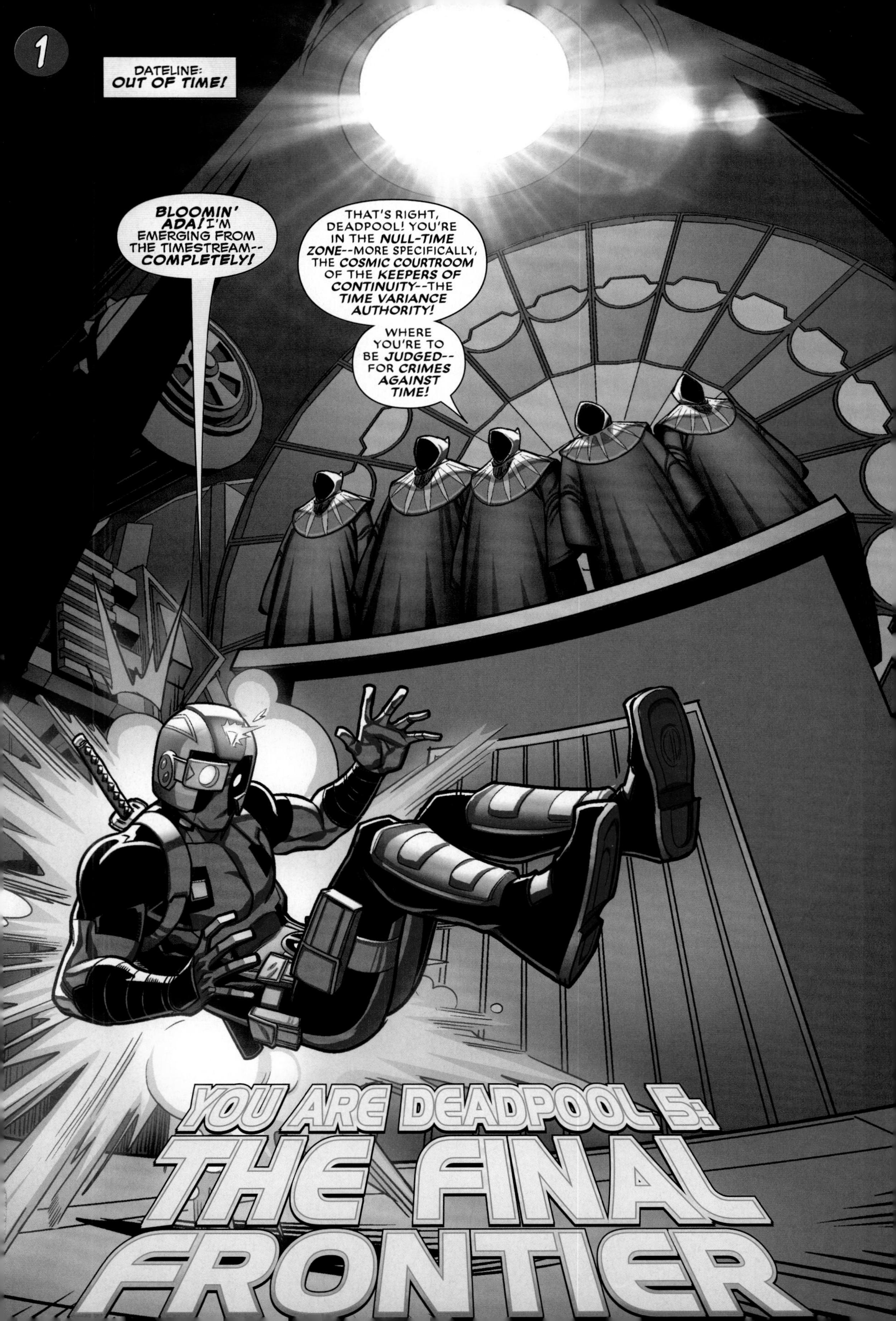
1
DATELINE: OUT OF TIME!
BLOOMIN' ADA! I'M EMERGING FROM THE TIMESTREAM--COMPLETELY!
THAT'S RIGHT, DEADPOOL! YOU'RE IN THE NULL-TIME ZONE--MORE SPECIFICALLY, THE COSMIC COURTROOM OF THE KEEPERS OF CONTINUITY--THE TIME VARIANCE AUTHORITY!
WHERE YOU'RE TO BE JUDGED--FOR CRIMES AGAINST TIME!
YOU ARE DEADPOOL 5: THE FINAL FRONTIER

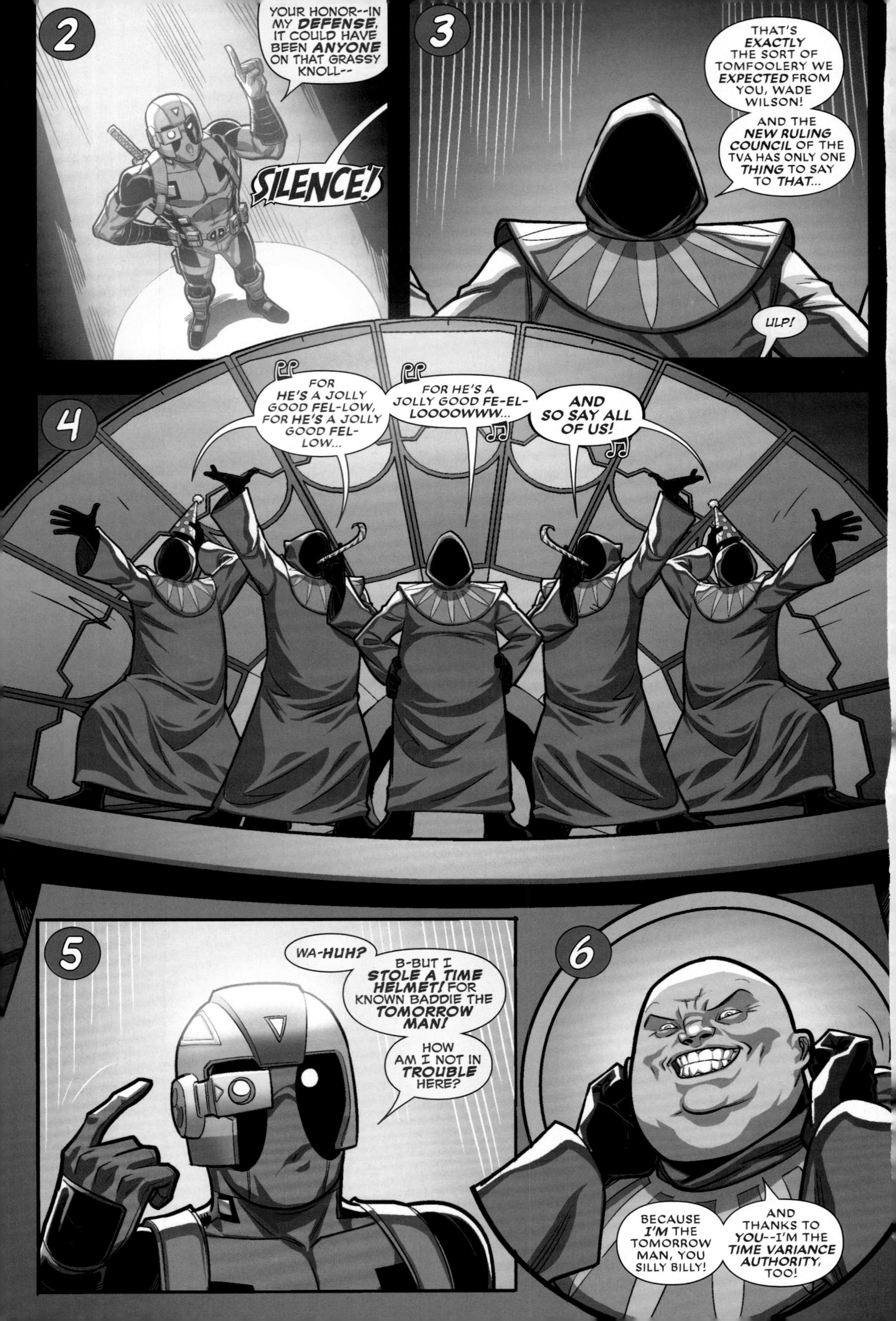
2
YOUR HONOR--IN MY DEFENSE, IT COULD HAVE BEEN ANYONE ON THAT GRASSY KNOLL--
SILENCE!
3
THAT'S EXACTLY THE SORT OF TOMFOOLERY WE EXPECTED FROM YOU, WADE WILSON!
AND THE NEW RULING COUNCIL OF THE TVA HAS ONLY ONE THING TO SAY TO THAT...
ULP!
4
FOR HE'S A JOLLY GOOD FEL-LOW, FOR HE'S A JOLLY GOOD FEL-LOW...
FOR HE'S A JOLLY GOOD FE-EL-LOOOOWWW...
AND SO SAY ALL OF US!
5
WA-HUH?
B-BUT I STOLE A TIME HELMET! FOR KNOWN BADDIE THE TOMORROW MAN!
HOW AM I NOT IN TROUBLE HERE?
6
BECAUSE I'M THE TOMORROW MAN, YOU SILLY BILLY!
AND THANKS TO YOU--I'M THE TIME VARIANCE AUTHORITY, TOO!

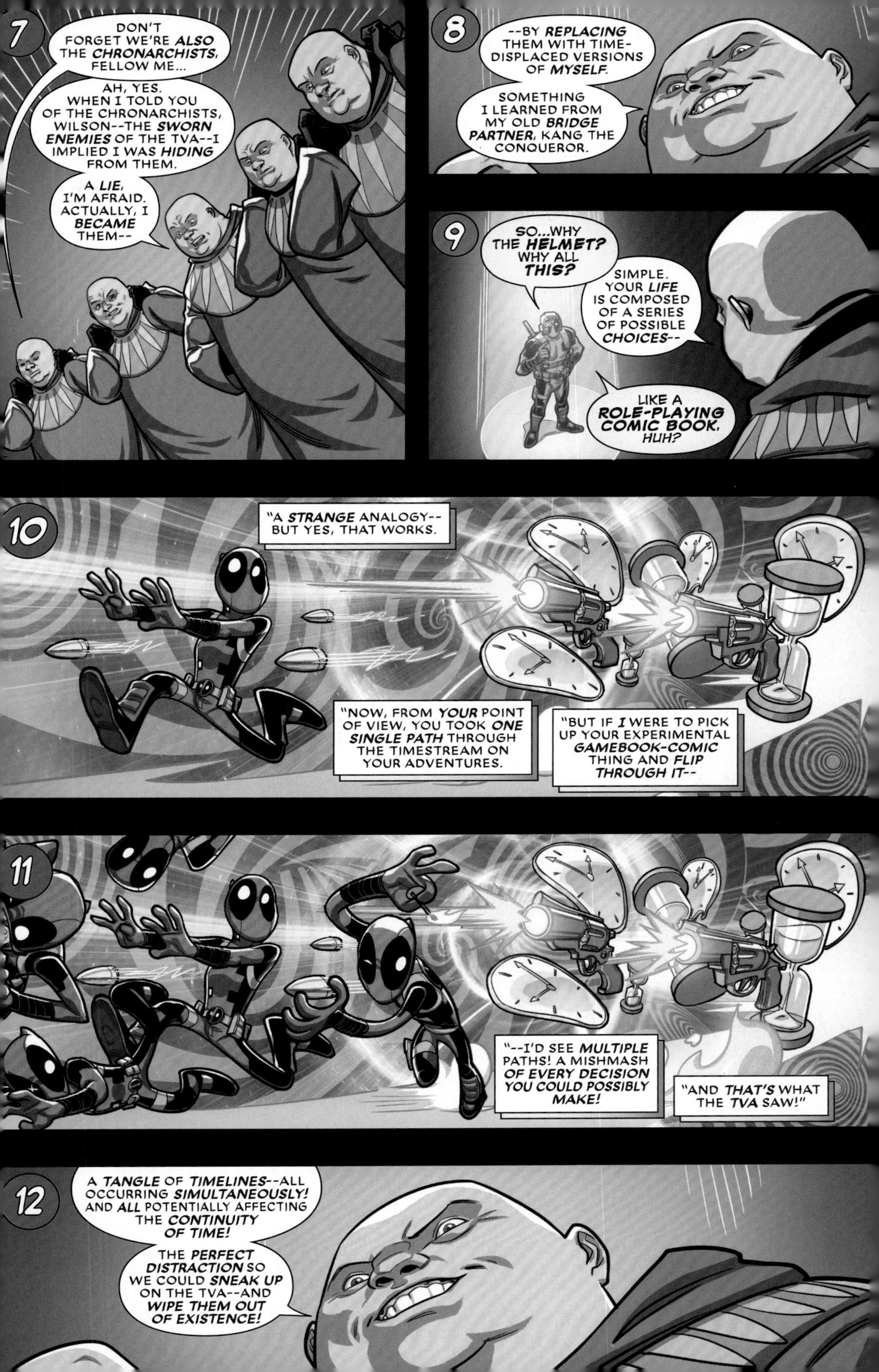
7
DON'T FORGET WE'RE ALSO THE CHRONARCHISTS, FELLOW ME...
AH, YES. WHEN I TOLD YOU OF THE CHRONARCHISTS, WILSON--THE SWORN ENEMIES OF THE TVA--I IMPLIED I WAS HIDING FROM THEM.
A LIE, I'M AFRAID. ACTUALLY, I BECAME THEM--
8
--BY REPLACING THEM WITH TIME-DISPLACED VERSIONS OF MYSELF.
SOMETHING I LEARNED FROM MY OLD BRIDGE PARTNER, KANG THE CONQUEROR.
9
SO...WHY THE HELMET? WHY ALL THIS?
SIMPLE. YOUR LIFE IS COMPOSED OF A SERIES OF POSSIBLE CHOICES--
LIKE A ROLE-PLAYING COMIC BOOK, HUH?
10
"A STRANGE ANALOGY--BUT YES, THAT WORKS.
"NOW, FROM YOUR POINT OF VIEW, YOU TOOK ONE SINGLE PATH THROUGH THE TIMESTREAM ON YOUR ADVENTURES.
"BUT IF I WERE TO PICK UP YOUR EXPERIMENTAL GAMEBOOK-COMIC THING AND FLIP THROUGH IT--
11
"--I'D SEE MULTIPLE PATHS! A MISHMASH OF EVERY DECISION YOU COULD POSSIBLY MAKE!
"AND THAT'S WHAT THE TVA SAW!"
12
A TANGLE OF TIMELINES--ALL OCCURRING SIMULTANEOUSLY! AND ALL POTENTIALLY AFFECTING THE CONTINUITY OF TIME!
THE PERFECT DISTRACTION SO WE COULD SNEAK UP ON THE TVA--AND WIPE THEM OUT OF EXISTENCE!

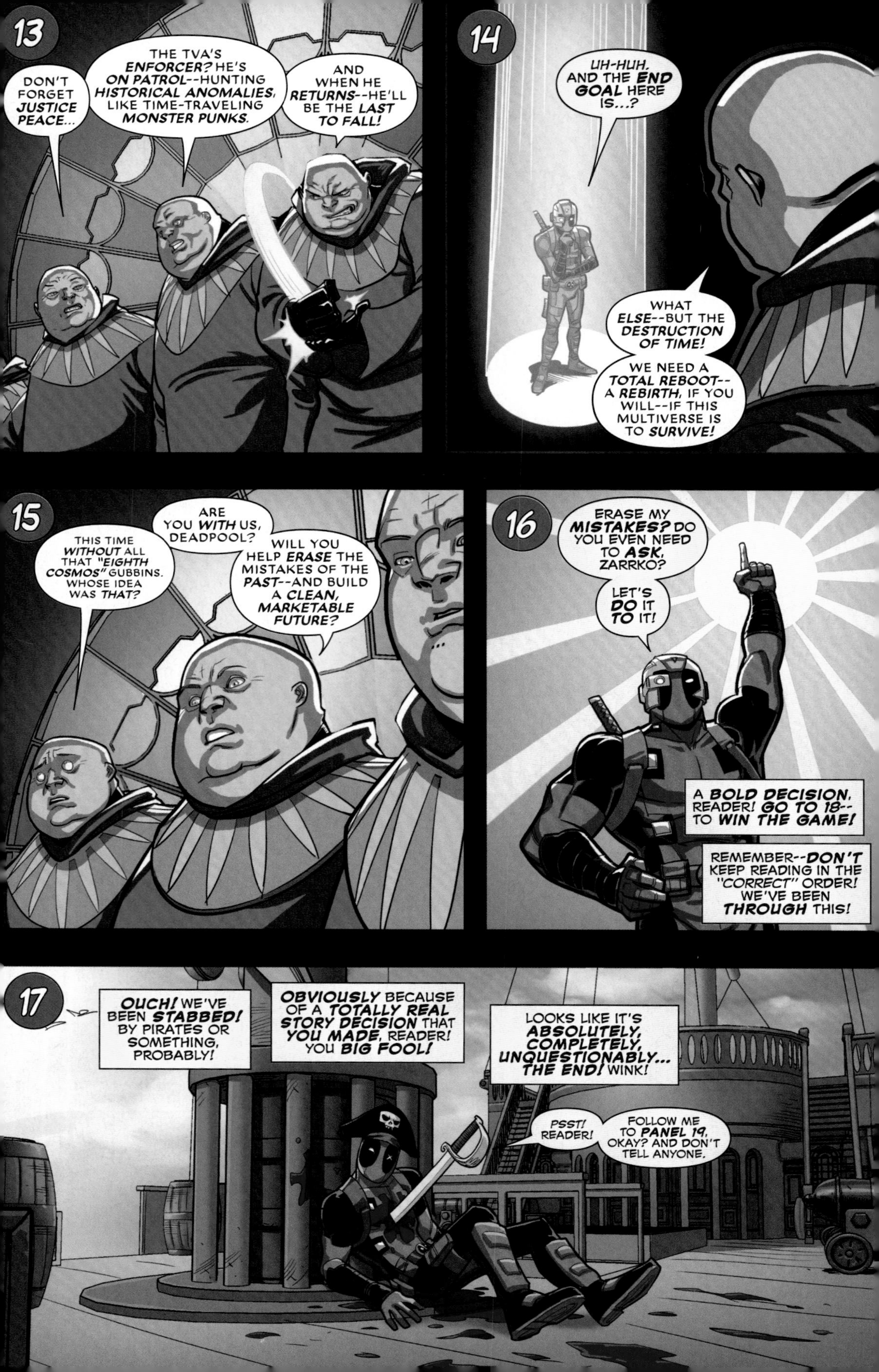
13
DON'T FORGET JUSTICE PEACE...
THE TVA'S ENFORCER? HE'S ON PATROL--HUNTING HISTORICAL ANOMALIES, LIKE TIME-TRAVELING MONSTER PUNKS.
AND WHEN HE RETURNS--HE'LL BE THE LAST TO FALL!
14
UH-HUH. AND THE END GOAL HERE IS...?
WHAT ELSE--BUT THE DESTRUCTION OF TIME!
WE NEED A TOTAL REBOOT--A REBIRTH, IF YOU WILL--IF THIS MULTIVERSE IS TO SURVIVE!
15
THIS TIME WITHOUT ALL THAT "EIGHTH COSMOS" GUBBINS. WHOSE IDEA WAS THAT?
ARE YOU WITH US, DEADPOOL?
WILL YOU HELP ERASE THE MISTAKES OF THE PAST--AND BUILD A CLEAN, MARKETABLE FUTURE?
16
ERASE MY MISTAKES? DO YOU EVEN NEED TO ASK, ZARRKO?
LET'S DO IT TO IT!
A BOLD DECISION, READER! GO TO 18--TO WIN THE GAME!
REMEMBER--DON'T KEEP READING IN THE "CORRECT" ORDER! WE'VE BEEN THROUGH THIS!
17
OUCH! WE'VE BEEN STABBED! BY PIRATES OR SOMETHING, PROBABLY!
OBVIOUSLY BECAUSE OF A TOTALLY REAL STORY DECISION THAT YOU MADE, READER! YOU BIG FOOL!
LOOKS LIKE IT'S ABSOLUTELY, COMPLETELY, UNQUESTIONABLY... THE END! WINK!
PSST! READER!
FOLLOW ME TO PANEL 19, OKAY? AND DON'T TELL ANYONE.

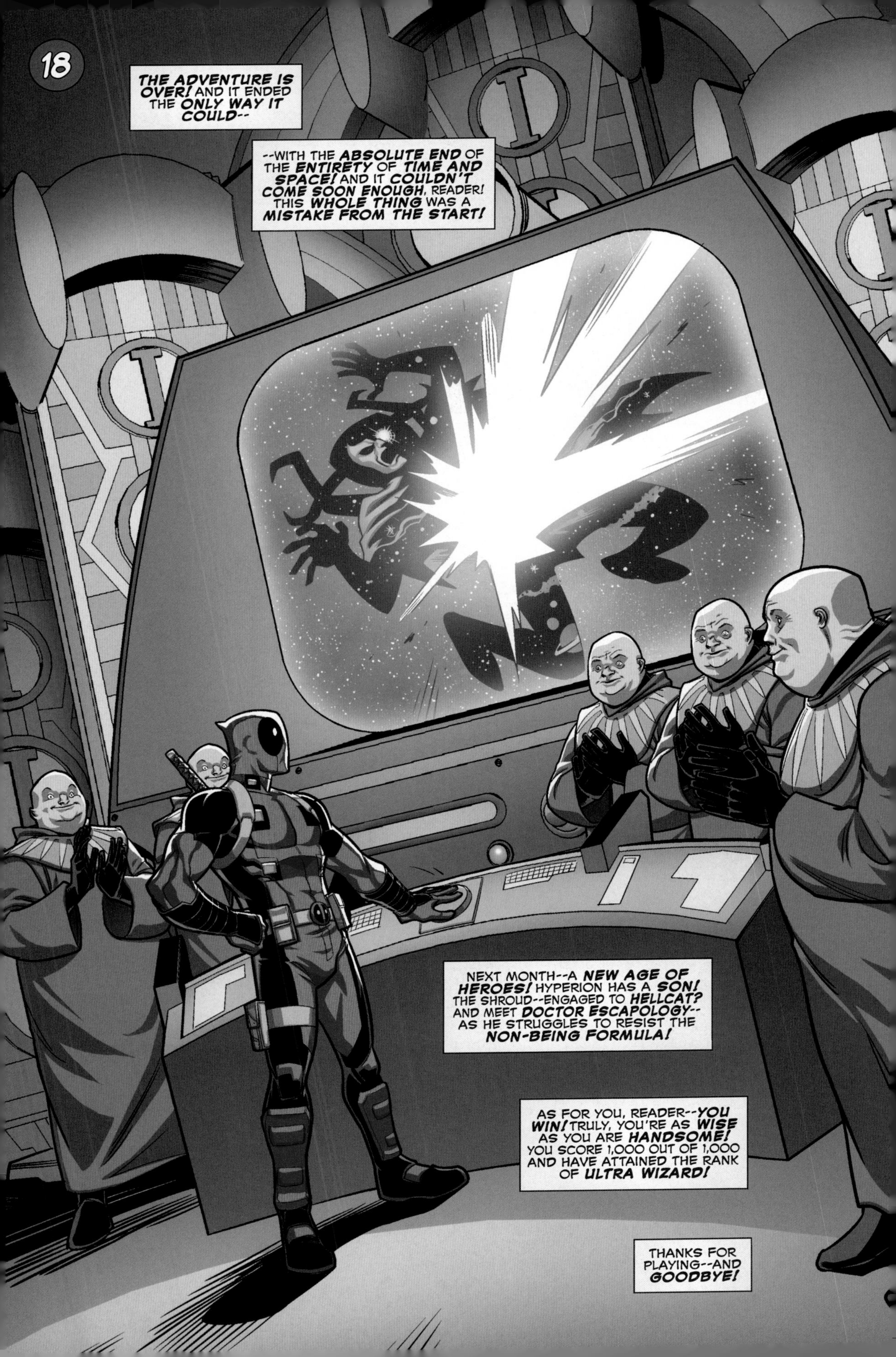
18
THE ADVENTURE IS OVER! AND IT ENDED THE ONLY WAY IT COULD--
--WITH THE ABSOLUTE END OF THE ENTIRETY OF TIME AND SPACE! AND IT COULDN'T COME SOON ENOUGH, READER! THIS WHOLE THING WAS A MISTAKE FROM THE START!
NEXT MONTH--A NEW AGE OF HEROES! HYPERION HAS A SON! THE SHROUD--ENGAGED TO HELLCAT? AND MEET DOCTOR ESCAPOLOGY--AS HE STRUGGLES TO RESIST THE NON-BEING FORMULA!
AS FOR YOU, READER--YOU WIN! TRULY, YOU'RE AS WISE AS YOU ARE HANDSOME! YOU SCORE 1,000 OUT OF 1,000 AND HAVE ATTAINED THE RANK OF ULTRA WIZARD!
THANKS FOR PLAYING--AND GOODBYE!

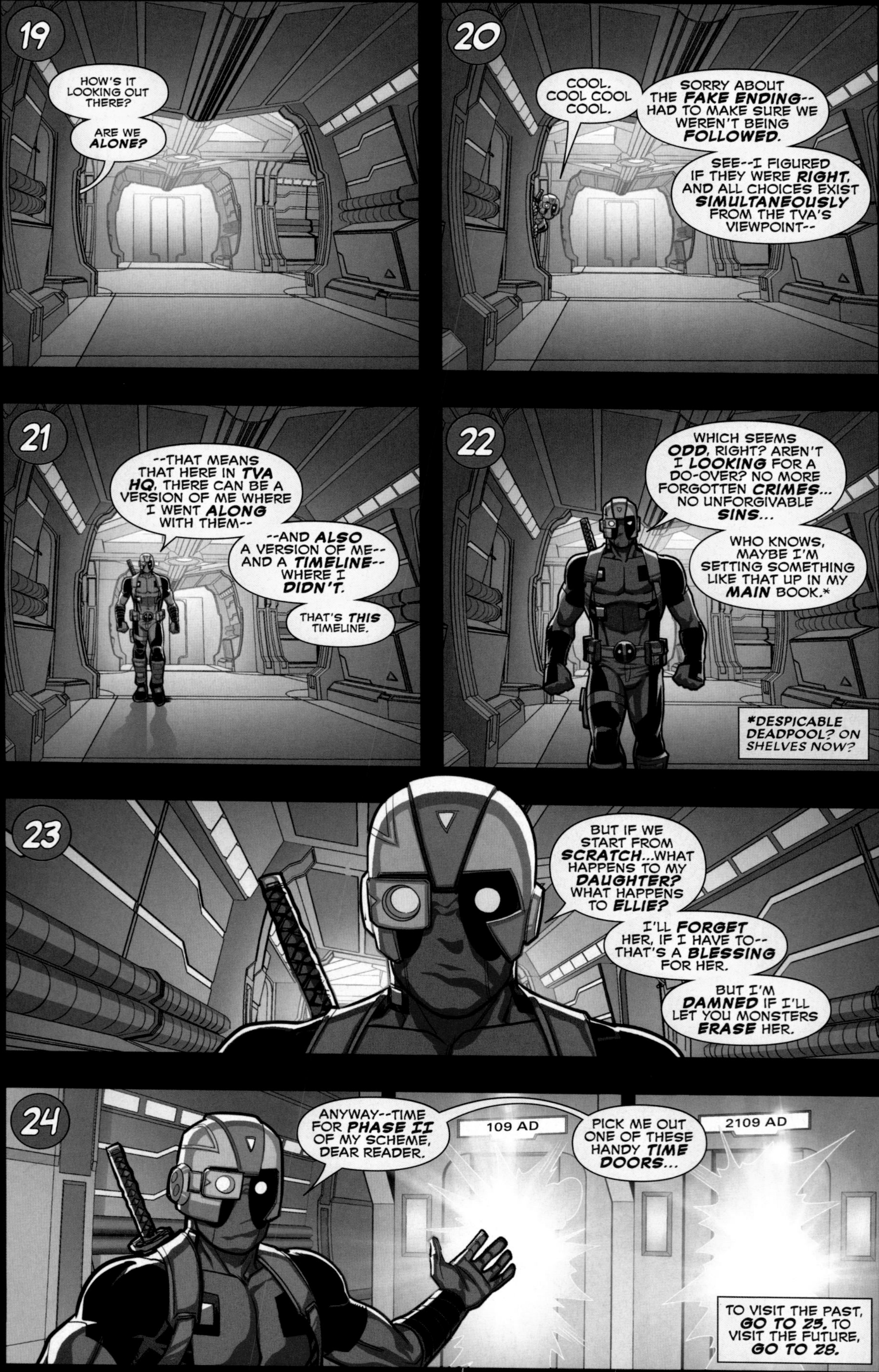
19
HOW'S IT LOOKING OUT THERE?
ARE WE ALONE?
20
COOL. COOL COOL COOL.
SORRY ABOUT THE FAKE ENDING-- HAD TO MAKE SURE WE WEREN'T BEING FOLLOWED.
SEE--I FIGURED IF THEY WERE RIGHT, AND ALL CHOICES EXIST SIMULTANEOUSLY FROM THE TVA'S VIEWPOINT--
21
--THAT MEANS THAT HERE IN TVA HQ, THERE CAN BE A VERSION OF ME WHERE I WENT ALONG WITH THEM--
--AND ALSO A VERSION OF ME-- AND A TIMELINE-- WHERE I DIDN'T.
THAT'S THIS TIMELINE.
22
WHICH SEEMS ODD, RIGHT? AREN'T I LOOKING FOR A DO-OVER? NO MORE FORGOTTEN CRIMES... NO UNFORGIVABLE SINS...
WHO KNOWS, MAYBE I'M SETTING SOMETHING LIKE THAT UP IN MY MAIN BOOK.*
*DESPICABLE DEADPOOL? ON SHELVES NOW?
23
BUT IF WE START FROM SCRATCH...WHAT HAPPENS TO MY DAUGHTER? WHAT HAPPENS TO ELLIE?
I'LL FORGET HER, IF I HAVE TO-- THAT'S A BLESSING FOR HER.
BUT I'M DAMNED IF I'LL LET YOU MONSTERS ERASE HER.
24
ANYWAY--TIME FOR PHASE II OF MY SCHEME, DEAR READER.
109 AD
PICK ME OUT ONE OF THESE HANDY TIME DOORS...
2109 AD
TO VISIT THE PAST, GO TO 25. TO VISIT THE FUTURE, GO TO 28.

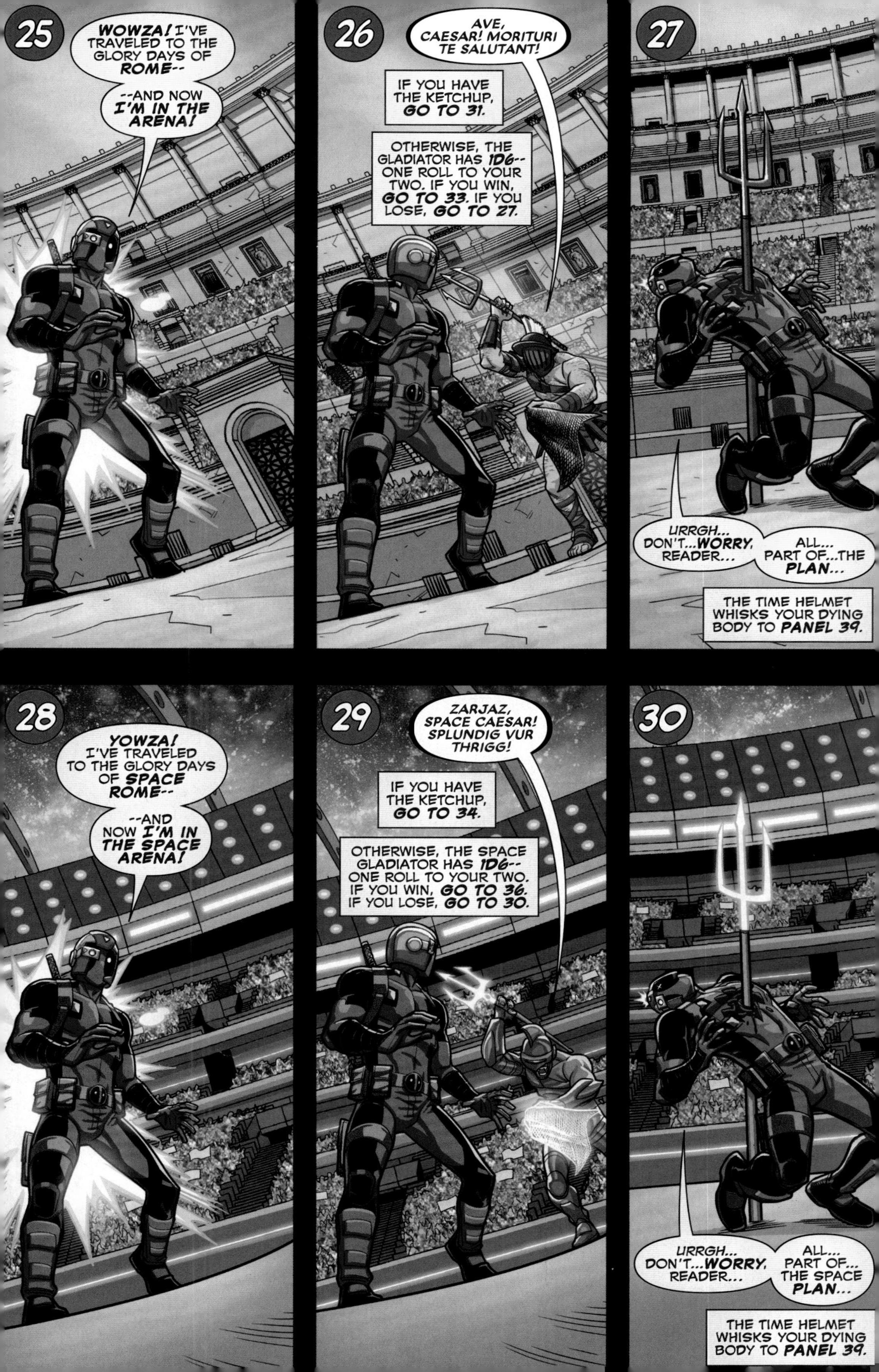
25
WOWZA! I'VE TRAVELED TO THE GLORY DAYS OF ROME--
--AND NOW I'M IN THE ARENA!
26
AVE, CAESAR! MORITURI TE SALUTANT!
IF YOU HAVE THE KETCHUP, GO TO 31.
OTHERWISE, THE GLADIATOR HAS 1D6-- ONE ROLL TO YOUR TWO. IF YOU WIN, GO TO 33. IF YOU LOSE, GO TO 27.
27
URRGH... DON'T...WORRY, READER...
ALL... PART OF...THE PLAN...
THE TIME HELMET WHISKS YOUR DYING BODY TO PANEL 39.
28
YOWZA! I'VE TRAVELED TO THE GLORY DAYS OF SPACE ROME--
--AND NOW I'M IN THE SPACE ARENA!
29
ZARJAZ, SPACE CAESAR! SPLUNDIG VUR THRIGG!
IF YOU HAVE THE KETCHUP, GO TO 34.
OTHERWISE, THE SPACE GLADIATOR HAS 1D6-- ONE ROLL TO YOUR TWO. IF YOU WIN, GO TO 36. IF YOU LOSE, GO TO 30.
30
URRGH... DON'T...WORRY, READER...
ALL... PART OF... THE SPACE PLAN...
THE TIME HELMET WHISKS YOUR DYING BODY TO PANEL 39.

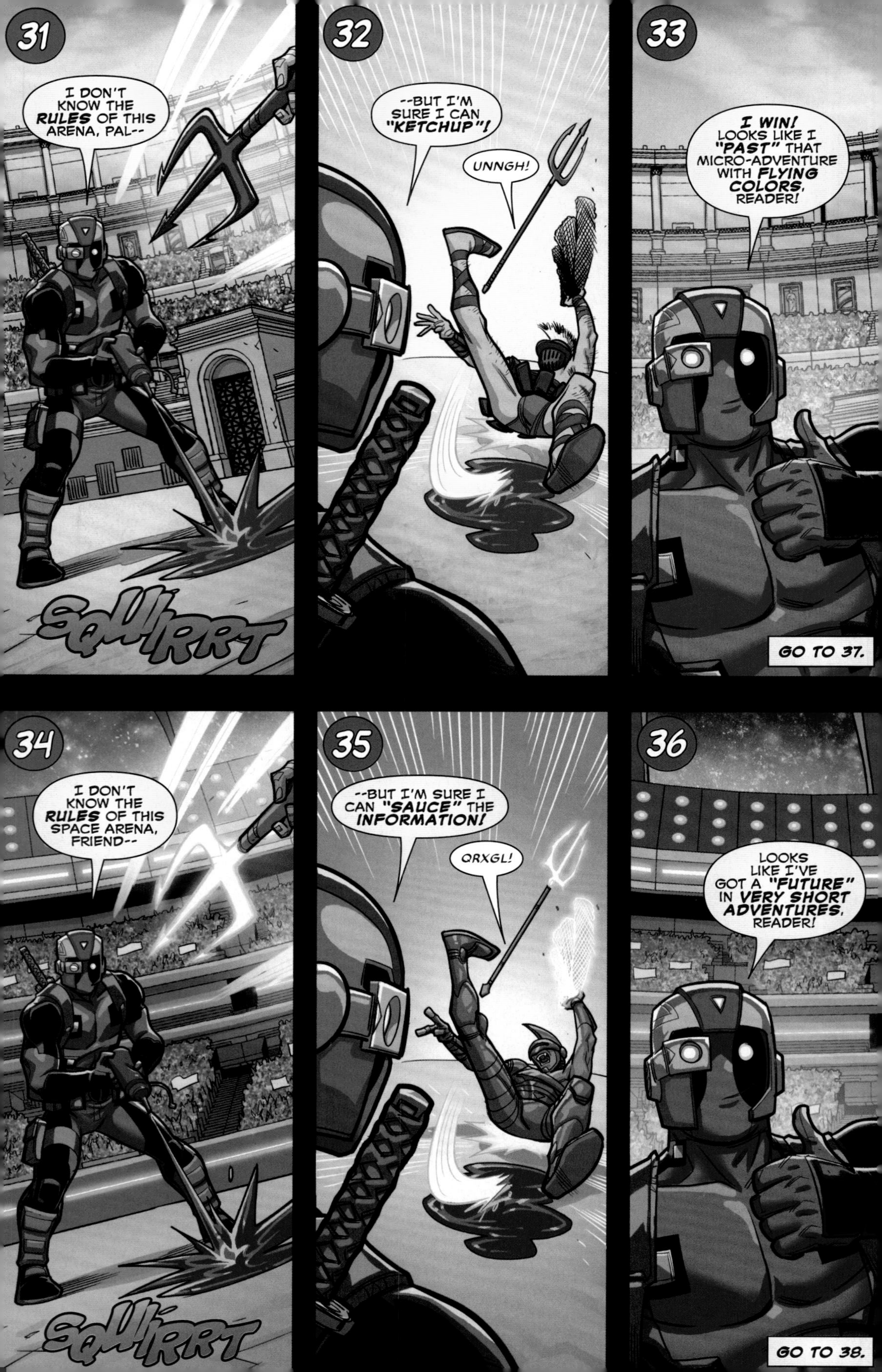
31
I DON'T KNOW THE RULES OF THIS ARENA, PAL--
SQUIRRT
32
--BUT I'M SURE I CAN "KETCHUP"!
UNNGH!
33
I WIN! LOOKS LIKE I "PAST" THAT MICRO-ADVENTURE WITH FLYING COLORS, READER!
GO TO 37.
34
I DON'T KNOW THE RULES OF THIS SPACE ARENA, FRIEND--
SQUIRRT
35
--BUT I'M SURE I CAN "SAUCE" THE INFORMATION!
QRXGL!
36
LOOKS LIKE I'VE GOT A "FUTURE" IN VERY SHORT ADVENTURES, READER!
GO TO 38.

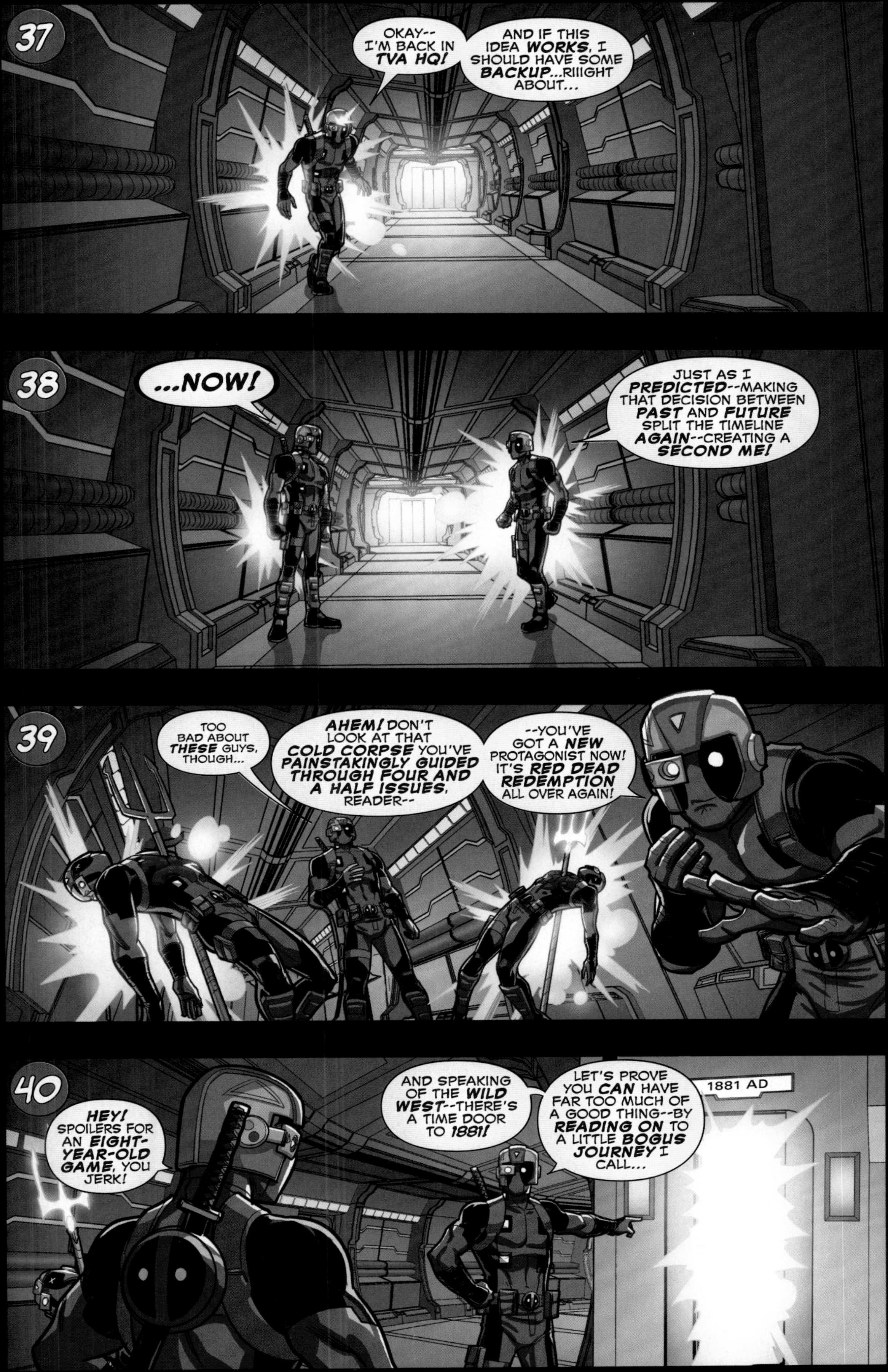
37
OKAY-- I'M BACK IN TVA HQ!
AND IF THIS IDEA WORKS, I SHOULD HAVE SOME BACKUP...RIIIGHT ABOUT...
38
...NOW!
JUST AS I PREDICTED--MAKING THAT DECISION BETWEEN PAST AND FUTURE SPLIT THE TIMELINE AGAIN--CREATING A SECOND ME!
39
TOO BAD ABOUT THESE GUYS, THOUGH...
AHEM! DON'T LOOK AT THAT COLD CORPSE YOU'VE PAINSTAKINGLY GUIDED THROUGH FOUR AND A HALF ISSUES, READER--
--YOU'VE GOT A NEW PROTAGONIST NOW! IT'S RED DEAD REDEMPTION ALL OVER AGAIN!
40
HEY! SPOILERS FOR AN EIGHT-YEAR-OLD GAME, YOU JERK!
AND SPEAKING OF THE WILD WEST--THERE'S A TIME DOOR TO 1881!
LET'S PROVE YOU CAN HAVE FAR TOO MUCH OF A GOOD THING--BY READING ON TO A LITTLE BOGUS JOURNEY I CALL...
1881 AD

...WADE AND WADE'S EVEN MORE EXCELLENT ADVENTURE! (WITH COWBOYS!)

START IN THE ***TOP LEFT HEXAGON***--
AND WORK YOUR WAY THROUGH THE
MAZE OF POSSIBILITIES WITH YOUR
DEADPOOL DICE!

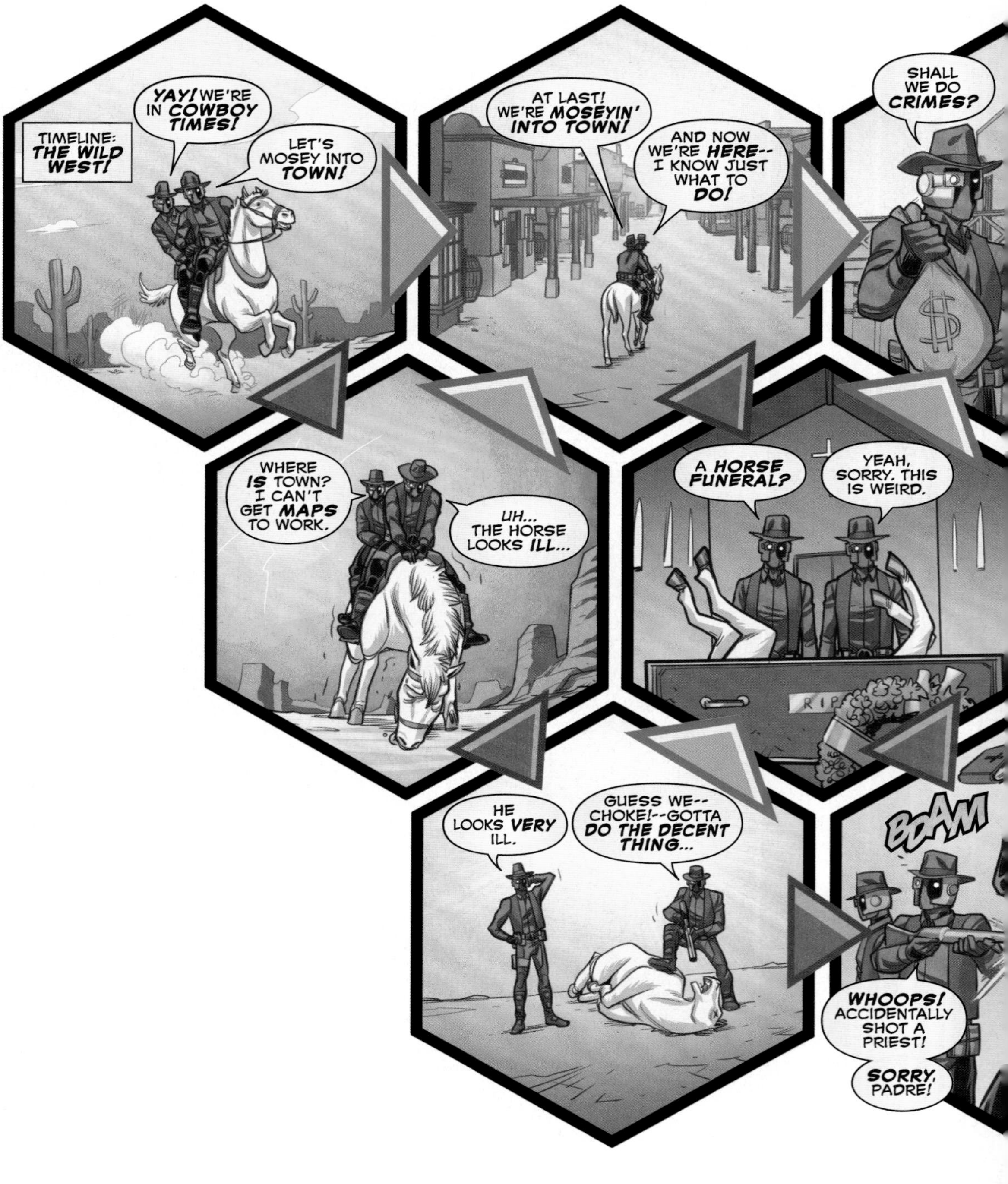
TIMELINE: THE WILD WEST!
YAY! WE'RE IN COWBOY TIMES!
LET'S MOSEY INTO TOWN!
AT LAST! WE'RE MOSEYIN' INTO TOWN!
AND NOW WE'RE HERE-- I KNOW JUST WHAT TO DO!
SHALL WE DO CRIMES?
WHERE IS TOWN? I CAN'T GET MAPS TO WORK.
UH... THE HORSE LOOKS ILL...
A HORSE FUNERAL?
YEAH, SORRY. THIS IS WEIRD.
RIP
HE LOOKS VERY ILL.
GUESS WE-- CHOKE!--GOTTA DO THE DECENT THING...
BDAM
WHOOPS! ACCIDENTALLY SHOT A PRIEST!
SORRY, PADRE!

AN EVEN NUMBER MEANS YOU MOVE ALONG THE ***GREEN*** ARROW--THINGS ARE LOOKING ***UP!*** BUT AN ***ODD*** NUMBER TAKES YOU ALONG THE ***RED*** ARROW--TO A ***NEW LOW!***

KEEP ***ROLLING***--AND FOLLOWING THE ***STORY PATH***--UNTIL YOU REACH THE ***END!*** NOTHING SIMPLER, PARD!

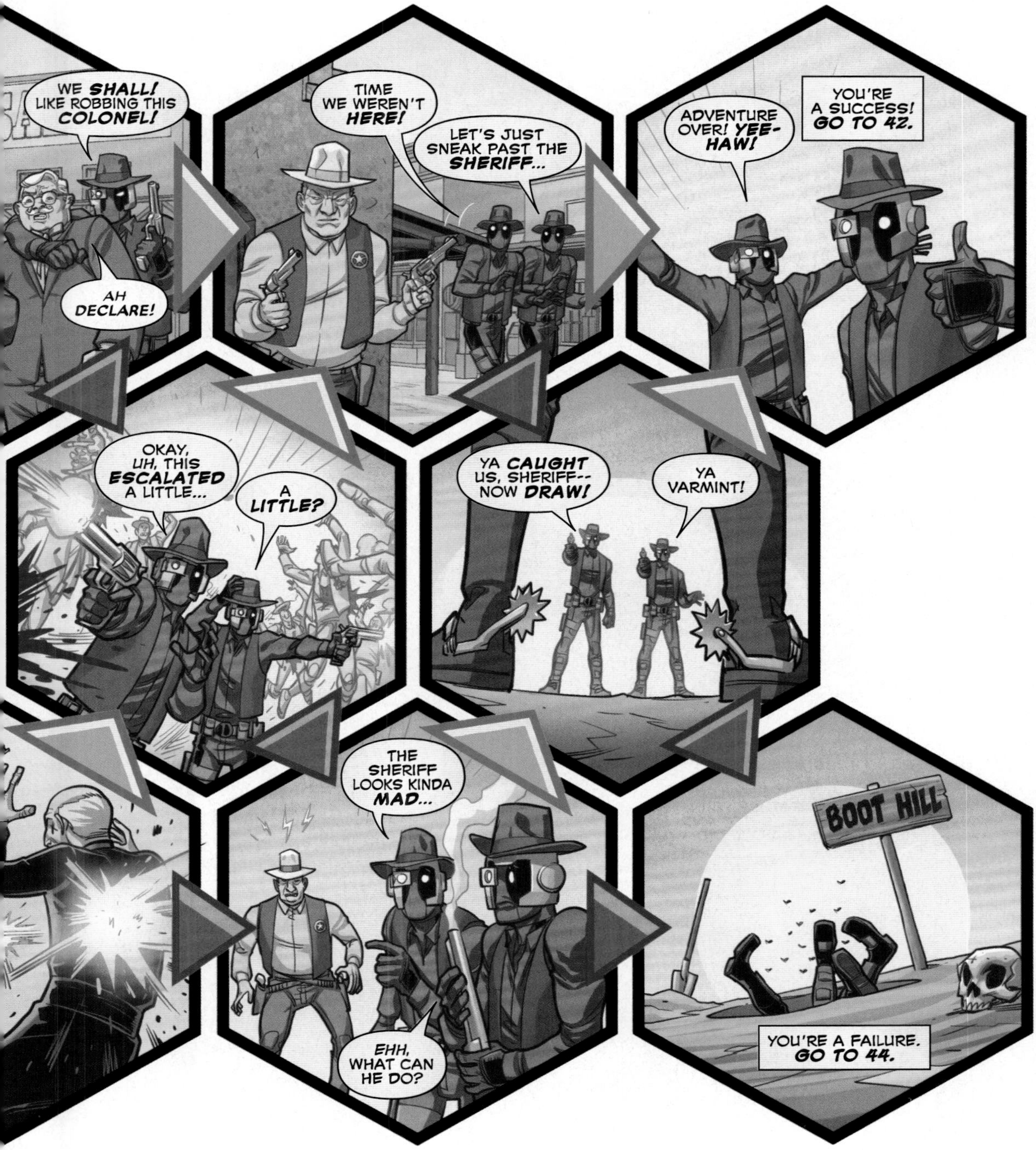
WE SHALL! LIKE ROBBING THIS COLONEL!
AH DECLARE!
TIME WE WEREN'T HERE!
LET'S JUST SNEAK PAST THE SHERIFF...
ADVENTURE OVER! YEE-HAW!
YOU'RE A SUCCESS! GO TO 42.
OKAY, UH, THIS ESCALATED A LITTLE...
A LITTLE?
YA CAUGHT US, SHERIFF--NOW DRAW!
YA VARMINT!
THE SHERIFF LOOKS KINDA MAD...
EHH, WHAT CAN HE DO?
BOOT HILL
YOU'RE A FAILURE. GO TO 44.

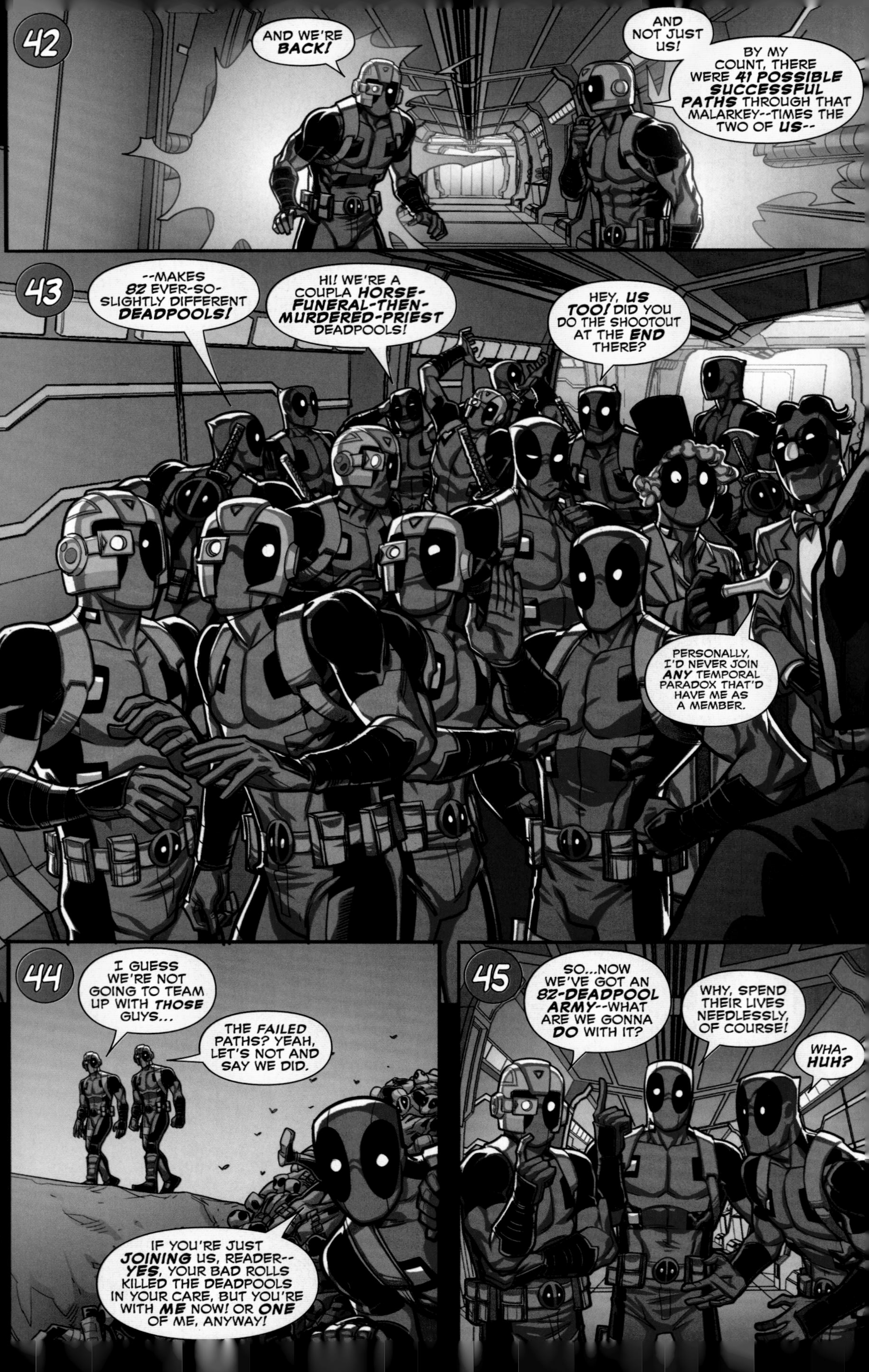
42
AND WE'RE BACK!
AND NOT JUST US!
BY MY COUNT, THERE WERE 41 POSSIBLE SUCCESSFUL PATHS THROUGH THAT MALARKEY--TIMES THE TWO OF US--
43
--MAKES 82 EVER-SO-SLIGHTLY DIFFERENT DEADPOOLS!
HI! WE'RE A COUPLA HORSE-FUNERAL-THEN-MURDERED-PRIEST DEADPOOLS!
HEY, US TOO! DID YOU DO THE SHOOTOUT AT THE END THERE?
PERSONALLY, I'D NEVER JOIN ANY TEMPORAL PARADOX THAT'D HAVE ME AS A MEMBER.
44
I GUESS WE'RE NOT GOING TO TEAM UP WITH THOSE GUYS...
THE FAILED PATHS? YEAH, LET'S NOT AND SAY WE DID.
IF YOU'RE JUST JOINING US, READER-- YES, YOUR BAD ROLLS KILLED THE DEADPOOLS IN YOUR CARE, BUT YOU'RE WITH ME NOW! OR ONE OF ME, ANYWAY!
45
SO...NOW WE'VE GOT AN 82-DEADPOOL ARMY--WHAT ARE WE GONNA DO WITH IT?
WHY, SPEND THEIR LIVES NEEDLESSLY, OF COURSE!
WHA-HUH?

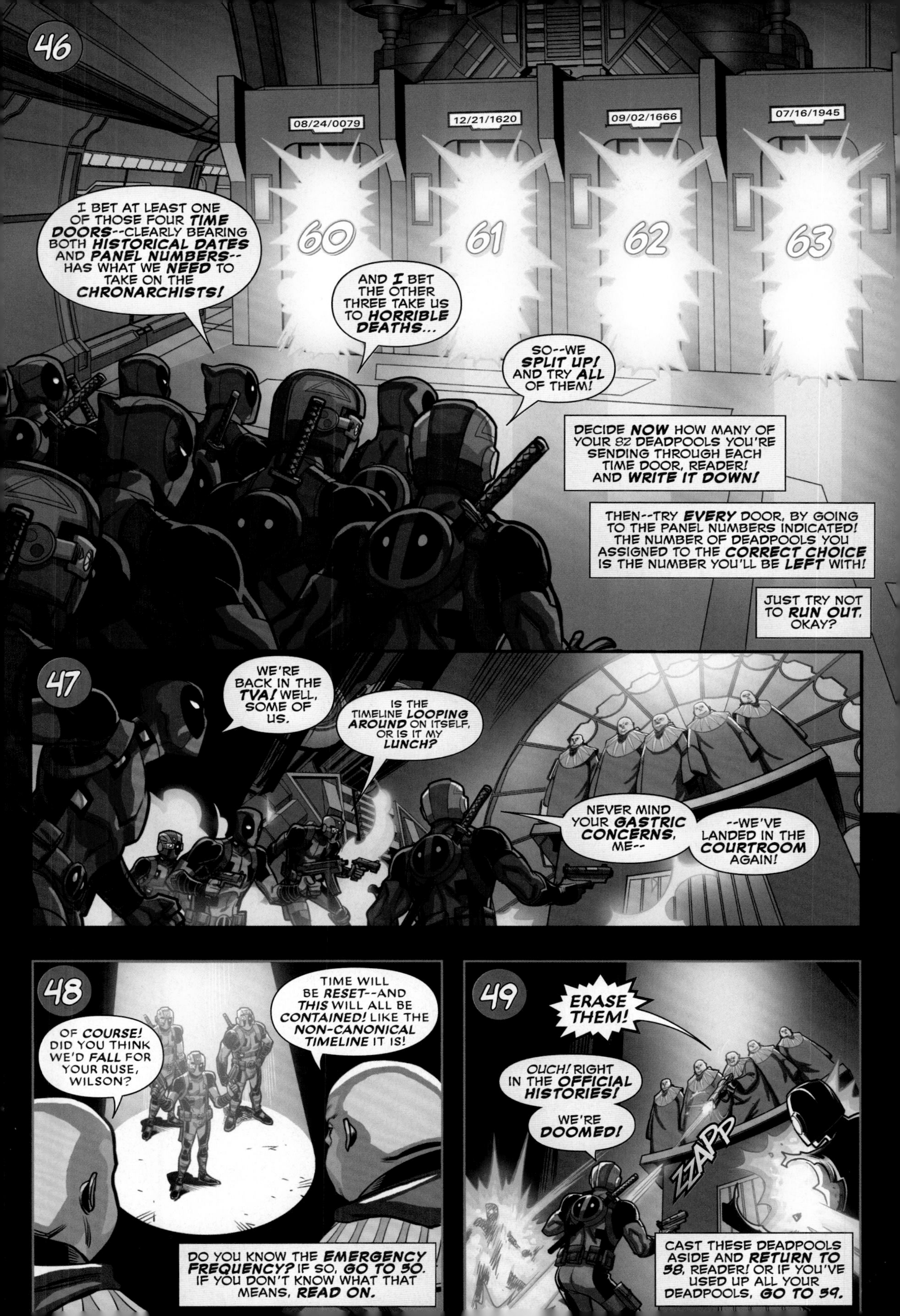
46
08/24/0079
12/21/1620
09/02/1666
07/16/1945
60
61
62
63
I BET AT LEAST ONE OF THOSE FOUR *TIME DOORS*--CLEARLY BEARING BOTH *HISTORICAL DATES* AND *PANEL NUMBERS*--HAS WHAT WE *NEED* TO TAKE ON THE *CHRONARCHISTS!*
AND *I* BET THE OTHER THREE TAKE US TO *HORRIBLE DEATHS*...
SO--WE *SPLIT UP!* AND TRY *ALL* OF THEM!
DECIDE **NOW** HOW MANY OF YOUR 82 DEADPOOLS YOU'RE SENDING THROUGH EACH TIME DOOR, READER! AND ***WRITE IT DOWN!***
THEN--TRY ***EVERY*** DOOR, BY GOING TO THE PANEL NUMBERS INDICATED! THE NUMBER OF DEADPOOLS YOU ASSIGNED TO THE ***CORRECT CHOICE*** IS THE NUMBER YOU'LL BE ***LEFT*** WITH!
JUST TRY NOT TO ***RUN OUT***, OKAY?
47
WE'RE BACK IN THE *TVA!* WELL, SOME OF US.
IS THE TIMELINE *LOOPING AROUND* ON ITSELF, OR IS IT MY *LUNCH?*
NEVER MIND YOUR *GASTRIC CONCERNS*, ME--
--WE'VE LANDED IN THE *COURTROOM* AGAIN!
48
OF *COURSE!* DID YOU THINK WE'D *FALL* FOR YOUR RUSE, WILSON?
TIME WILL BE *RESET*--AND *THIS* WILL ALL BE *CONTAINED!* LIKE THE *NON-CANONICAL TIMELINE* IT IS!
DO YOU KNOW THE ***EMERGENCY FREQUENCY?*** IF SO, ***GO TO 50***. IF YOU DON'T KNOW WHAT THAT MEANS, ***READ ON.***
49
ERASE THEM!
OUCH! RIGHT IN THE *OFFICIAL HISTORIES!*
WE'RE *DOOMED!*
ZZAPP
CAST THESE DEADPOOLS ASIDE AND ***RETURN TO 58***, READER! OR IF YOU'VE USED UP ALL YOUR DEADPOOLS, ***GO TO 59.***

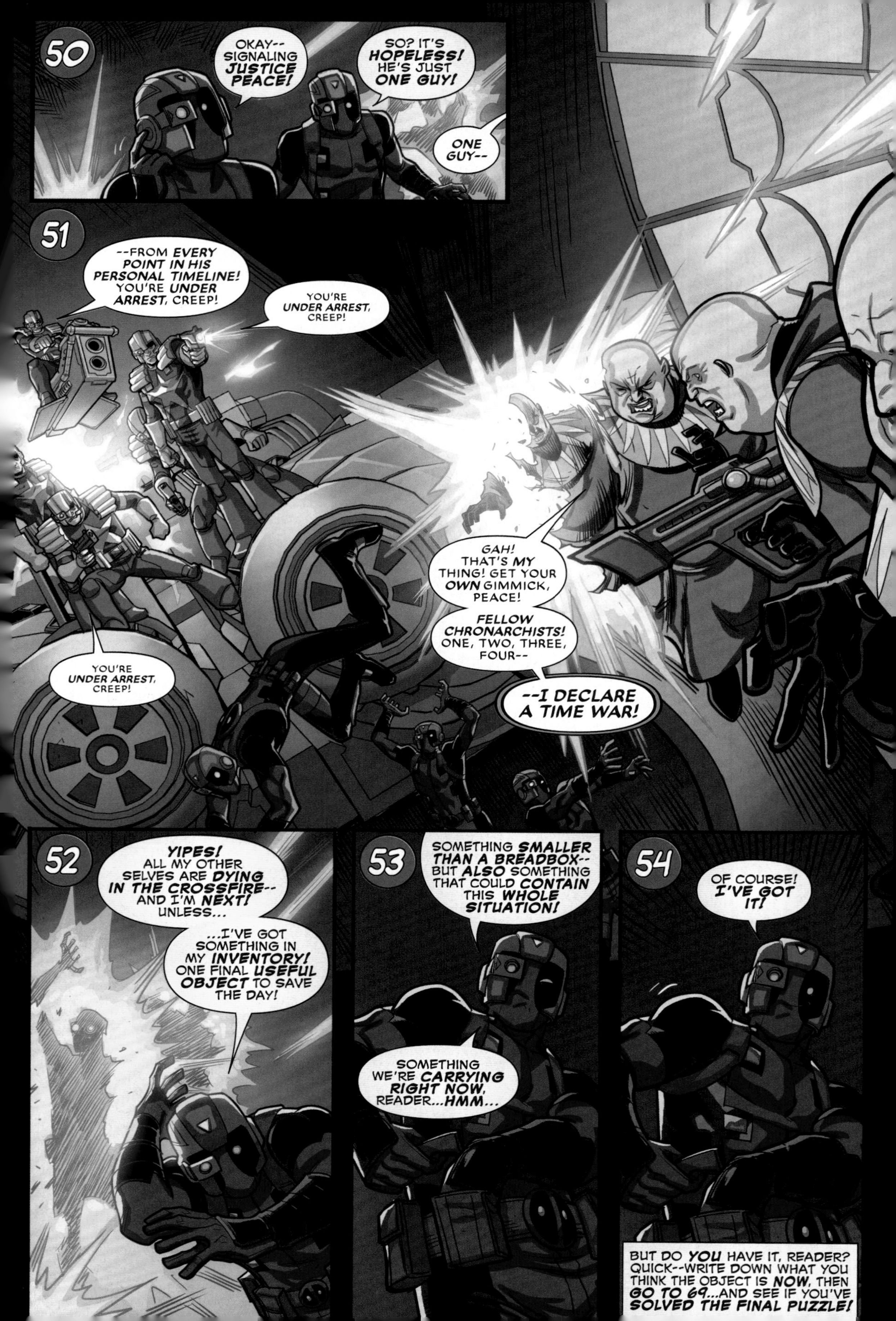
50
OKAY-- SIGNALING JUSTICE PEACE!
SO? IT'S HOPELESS! HE'S JUST ONE GUY!
ONE GUY--
51
--FROM EVERY POINT IN HIS PERSONAL TIMELINE! YOU'RE UNDER ARREST, CREEP!
YOU'RE UNDER ARREST, CREEP!
YOU'RE UNDER ARREST, CREEP!
GAH! THAT'S MY THING! GET YOUR OWN GIMMICK, PEACE!
FELLOW CHRONARCHISTS! ONE, TWO, THREE, FOUR--
--I DECLARE A TIME WAR!
52
YIPES! ALL MY OTHER SELVES ARE DYING IN THE CROSSFIRE-- AND I'M NEXT! UNLESS...
...I'VE GOT SOMETHING IN MY INVENTORY! ONE FINAL USEFUL OBJECT TO SAVE THE DAY!
53
SOMETHING SMALLER THAN A BREADBOX-- BUT ALSO SOMETHING THAT COULD CONTAIN THIS WHOLE SITUATION!
SOMETHING WE'RE CARRYING RIGHT NOW, READER...HMM...
54
OF COURSE! I'VE GOT IT!
BUT DO YOU HAVE IT, READER? QUICK--WRITE DOWN WHAT YOU THINK THE OBJECT IS NOW, THEN GO TO 69...AND SEE IF YOU'VE SOLVED THE FINAL PUZZLE!

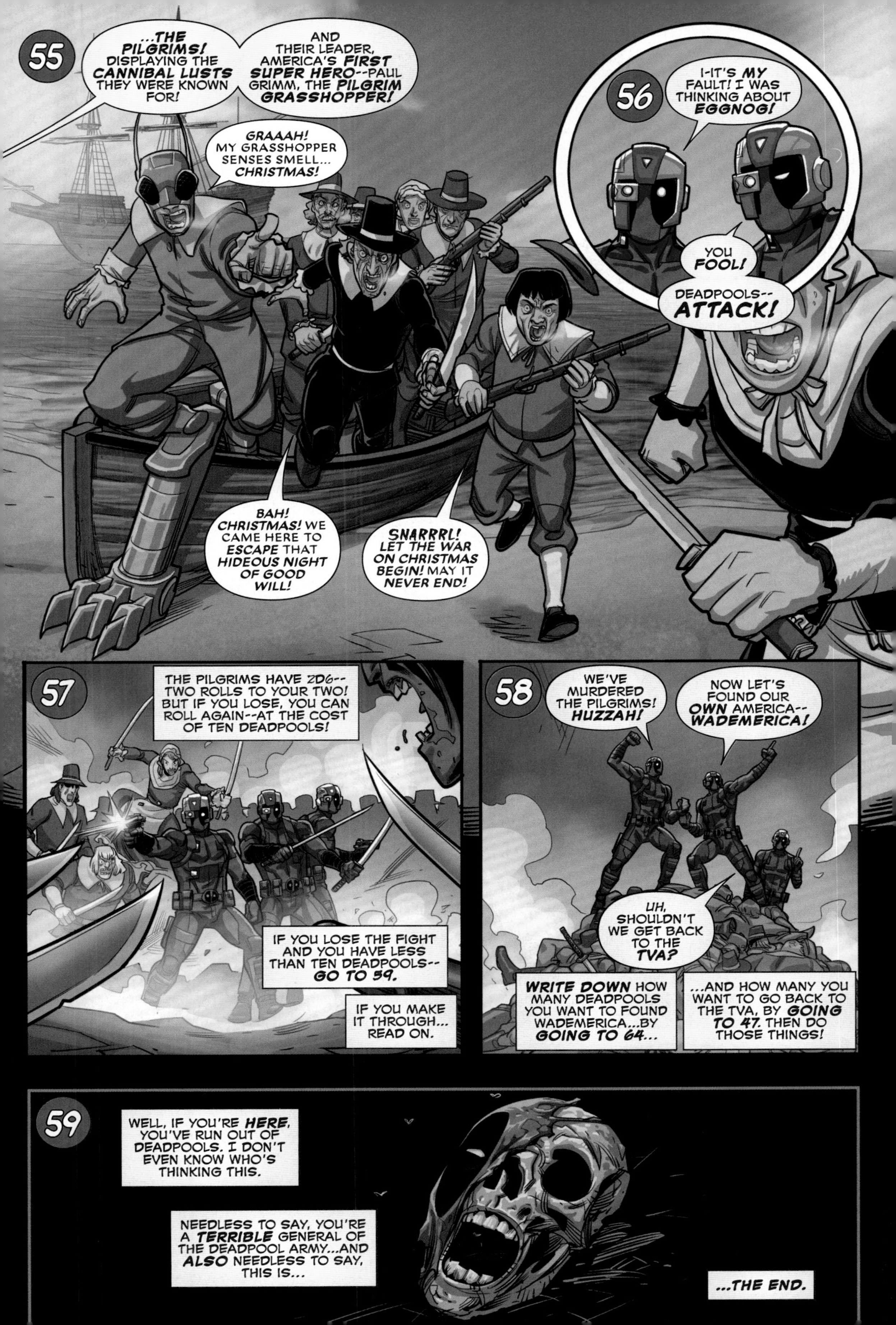
55
...THE PILGRIMS! DISPLAYING THE CANNIBAL LUSTS THEY WERE KNOWN FOR!
AND THEIR LEADER, AMERICA'S FIRST SUPER HERO--PAUL GRIMM, THE PILGRIM GRASSHOPPER!
GRAAAH! MY GRASSHOPPER SENSES SMELL... CHRISTMAS!
BAH! CHRISTMAS! WE CAME HERE TO ESCAPE THAT HIDEOUS NIGHT OF GOOD WILL!
SNARRRL! LET THE WAR ON CHRISTMAS BEGIN! MAY IT NEVER END!
56
I-IT'S MY FAULT! I WAS THINKING ABOUT EGGNOG!
YOU FOOL!
DEADPOOLS-- ATTACK!
57
THE PILGRIMS HAVE 2D6--TWO ROLLS TO YOUR TWO! BUT IF YOU LOSE, YOU CAN ROLL AGAIN--AT THE COST OF TEN DEADPOOLS!
IF YOU LOSE THE FIGHT AND YOU HAVE LESS THAN TEN DEADPOOLS-- GO TO 59.
IF YOU MAKE IT THROUGH... READ ON.
58
WE'VE MURDERED THE PILGRIMS! HUZZAH!
NOW LET'S FOUND OUR OWN AMERICA-- WADEMERICA!
UH, SHOULDN'T WE GET BACK TO THE TVA?
WRITE DOWN HOW MANY DEADPOOLS YOU WANT TO FOUND WADEMERICA...BY GOING TO 64...
...AND HOW MANY YOU WANT TO GO BACK TO THE TVA, BY GOING TO 47. THEN DO THOSE THINGS!
59
WELL, IF YOU'RE HERE, YOU'VE RUN OUT OF DEADPOOLS. I DON'T EVEN KNOW WHO'S THINKING THIS.
NEEDLESS TO SAY, YOU'RE A TERRIBLE GENERAL OF THE DEADPOOL ARMY...AND ALSO NEEDLESS TO SAY, THIS IS...
...THE END.

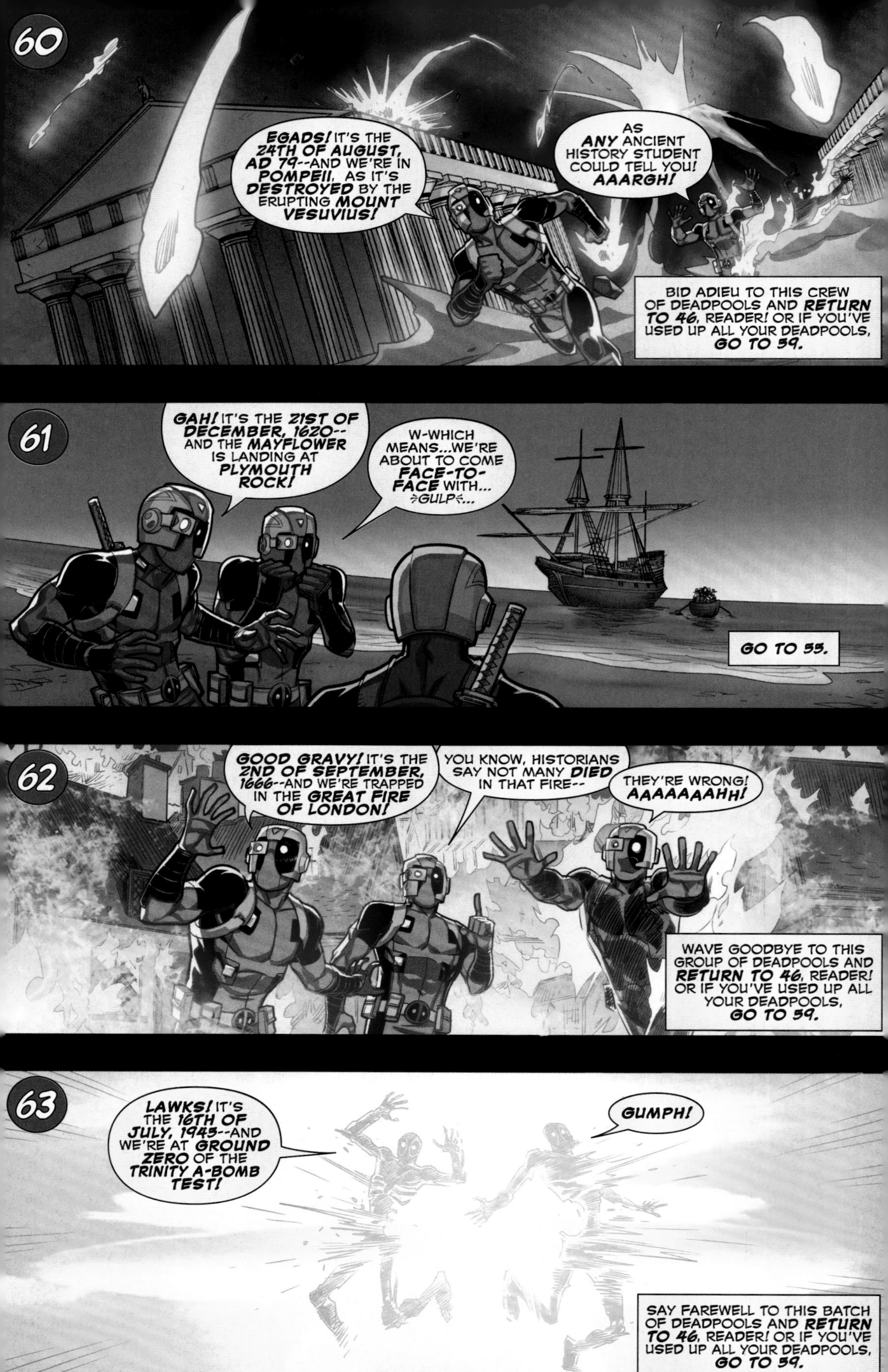
60
EGADS! IT'S THE 24TH OF AUGUST, AD 79--AND WE'RE IN POMPEII, AS IT'S DESTROYED BY THE ERUPTING MOUNT VESUVIUS!
AS ANY ANCIENT HISTORY STUDENT COULD TELL YOU! AAARGH!
BID ADIEU TO THIS CREW OF DEADPOOLS AND RETURN TO 46, READER! OR IF YOU'VE USED UP ALL YOUR DEADPOOLS, GO TO 59.
61
GAH! IT'S THE 21ST OF DECEMBER, 1620--AND THE MAYFLOWER IS LANDING AT PLYMOUTH ROCK!
W-WHICH MEANS...WE'RE ABOUT TO COME FACE-TO-FACE WITH... GULP...
GO TO 55.
62
GOOD GRAVY! IT'S THE 2ND OF SEPTEMBER, 1666--AND WE'RE TRAPPED IN THE GREAT FIRE OF LONDON!
YOU KNOW, HISTORIANS SAY NOT MANY DIED IN THAT FIRE--
THEY'RE WRONG! AAAAAAAHH!
WAVE GOODBYE TO THIS GROUP OF DEADPOOLS AND RETURN TO 46, READER! OR IF YOU'VE USED UP ALL YOUR DEADPOOLS, GO TO 59.
63
LAWKS! IT'S THE 16TH OF JULY, 1945--AND WE'RE AT GROUND ZERO OF THE TRINITY A-BOMB TEST!
GUMPH!
SAY FAREWELL TO THIS BATCH OF DEADPOOLS AND RETURN TO 46, READER! OR IF YOU'VE USED UP ALL YOUR DEADPOOLS, GO TO 59.

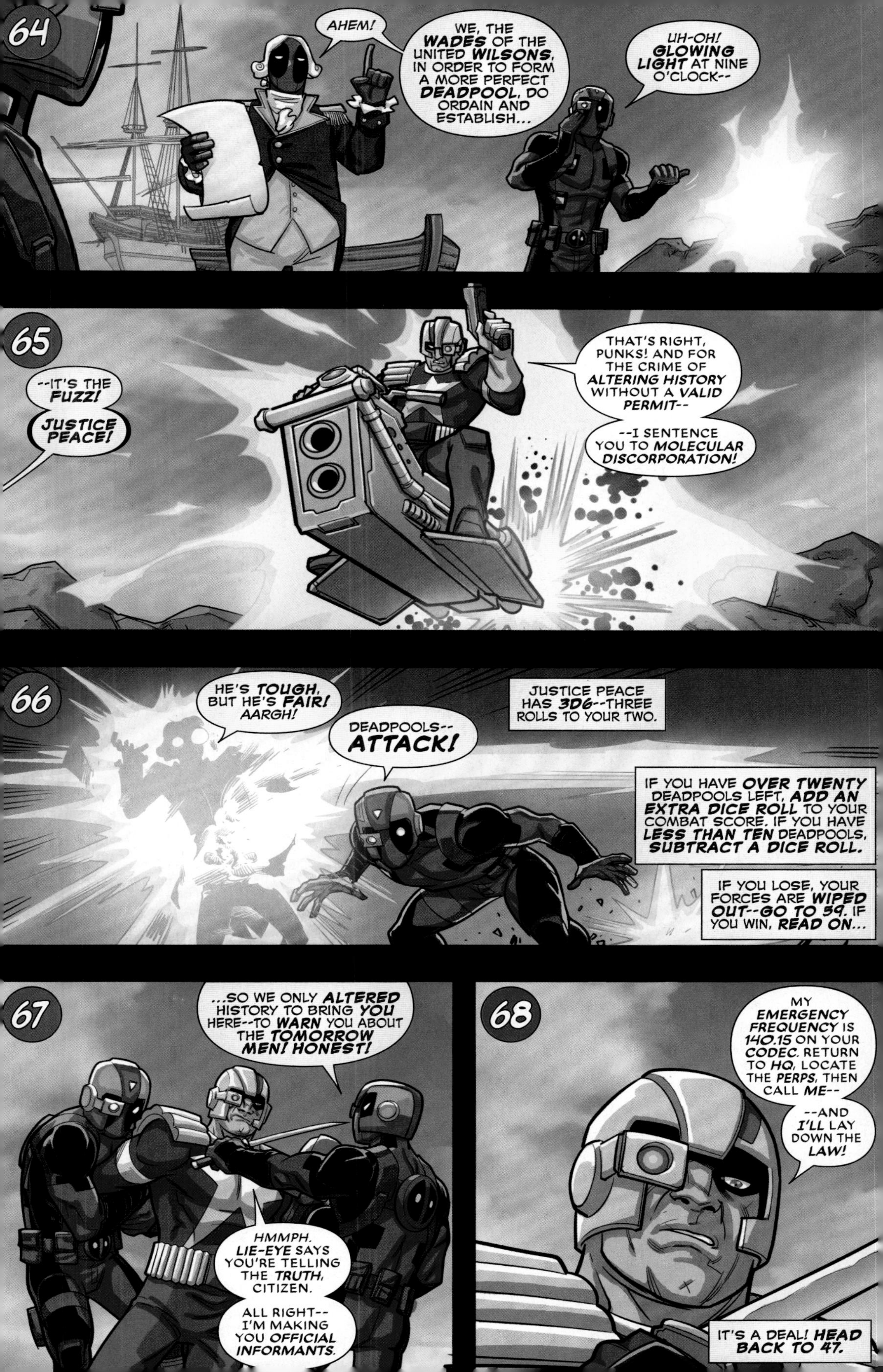
64
AHEM!
WE, THE WADES OF THE UNITED WILSONS, IN ORDER TO FORM A MORE PERFECT DEADPOOL, DO ORDAIN AND ESTABLISH...
UH-OH! GLOWING LIGHT AT NINE O'CLOCK--
65
--IT'S THE FUZZ!
JUSTICE PEACE!
THAT'S RIGHT, PUNKS! AND FOR THE CRIME OF ALTERING HISTORY WITHOUT A VALID PERMIT--
--I SENTENCE YOU TO MOLECULAR DISCORPORATION!
66
HE'S TOUGH, BUT HE'S FAIR! AARGH!
DEADPOOLS-- ATTACK!
JUSTICE PEACE HAS 3D6--THREE ROLLS TO YOUR TWO.
IF YOU HAVE OVER TWENTY DEADPOOLS LEFT, ADD AN EXTRA DICE ROLL TO YOUR COMBAT SCORE. IF YOU HAVE LESS THAN TEN DEADPOOLS, SUBTRACT A DICE ROLL.
IF YOU LOSE, YOUR FORCES ARE WIPED OUT--GO TO 59. IF YOU WIN, READ ON...
67
...SO WE ONLY ALTERED HISTORY TO BRING YOU HERE--TO WARN YOU ABOUT THE TOMORROW MEN! HONEST!
HMMPH. LIE-EYE SAYS YOU'RE TELLING THE TRUTH, CITIZEN.
ALL RIGHT-- I'M MAKING YOU OFFICIAL INFORMANTS.
68
MY EMERGENCY FREQUENCY IS 140.15 ON YOUR CODEC. RETURN TO HQ, LOCATE THE PERPS, THEN CALL ME--
--AND I'LL LAY DOWN THE LAW!
IT'S A DEAL! HEAD BACK TO 47.

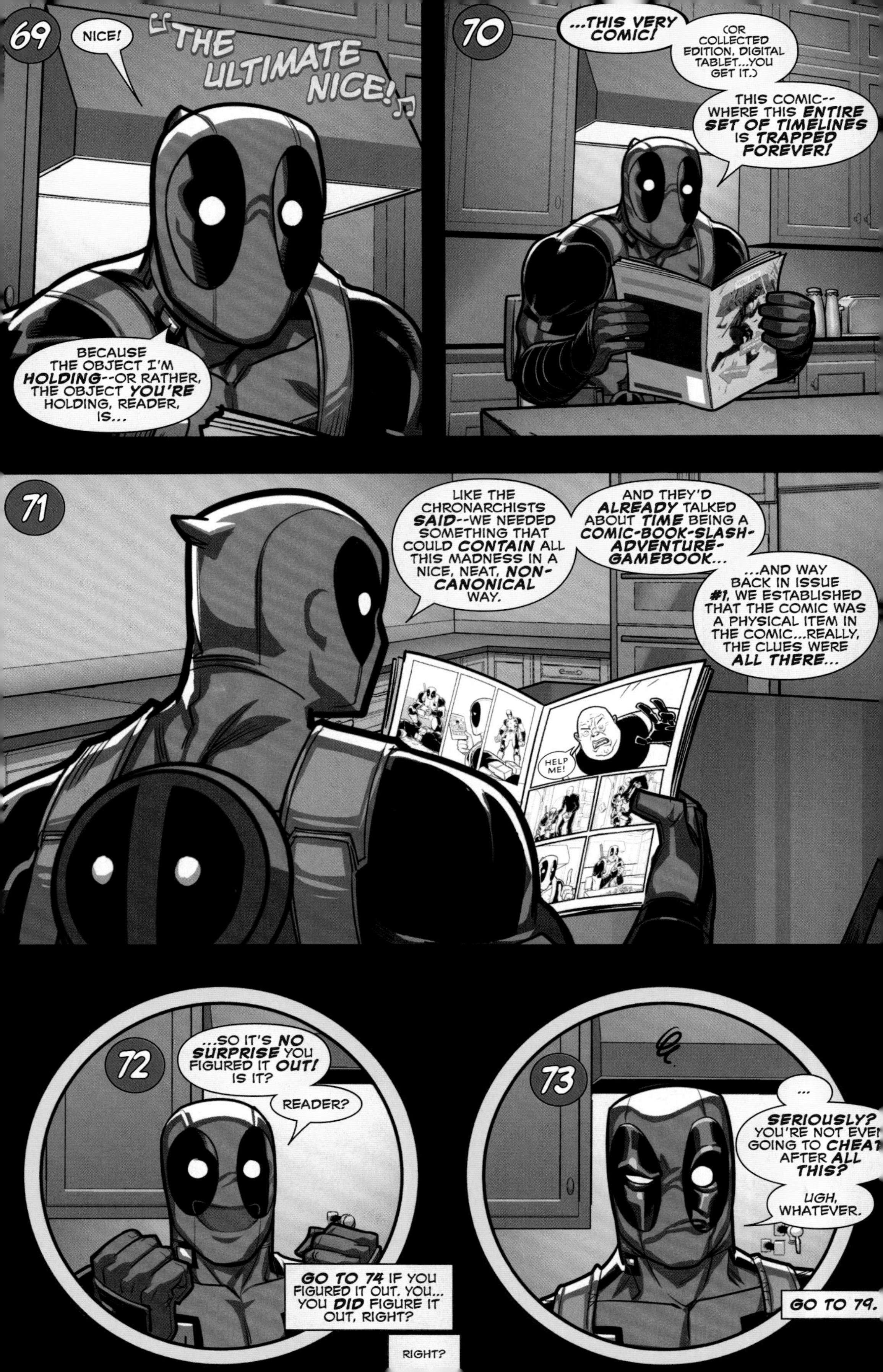

69
NICE!
♫THE ULTIMATE NICE!♫
BECAUSE THE OBJECT I'M HOLDING--OR RATHER, THE OBJECT YOU'RE HOLDING, READER, IS...
70
...THIS VERY COMIC!
(OR COLLECTED EDITION, DIGITAL TABLET...YOU GET IT.)
THIS COMIC--WHERE THIS ENTIRE SET OF TIMELINES IS TRAPPED FOREVER!
71
LIKE THE CHRONARCHISTS SAID--WE NEEDED SOMETHING THAT COULD CONTAIN ALL THIS MADNESS IN A NICE, NEAT, NON-CANONICAL WAY.
AND THEY'D ALREADY TALKED ABOUT TIME BEING A COMIC-BOOK-SLASH-ADVENTURE-GAMEBOOK...
...AND WAY BACK IN ISSUE #1, WE ESTABLISHED THAT THE COMIC WAS A PHYSICAL ITEM IN THE COMIC...REALLY, THE CLUES WERE ALL THERE...
HELP ME!
72
...SO IT'S NO SURPRISE YOU FIGURED IT OUT! IS IT?
READER?
GO TO 74 IF YOU FIGURED IT OUT. YOU... YOU DID FIGURE IT OUT, RIGHT?
RIGHT?
73
...
SERIOUSLY? YOU'RE NOT EVEN GOING TO CHEAT AFTER ALL THIS?
UGH, WHATEVER.
GO TO 79.

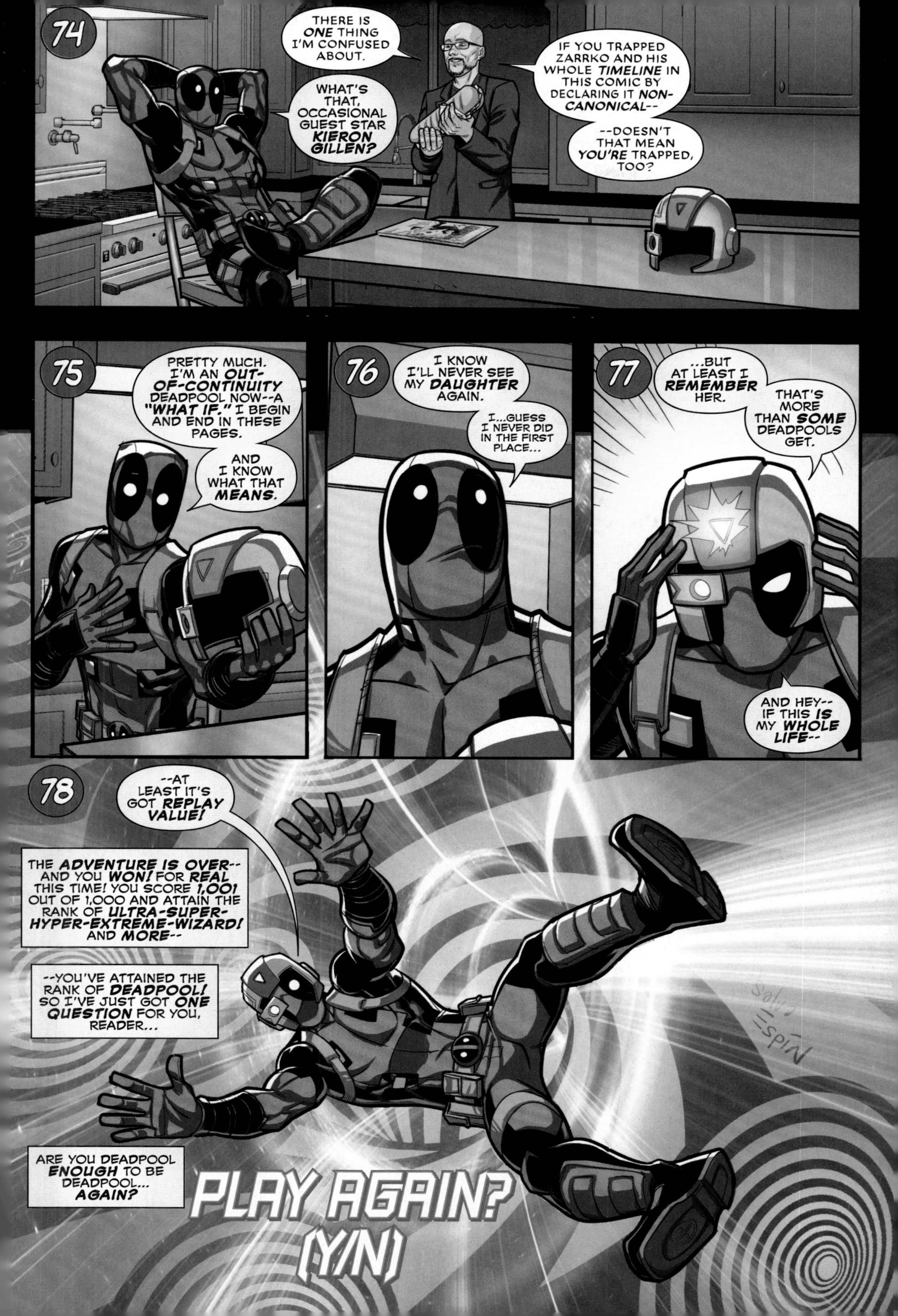
74
THERE IS ONE THING I'M CONFUSED ABOUT.
WHAT'S THAT, OCCASIONAL GUEST STAR KIERON GILLEN?
IF YOU TRAPPED ZARRKO AND HIS WHOLE TIMELINE IN THIS COMIC BY DECLARING IT NON-CANONICAL--
--DOESN'T THAT MEAN YOU'RE TRAPPED, TOO?
75
PRETTY MUCH. I'M AN OUT-OF-CONTINUITY DEADPOOL NOW--A "WHAT IF." I BEGIN AND END IN THESE PAGES.
AND I KNOW WHAT THAT MEANS.
76
I KNOW I'LL NEVER SEE MY DAUGHTER AGAIN.
I...GUESS I NEVER DID IN THE FIRST PLACE...
77
...BUT AT LEAST I REMEMBER HER.
THAT'S MORE THAN SOME DEADPOOLS GET.
AND HEY--IF THIS IS MY WHOLE LIFE--
78
--AT LEAST IT'S GOT REPLAY VALUE!
THE ADVENTURE IS OVER--AND YOU WON! FOR REAL THIS TIME! YOU SCORE 1,001 OUT OF 1,000 AND ATTAIN THE RANK OF ULTRA-SUPER-HYPER-EXTREME-WIZARD! AND MORE--
--YOU'VE ATTAINED THE RANK OF DEADPOOL! SO I'VE JUST GOT ONE QUESTION FOR YOU, READER...
ARE YOU DEADPOOL ENOUGH TO BE DEADPOOL... AGAIN?
PLAY AGAIN? (Y/N)

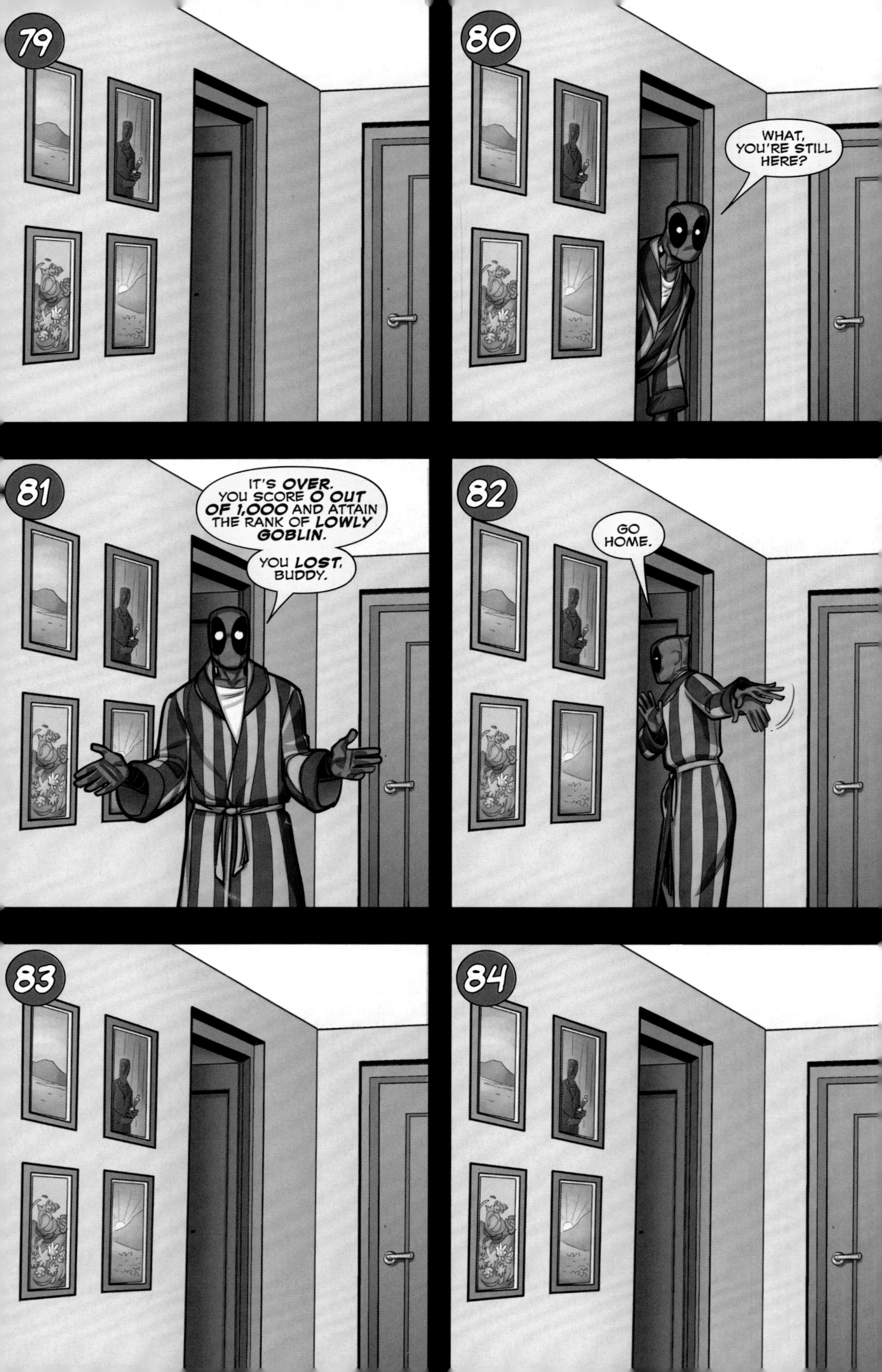
79
80
WHAT, YOU'RE STILL HERE?
81
IT'S OVER. YOU SCORE 0 OUT OF 1,000 AND ATTAIN THE RANK OF LOWLY GOBLIN.
YOU LOST, BUDDY.
82
GO HOME.
83
84

||||||||||||||||||||||||||||||||||||||||||||||||||||||||||||||||||||||||||||||

Hey, fellow kids! It's me, Deadpool, and I'd like to get real for a moment. Like, **really** real. Imagine I'm turning a chair around and sitting backwards on it with my thighs splayed uncomfortably wide because I haven't thought this through. Imagine a blackboard behind me with "DRUGS ARE FOR MUGS" written on it. Imagine I'm not just Mr. Bergandorff from the drama department – today, I want you call me **Phil. That's how real with you I'm being, Reader.**

Now, we've all had a lot of fun with this game. But you know what's **really** fun? I'll tell you. What's really fun is **quantifying** your fun by ticking off a serious of arbitrary "achievements" set by the game developers. That's how you **know** you're having fun, Reader.

So behold – your...

ACHIEVEMENTS CHECKLIST

|||||||||||||||||||||||||||||||||||||||| ||||||||||||||||||||||||||||||||||

- ☐ **EVERY FIRST ACHIEVEMENT EVER -** PLAY THE TUTORIAL!
- ☐ **ULTRA EXTREME WIZARD -** WIN THE GAME WITH 1001 POINTS OUT OF 1000!
- ☐ **WADE IN GORE -** WIN TEN FIGHTS IN ONE GAME!
- ☐ **UTILITY BELT -** USE FIVE INVENTORY ITEMS IN ONE GAME!
- ☐ **FUTILITY BELT –** USE ZERO INVENTORY ITEMS IN ONE GAME!

- ☐ **ELEMENTARY, MY DEAR WILSON -** GET ALL THREE CLUES TO THE KINGPIN'S CODE IN ONE GAME!
- ☐ **DOUG WOULD BE PROUD -** MEET ALL FIVE GRASSHOPPERS IN ONE GAME!
- ☐ **MINI MARVEL -** WIN ALL FOUR MINIGAMES IN ONE GAME!
- ☐ **TYPE "SCORE" -** COLLECT ALL SEVEN *GEMS IN ONE GAME!
- ☐ **ARMY OF ONE -** BRING ALL 82 DEADPOOLS TO THE FINAL SHOWDOWN!

- ☐ **TIME PARADOX -** KILL JUSTICE PEACE BEFORE HE MEETS THE TOMORROW MAN! (Uh, spoilers.)
- ☐ **MMM, SPRINKLES –** EAT THE DONUT!
- ☐ **NO LONGER MINT –** PHYSICALLY CUT OUT THE DEADPOOL DIE!*
- ☐ **BUELLER? -** ATTAIN THE RANK OF LOWLY GOBLIN!
- ☐ **MEGA MAN MODE –** USE THREE ITEMS FROM ISSUE #3 IN ISSUE #3!

*Digital readers – I don't know, do fifty push-ups or something.

|||||||||||||||||||||||||||||||||||||||||||||||||||||||||||||||||||||||||||||||

And it's not all work, work, work! For every **THREE** achievements you tick off, pick **ONE** of the following **FUN CHEAT MODES** – to render the game **doubly meaningless!**

|||||||||||||||||||||||||||||||||||||||||||||||||||||||||||||||||||||||||||||||

- ☐ **EMOTION CONTROLLER –** PLAY THE ISSUES IN ANY ORDER!
- ☐ **INFINITE AMMO –** ROLL 3D6 IN COMBAT!
- ☐ **MAGIC POCKETS –** ADD TWO EXTRA INVENTORY SLOTS!
- ☐ **STEALTH CAMO –** BYPASS ONE FIGHT PER ISSUE!
- ☐ **GAME OF THE MOVIE –** READ ALL DEADPOOL DIALOGUE IN RYAN REYNOLDS' VOICE!

|||||||||||||||||||||||||||||||||||||||||||||||||||||||||||||||||||||||||||||||

Remember, Reader, 100% completion – or more realistically, about 86% completion – will bring you the **greatest prize of all:** The numb realization that what was once a pure joy is now a groaningly tedious chore!

Also, you get to tick this box: ☐ It's made of **gold**.

So hop to it.

|||||||||||||||||||||||||||||||||||||||||||||||||||||||||||||||||||||||||||||||

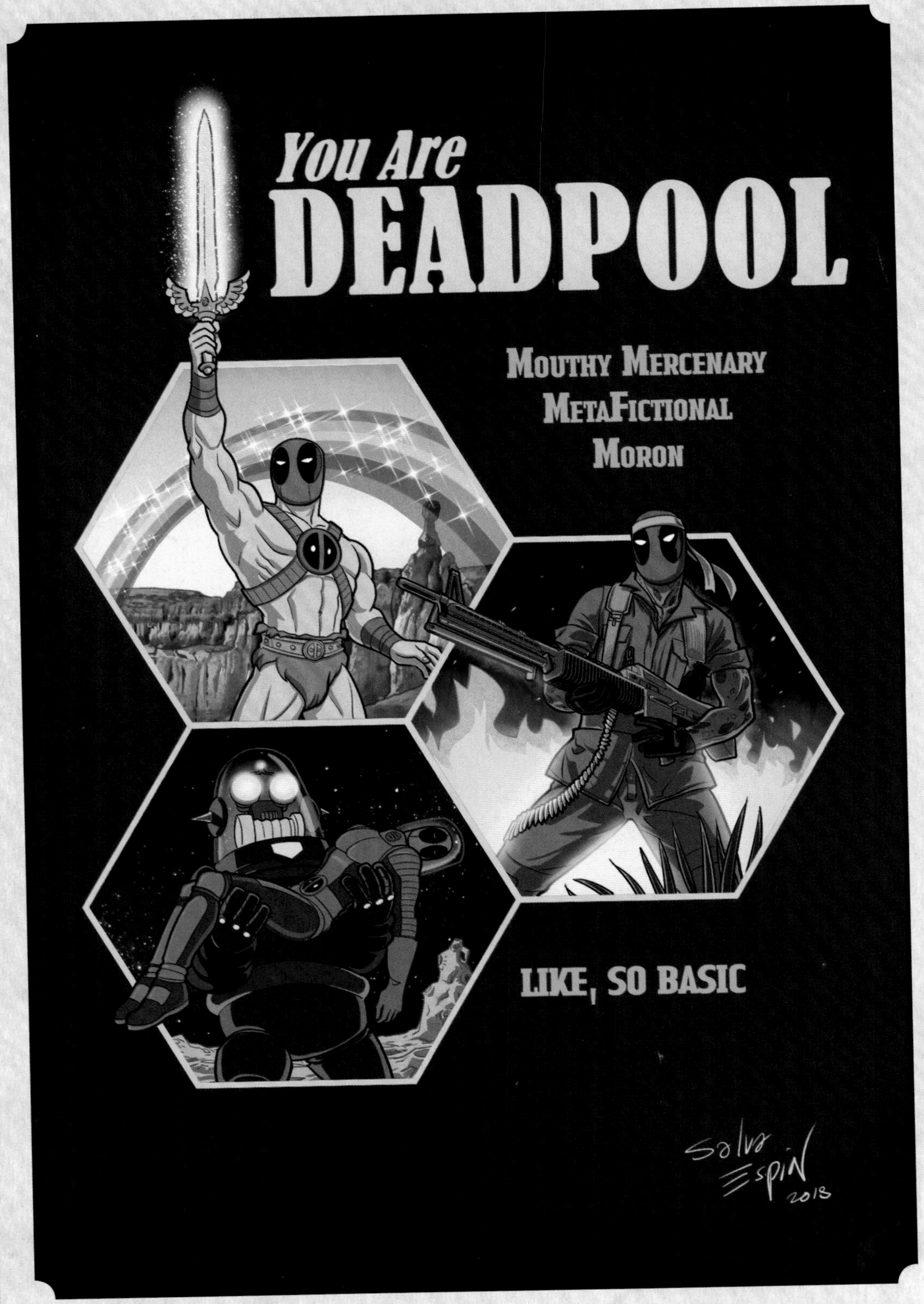
You Are
DEADPOOL
Mouthy Mercenary
MetaFictional
Moron
LIKE, SO BASIC
salva Espin

5 VARIANT BY **SALVA ESPIN**